THE POVERTY INDUSTRY

FAMILIES, LAW, AND SOCIETY SERIES

General Editor: Nancy E. Dowd

The Poverty Industry

*The Exploitation of America's
Most Vulnerable Citizens*

Daniel L. Hatcher

NEW YORK UNIVERSITY PRESS
New York

NEW YORK UNIVERSITY PRESS
New York
www.nyupress.org

First published in paperback in 2019

References to Internet websites (URLs) were accurate at the time of writing. Neither the author nor New York University Press is responsible for URLs that may have expired or changed since the manuscript was prepared.

ISBN: 978-1-4798-7472-9 (hb)

ISBN: 978-1-4798-2697-1 (pb)

For Library of Congress Cataloging-in-Publication data, please contact the Library of Congress.

New York University Press books are printed on acid-free paper, and their binding materials are chosen for strength and durability. We strive to use environmentally responsible suppliers and materials to the greatest extent possible in publishing our books.

Manufactured in the United States of America

10 9 8 7 6 5 4 3 2 1

Also available as an ebook

For my parents, James and Barbara, and for my children, Landon, Raina, and Ava

CONTENTS

ACKNOWLEDGMENTS

I would like to begin by acknowledging and thanking my past clients who inspire my advocacy, writing, and teaching: low-income mothers and fathers striving for economic stability; disabled individuals fighting for their rights; aging adults seeking the quality of treatment they deserve; and the many foster children I represented—who are now adults—and who I deeply hope have beat the odds and are doing well.

I am grateful for the opportunity provided by NYU Press, and for the wonderful support from Clara Platter and Constance Grady. I am also grateful to Deborah Gershenowitz, formerly at NYU Press, who initially encouraged me to write this book.

I am lucky to teach at the University of Baltimore School of Law, and thankful for the leadership and support from Dean Ronald Weich. The Dean, the school, the faculty, and staff have provided me with excellent support and encouragement in writing this book. I also could not be more grateful for the opportunity to teach in the University of Baltimore's outstanding clinical program. I am always inspired by the enthusiasm of the clinic's wonderful faculty, staff, and students. Many of my colleagues provided me with invaluable feedback and encouragement in the writing process, both in this book and prior articles that ultimately led me to write this book. Special thanks to Professors who reviewed my prior scholarship, including Jane Murphy, Robert Rubinson, Michael I. Meyerson, Christopher J. Peters, and Elizabeth J. Samuels. I am fortunate to teach with Professor Michele Gilman in the Civil Advocacy Clinic, and I credit her with helping me learn how to translate my grounding in advocacy into teaching and scholarship. I also thank my administrative assistant, Rosalind Williams, and my research assistant, Alexa Curley, for their very helpful and insightful work and support during the writing process.

Professors Nancy Dowd and Barbara Bennett Woodhouse provided me with mentorship, support, and helpful feedback from the very beginning of my initial book proposal. I can't thank them enough. And I am also thankful for past comments and support from Professors Karen Syma Czapanskiy, Martin Guggenheim, David Super, Leigh Goodmark, and Bruce A. Boyer. I also thank Ezra Rosser and the American University Washington College of Law for the opportunity to present portions of this book and to benefit from participants' comments and feedback. Portions of my earlier articles appearing in the *Wake Forest Law Review*, *Arizona Law Review*, *New Mexico Law Review*, *Cardozo Law Review*, and the *Brooklyn Law Review* provided foundational research and material for this book. I thank the excellent staffs at those journals. Further, I am grateful for assistance creating charts from Marcelo Agudo.

I would like to thank all my former colleagues from the Maryland Legal Aid Bureau and Children's Defense Fund. Special thanks to Rhonda Lipkin, Hannah Lieberman, Joan Little, Wilhelm Joseph, and Deborah Weinstein—their mentorship and encouragement led me to where I am today.

I also am incredibly thankful for family and friends. All were supportive, and many also provided helpful suggestions, including David Hatcher, Pam Wallis, Kella Hatcher, R. J. Wallis, Judi Marzullo, Caterina Hatcher, Walter Helmke, and Rowene Helmke. And I want to thank Mark Helmke, who went out of his way to encourage and help me early on regarding how to seek media coverage and foster interest in my writing and advocacy, and who left us too early. He is deeply missed.

And finally, I want to especially thank my parents, James L. and Barbara J. Hatcher, and my children, Landon, Raina, and Ava—to whom this book is dedicated. They have showered me with their pride, support, and helpful suggestions. My parents inspired my life path, including my desire to serve the vulnerable populations discussed in this book. I learned from my mother's giving nature and her passion for reaching out to those who are less fortunate or simply different. While writing, I have been surrounded by beautiful furniture creations made by my father (with me often serving as his apprentice), and I was inspired by his wonderful views on life—including in his excellent book, *Going to Camp: A Memoir of Twin Boys' Quest for Education in the Rural South*. And my children also inspire me every day, with their amazing qualities and insights—and their passions for learning and living life true to who they are. They have encouraged me with fascinating questions about my writing, and have been incredibly supportive and patient during the countless hours I have devoted to this book.

Introduction

Alex was taken into foster care at age twelve after his mother's death. Over a six-year period, he was moved at least twenty times between temporary placements and group homes. Soon after losing his mother, Alex learned his older brother might be able to care for him, but then his brother died. There were also hopes that Alex could go to live with his father, but then his father died as well.

Unknown to Alex, he was eligible to receive Social Security survivor benefits after his father died. These funds could have provided an invaluable benefit to Alex, supplying an emotional connection to his deceased father and financial resources to help with his difficult transition out of foster care.

But without telling Alex, the Maryland foster care agency applied for the survivor benefits on his behalf and to become his representative payee. Then, although obligated to only use the benefits for the child's best interests, the agency took every payment from Alex. The agency didn't tell Alex it was applying for the funds, and didn't tell him when the agency took the money for itself. Alex struggled during his years in foster care, left foster care penniless, and continued to struggle on his own. And after taking Alex's funds, the agency hired a private revenue contractor to learn how to obtain more resources from foster children.

This book will tell the story of how states and their human service agencies are partnering with private companies to form a vast poverty industry, turning America's most vulnerable populations into a source of revenue. My intention is to reveal how the resulting industry is strip-mining billions in federal aid and other funds from impoverished families, abused and neglected children, and the disabled and elderly poor. As the vulnerable struggle, as advocates strive to assist in their struggle, and as policy experts across the political spectrum debate the best structure for governmental aid programs, a massive siphoning of the safety net is occurring behind the scenes.

1

An industry is usually defined as a category of private companies providing similar goods or services, such as the coal mining industry. The poverty industry, however, includes both companies and government entities: the private sector is partnering with state and local governments to use the vulnerable as a resource for extracting funds. Similar to how the coal mining industry mines rock for coal ore that can be converted into profit, the poverty industry mines children and the poor for aid funds and resources that are converted into private profit and government revenue.

For example, "revenue maximization" contractors help foster care agencies take over a quarter of a billion dollars each year from abused and neglected children. The agencies and contractors seek to increase the number of foster children who are designated as disabled in order to obtain their disability benefits. They also search for children with deceased parents and take their survivor benefits.

Following the story of Alex, the Maryland agency planned to expand this strategy, contracting with MAXIMUS, Inc. to develop recommendations about how to maximize the claiming of children's disability and survivor benefits as government revenue. In a section titled "Current and Potential Revenue Acquisition," the MAXIMUS report describes foster children as a "revenue generating mechanism."[1]

The practice Alex encountered is an example of how states and their contractors often look to the vulnerable less in terms of how to best serve their needs but rather in terms of how to best use them in strategies to bolster state coffers. Then, after diverting their aid funds and resources, the poverty industry often leaves the poor with inadequate care and services. The poverty industry profits from poverty as the needy are left with unmet needs.

The revenue strategies begin with state human service agencies. Facing shrinking budgets, the agencies subvert their service missions to their own fiscal interests and turn their intended beneficiaries into revenue tools. This effort by cash-strapped agencies—even taking assets from abused and neglected children—is asserted to be for the greater good because increased agency funds will lead to improved agency services. Agencies created to serve the vulnerable are using their power to extract revenue from the vulnerable, under the guise of adding fiscal capacity to serve the vulnerable.

But the rationale fails. The notion that human service agencies should fund themselves by taking resources from populations they exist to serve is counterintuitive at best. Also, the revenue strategies often do not provide the agencies with additional fiscal capacity. While the agencies are searching for funds, their parent states are as well. Funds extracted from children and the poor are often rerouted into general state coffers rather than used to increase agency funding. Human service agencies extract funds from their own impoverished beneficiaries, states take aid funds from their agencies, and the private contractors in turn take their cut.

The revenue tactics are vast in scope but largely unknown to the public. Therefore, it is my intent in this book to make plain how this money is disappearing, who it winds up benefiting, and who is ultimately hurt.

In part 1, two chapters lay out the background and conflict leading to the emergence of the poverty industry. Chapter 1 introduces the vulnerable populations discussed in this book, provides the historical foundations of the purpose of human service agencies that exist to serve those populations, and explains how the agencies have often prioritized their own finances over the interests of their beneficiaries. The purpose of human service agencies has come into conflict with the fiscal self-interests of the agencies, a theme that continues throughout the book.

Chapter 2 exposes the scope and impact of the poverty industry, which has grown as a result of the conflict discussed in chapter 1. The chapter explains fiscal federalism, the economic structure in which the federal government provides aid funds to help states operate programs for the poor. However, the intended collaboration has turned to tension and distrust as the states hire contractors to help maximize and divert the federal aid through illusory revenue strategies. And while contracting with states to increase the federal funds, private companies often contract with the federal government to reduce payout of those same federal dollars.

The poverty industry is thus undermining the structure of America's largest aid programs. The result is akin to an "iron triangle," a political science model that describes the self-serving interrelationships between government and private interests. Warned against by President Eisenhower in his farewell address, the military-industrial complex is an example of such an iron triangle, with public funds diverted to benefit defense contractors and agency self-interests. Similarly, the iron triangle caused by the poverty industry—or the poverty-industrial complex—is diverting public funds intended to help children and the poor.

Moreover, poverty industry companies do much more than maximize revenue. Private contractors now provide services in virtually every aspect of government aid programs. Much like its military-based predecessor, the poverty-industrial complex is rife with potential conflicts of interest, pay-to-play tactics, and a revolving door of personnel.

Part 2 of the book includes three chapters that describe specific revenue strategies. These examples differ in details but are linked by common threads: human service agencies are using the impoverished as a revenue tool; a growing private sector is aiding and profiting from the practices; and defenseless populations are harmed as a result.

Chapter 3 describes the first example, in which foster care agencies are hiring private companies to help obtain disability and survivor benefits from abused and neglected children. Rather than using the funds to help the children, the money is diverted to agency revenue or to state general coffers. Some foster care agencies take even more, such as taking Veteran's Assistance benefits belonging to a child after a parent serves and dies in the military. The Maryland foster care agency drafted a regulation allowing it to take *all* resources from foster children: "the child's own benefits, insurance, cash assets, trust accounts" and even the child's own earnings—everything. And a Nebraska regulation allows the agency to even take a foster child's burial space.

Public records detailing the practices were obtained from state freedom of information act requests, and are summarized in chapter 3. The records show foster children being used almost as minerals on a revenue maximization conveyor belt: describing the children as "units"; plugging the children into "data match algorithms," "predictive analytics," and "data mining"; and prioritizing and "dissecting" the population of foster children in terms of which children will bring in the most money.

Chapter 4 sets out the second example revenue strategy, where the poverty industry has turned its sights on federal healthcare funds. Often with assistance of revenue maximization consultants, states develop illusory budget maneuvers to claim billions in increased federal Medicaid funds. The federal aid is then often diverted to bolster state general coffers rather than to the intended Medicaid related services for children and the poor. For example, while governor of New Hampshire, Judd Gregg initiated a shell game that became known in the state as "Mediscam"—a scheme also used by his successors and by many other states—in which the state's public hospitals serving the poor have been used to claim more than $2 billion in increased federal Medicaid funds that were converted into state revenue.

In the third poverty industry strategy, explained in chapter 5, child support agencies are teaming up with private contractors to convert child support into government revenue. In addition to diverting Social Security benefits, state agencies also take child support payments from foster children. Also, poor mothers applying for public assistance are forced to sue the poor fathers for child support obligations that are rerouted to the government coffers. Already fragile families are further weakened, as impoverished parents are pit against each other. Children lose out as their child support payments are diverted to the government, and private companies profit from the harm.

Part 3 is comprised of two chapters, first addressing how the poverty industry practices are expanding and then considering how to reel the industry in. Chapter 6 illustrates how the practices in the earlier chapters just scratch the surface of the growing web of revenue strategies that take advantage of the vulnerable. For example, a scheme using nursing homes was developed in Indiana where the state's largest public hospital system has bought up for-profit nursing homes, used them to increase federal Medicaid payments, and then diverted the aid for other purposes rather than improving care to the nursing homes' residents.

Further, in another strategy discussed in chapter 6, for-profit nursing homes are sedating the elderly with psychotropic drugs in order to reduce staffing needs and maximize profit. And similar fiscal motives have led to alarming growth in the use of psychotropic drugs for children in foster care and juvenile detention facilities. Simultaneously, pharmacies have profited by illegally promoting the use of their psychotropic drugs to these nursing home residents and institutionalized children for off-label uses, including illegal incentives to doctors.

Also discussed in chapter 6, states and counties are working with private companies to turn courts serving the poor into revenue generators. Low-income defendants are first saddled with unmanageable court fines and fees, then the courts partner with private collections agencies, probation companies, and companies that manufacture electronic monitoring devices—all tacking on more and more fees to the debts owed by the poor. Collections can provide funding for the courts or are often routed to the general funds of the state or local governments. If the poor don't pay, they go to jail, like the old debtors' prisons that were abolished long ago. An Alabama judge told poor litigants they must sell their blood to pay court fines, or face jail time.[2] Poor debtors in Mississippi have been forced into penal farms to work off court fines at a rate of $58 a day.[3]

And the poverty industry keeps growing. Non-profit hospitals contract with private companies to use a discount drug program intended to increase access to medications for the poor as hospital revenue. Companies that provide hospice care, services intended to aid the dying, are targeting patients who may not actually be dying in order to maximize profits from government aid.

This book seeks to spur public focus and scrutiny that has long been lacking. The details, scope, and impact of the poverty industry are exposed, and understanding of the industry's revenue tactics is provided. The book explains where laws are possibly being broken, and where laws are inadequately crafted or implemented to halt the harmful practices. The concluding chapter provides a road map for reforms necessary to realign the practices of human service agencies with their intended missions, and to help ensure that any involvement of the private sector is consistent with those aims. These reforms will help strengthen the social fabric, prevent misuse of public funds, and lead to improved services for America's most vulnerable individuals and families.

Use of the term "vulnerable" in this book to describe the populations who are used in revenue strategies is not intended to imply weakness. To the contrary, I continue to be amazed by the strength and determination of the families, children, and individuals struggling to overcome their difficult life circumstances. To quote Martha Albertson Fineman, "[v]ulnerability is the characteristic that positions us in relation to each other as human beings and also suggests a relationship of responsibility between the state and its institutions and the individual."[4] We are all vulnerable, and we are all interdependent—both with each other and with the government systems that support us. Some of us, however, face greater disadvantage, trauma, and difficulty than others. These are the vulnerable populations considered in this book.

When our interdependence with each other and with our government institutions is recognized in a positive way, the opportunity and support from that interdependence can provide a tremendous benefit. But when the vulnerability of those who are struggling the most is instead used for the gain of others, we are all ultimately harmed. This, unfortunately, is what has been occurring through the practices of the poverty industry—a partnership of government and private companies that is using the vulnerable to serve itself.

To be clear, I do not support arguments to cut aid programs. To the contrary, the analysis and exposed practices call out for policy reform in order to strengthen aid programs and increase targeted funding so that needed assistance truly gets to those in need. States and their human service agencies are cash-strapped and need more revenue, but diverting resources intended to help children and the poor is not the answer.

PART I

How the Poverty Industry Is Siphoning Aid
from the Vulnerable

1

Agency Purpose versus Agency Self-Interest

Conflict in Serving the Vulnerable

"They're my advocates? No they're not. To me, they're
against me."
—Quote from teenage foster child about a foster care
agency taking his Social Security survivor benefits[1]

Alex and Ryan share unfortunate histories in the Maryland foster care
system.[2] Both boys, now young men, were shuffled between multiple
placements and they struggled with the transition to adulthood. Both
Alex and Ryan suffered through their parents' deaths while in state custody, and then had the only remaining connection to their deceased
parents—their Social Security survivor benefits—taken by the foster
care agency without their knowledge.

As described in the introduction, Alex was twelve when he entered
foster care following his mother's death. During his six years in foster
care, Alex was moved several times between temporary placements.
Soon after losing his mother, Alex's father also died. Unknown to Alex,
he was then eligible to receive Social Security survivor benefits. The
Baltimore County Department of Social Services (BCDSS) was charged
with protecting Alex's interests, but the agency sidestepped that obligation when it saw the potential money it could obtain from the boy. Without telling Alex, the agency applied for the survivor benefits on Alex's
behalf, applied to become his representative payee to gain access to the
funds, and then took every payment Alex received.

If the agency applied fiduciary discretion to use Alex's money in his
best interests, the payments could have been used to help him prepare
for the difficult transition to independence: saved for college or to pay
for vocational training; used to purchase specialized tools or equipment
for Alex's future chosen profession; saved to help pay future rent or to

purchase a car—now virtually a necessity for independent living; or simply conserved in a savings account for the many unforeseen expenses that Alex would encounter. However, the agency ignored Alex's needs and simply took the boy's money.

Ryan's experiences were very similar to those of Alex. Ryan did not understand how the Baltimore City foster care agency could take his survivor benefits that were left to him by his deceased father. He expressed frustration, but also determination: *"You know, the thing is, they are survivor benefits. I am a survivor."*[3] And he explained his feelings in more detail:

> When I first wanted to move where I am now, they didn't want to do it, meaning they were fighting me. They thought I was better where I was in a group home, than be in a foster home where I was in a much better school, and getting the help I needed. For now, they're supposed to be here for me, but everything that benefits me they're fighting. My parents have passed away, you know. I loved my parents to death. I just lost my big brother. If my parents pass away, they would want me to have their work benefits, and DSS, they don't need it . . . You know, the thing is, they are survivor benefits. I am a survivor . . . Everyone's passed away, besides my Aunt. I wish that I'd be able to get this, so I can move on with my life, and stop having to fight for everything that benefits me. That's what they (BCDSS) have been doing. They're my advocates? No they're not. To me, they're against me.[4]

Both Alex and Ryan filed court actions in an effort to stop the agencies from taking their money. The boys' cases are discussed in more detail in chapter 3, and illustrate the lengths to which a child welfare agency will go to convert a child's funds into agency revenue. The details provide a stark example of a human service agency turning its power against the interests of its child beneficiaries by ignoring its legal and ethical obligations.

The experiences of Alex and Ryan are unfortunately emblematic of tens of thousands of foster children across the country who are being used in the same revenue strategy. And their experiences are also emblematic of the numerous other methods developed by states and their agencies, with the assistance of private contractors, to convert funds intended to help struggling families and individuals into state revenue and private profit. The boys' experiences thus provide an excellent backdrop to consider the conflict between the intended benign purpose and fiscal self-interests of agencies created to serve the vulnerable.

The Vulnerable

Impoverished and Fragile Families

By 2009, after the financial crisis hit, circumstances facing vulnerable populations were already looking grim. Cities participating in the 2009 U.S. Conference of Mayors Hunger and Homelessness Survey reported a 26 percent average increase in demand for hunger assistance, the largest increase in almost 20 years—including an increase in hunger assistance requests from middle-class families who used to donate food. More than three out of every four cities reported an increase in family homelessness.[5]

By 2012, circumstances for low-income families were worsening. More than 70 percent of cities reported increases in family homelessness, and almost two-thirds of cities were turning away homeless families with children from emergency shelters due to lack of resources.[6] By 2013, family homelessness again increased, emergency food assistance requests continued to increase, and the percentage of the total food assistance requests coming from families increased to almost 60 percent.[7]

According to 2012 census data, 9.5 million families in the U.S. were living below the poverty line, up from 7.7 million families in 2005. The families living in poverty included 33.1 million individuals (adults and children) within those families—so an average family size of about 3.5 individuals. Almost one out of 4 children under six years of age were living in families under the poverty threshold.

And the numbers are likely underestimated because the official poverty line is recognized as being too low for what families actually need. The poverty line is based on how much money families spent on food in the 1950s. Mollie Orshansky was working for the Social Security Administration and she was assigned to report on child poverty. There was no measure at the time, so she created her own by using a Department of Agriculture report from 1955 that found families spent about a third of their income on food. Her approach was to determine the amount a poor household spent on food, and multiply it by three. To determine the amount, she used the cheapest estimated food plan developed by the Department of Agriculture only for "temporary or emergency use":

> Orshansky based her poverty thresholds on the economy food plan—the cheapest of four food plans developed by the Department of Agriculture. The actual combinations of foods in the food plans, devised by Agriculture Department dietitians using complex procedures, constituted nutritionally adequate diets; the Agriculture Department described the economy food plan as being "designed for temporary or emergency use when funds are low."[8]

Thus, because the official poverty line is too low, families and children who are a little above the poverty line still face incredible difficulties. Families up to 150 percent of the poverty line, if not higher, are often classified as low-income. In 2012, 35 percent of children in the United States lived below 150 percent of the poverty line.

Abused and Neglected Children

Studies show a strong link between poverty and foster care. For example, the Third National Incidence Study of Child Abuse and Neglect found that children in families with annual incomes below $15,000 were much more likely to experience maltreatment than those in families making $30,000 or more—not just twice as much, but 22 times more likely to experience maltreatment. The most common form of maltreatment is neglect, with almost four-fifths (78.3 percent) of maltreated children experiencing neglect rather than some form of physical or mental abuse according to a 2012 federal report. Children in poor families are forty-four times as likely to experience some form of neglect.

Further, the parents of abused and neglected children often face numerous difficulties in addition to poverty, including homelessness, domestic violence, poor education, substance abuse, mental illness, and lack of healthcare. State practices often treat such circumstances of poverty as grounds for child removal.

As the parents of foster children struggle, the children face even more difficulties both in foster care and as they try to transition to independence when aging out of the system. Children in the child welfare system can encounter insufficient services, underfunded agencies, overworked caseworkers, chaotic juvenile courts, poorly run group homes, and inadequately monitored placements. And children removed from their families due to abuse or neglect unfortunately sometimes encounter abuse or neglect again after entering the foster care system.

Then, as the children age out of care, the difficulties continue. The statistics facing former foster children are daunting. More than half of the children experience unemployment, almost three-fifths make less than $10,000 in annual income, 43 percent lack health insurance, 25 percent experience homelessness, 25 percent don't graduate from high school, just 2 percent obtain a bachelor's degree, and almost 70 percent of young women receive food stamps.[9] And former foster boys in particular encounter barriers to employment and difficulties tied to involvement with the criminal justice system. A 2010 study found that by age 24, nearly 60 percent of former foster males had been convicted of a crime, and by age 26 almost 75 percent of the young men had been incarcerated and 82 percent had been arrested.[10]

The Disabled Poor

About 28 percent of disabled individuals are living below the poverty line according to 2010 census data. Further, while people's circumstances can change and they can fluctuate in and out of poverty, disabled individuals who are poor are more likely to stay persistently poor.

Of those who are disabled, the mentally ill face a particularly difficult connection with poverty. If you suffer from mental illness, you are more likely to be poor. And if you are poor, you are more likely to suffer from mental illness. The causal connection travels both ways and can form a vicious cycle. For example, cities in the 2012 U.S. Conference of Mayors Hunger and Homelessness Survey reported that an average of 30 percent of the homeless were severely mentally ill, and almost 20 percent of the homeless were physically disabled. Also, a strong connection exists between mental illness and substance abuse. According to the Journal of the American Medical Association, about half of people with mental illness also struggle with addiction to alcohol or drugs. According to the Bureau of Justice Statistics, more than half of all prison and jail inmates struggle with mental health issues.[11] And it's worse for women, with almost three-quarters of women in state prisons suffering from mental health problems.

However, despite the enormous need, state funding for the mentally ill has been slashed. After the financial crisis of 2008, when economic struggles for individuals and families intensified, mental health services declined. A report by the National Alliance on Mental Illness found that states cut in excess of $1.6 billion in funds for mental health services from FY2009 to FY2012.[12]

The Elderly Poor

Under a new poverty measure developed by the Census Bureau that takes into account out-of-pocket medical care costs, more than 15 percent of the 41 million elderly in the United States are living in poverty. Almost half of the elderly are struggling to live on less than 200 percent of the poverty level.[13] Deep or extreme poverty—defined as income of less than $5,700 per year—has also increased among the elderly. According to a report by the National Women's Law Center, deep poverty increased by 23 percent among elderly men and 18 percent for elderly women from 2011 to 2012.[14]

Further, the conditions of housing and care for low-income aging adults can often be described as dismal. Poor quality care and low staffing levels often plague nursing facilities for older Americans. Nursing homes use psychotropic drugs for off-label uses at alarming rates, often to sedate the elderly as a way to reduce staffing needs and increase profits. And needed care is often lacking. For example, according to the *New York Times*, a Wisconsin study found that dental care for nursing home residents was so bad that almost a third of the residents had teeth that were broken to the gums, with the roots visible.[15] Similarly, a study in upstate New York found that only 16 percent of nursing home residents received any oral care whatsoever.[16] A 2013 audit by the U.S. Department of Health and Human Services Office of Inspector General (OIG) found that in 37 percent of stays in skilled nursing facilities, the facilities did not provide needed services or failed to develop required care plans. The

OIG audit also "found a number of egregious examples of poor quality care that were related to wound care, medication management, and therapy." For example:

> Another beneficiary was given an antipsychotic drug when she did not have a diagnosis for psychosis and her care plan did not indicate that she had a mood disorder. The physician noted that the beneficiary was confused while on the drug, but he still increased the dosage. A month later, the beneficiary's family complained that the physician and SNF staff were trying to sedate the beneficiary with the drug.[17]

A 2014 OIG audit examined "adverse events," which harm a patient or resident as a result of medical errors, poor conditions/treatment, and failure to provide needed care—among other reasons. The audit found that among Medicare beneficiaries staying at skilled nursing facilities for only short stays (35 days or less), 22 percent of the residents suffered from at least one adverse event while in care.[18]

The difficulties these populations face cause greater interdependence, including greater need for government services. The vulnerability also causes the already struggling children, families, and adults to be even more susceptible to harm—and unfortunately more susceptible to being used rather than helped. These are the populations who have been used by the poverty industry, in which the purpose of human service agencies is subverted to the search for money.

Agency Purpose

The purpose of human service agencies is not difficult to understand: to help those in need. However, the use of such government power has not always adhered to that humanitarian aim.[19] The purpose and power of state human service agencies derives from the old English doctrine of *parens patriae*, translated as the inherent role of the state as parent of the country. Through this parental role, the state takes on an obligation to protect those who are unable to protect themselves.

Although the doctrine is frequently considered in this chapter in the context of children, often the most vulnerable among us, the discussion is also applicable to understanding the conflict between the purpose and self-interests of state agencies serving any vulnerable population—including children, families, the elderly, and impoverished and disabled adults. Further, the doctrine should also be considered within the broader purpose of government, often described in terms of protecting and maximizing the general welfare of a government's citizenry.

The parens patriae doctrine dates back to feudal England, during the medieval time of lords, knights, and kings, and has an unfortunate conflicted beginning. Early use of the doctrine included the pure aim of aiding those in need, but which was pitted against the self-interested fiscal motive of obtaining riches to sustain the crown.

Historical use of the power was partly benevolent, in which the king provided assistance to some citizens who could not care for themselves. For the mentally impaired, then termed "idiots and lunatics," the king provided assistance without self-interested fiscal motives: "[I]in the seventeenth century the king's relation to idiots and lunatics was that of guardian to ward, that the guardianship was a duty of care rather than a source of profit."[20] However, regarding children, the king applied the parens patriae doctrine with selfish intent. He did not use the protective power for all children, but focused on children of landed gentry with estates that could be taken. The resulting wardships were not aimed at protecting the children, but rather using them. For example, the wardships were used in the feudal tenurial system in which the guardians—usually a lord, or the king directly—had rights with regard to the male and female wards. And such rights were abused for financial gain: "In the case of wards of the crown, it was the practice of the Court of Wards and Liveries to sell both the wardship and marriage rights, and that these wardships went as often to strangers as to mothers or families of minor heirs indicates that this type of wardship was administered with a financial rather than a humanitarian motive."[21]

Thus, the government power to help vulnerable populations was conflicted from its feudal beginnings. Fortunately, public enlightenment and revulsion to such sale of wardship and marriage rights eventually led to the end of the practice in England. But the conflict between government purpose and self-interest continued in America.

America also adopted the parens patriae doctrine, and exercise of the power has been conflicted here as well. The doctrine was established by early American courts as the foundational authority and duty of states to protect the interests of vulnerable children and adults. The parens patriae doctrine and fiduciary purpose of human service agencies is often embedded in statutory and regulatory language and policy statements. For example, the Maryland Department of Human Resources explains why the agency exists:

> The Maryland Department of Human Resources (DHR) is the state's primary social service provider, serving over one million people annually. The Department, through its 24 local departments of social services, aggressively pursues opportunities to assist people in economic need, provide preventive services, and protect vulnerable children and adults.[22]

The core purpose of human service agencies in America is therefore clear, whether found in the parens patriae doctrine or in state policy: to protect and serve the vulnerable. And in carrying out that duty, the agencies' fiduciary obligation is also clear: to never place their own self-interests over the interests of the populations that the agencies exist to serve.

However, despite the clarity of the agency service mandate, the conflict between agency purpose and agency self-interest found fertile ground to grow in America. Under confidential and bureaucratic agency practices, and a lack of due process protections, human service agencies have often prioritized their own fiscal interests over the interests of their beneficiaries. The agencies and their parent states have sometimes lost sight of Thomas Jefferson's simple but crucial principle regarding the purpose of government: that "government exists for the interests of the governed, not for the governors."

Agency Self-Interest

Human service agencies created to look outward toward helping those in need are simultaneously turning inward toward their own self-preservation and agency finances. As a result, agencies often flip the Jeffersonian principle regarding the purpose of government. Rather than only determining the best strategies to serve the interests of their beneficiaries, the agencies often develop strategies to use the vulnerable as a means of serving themselves.

For example, despite the growing recognition of children's rights, human service agencies created to protect those rights often look back toward feudal England when children were considered property and a source of funds. The agencies seek to hide their actions from public view, often fight to diminish the rights of those they serve, and maneuver to place their own fiscal self-interests over the interests of their beneficiaries.

Agency confidentiality has permitted short-changed due process rights for children and other vulnerable individuals, and has kept the public largely in the dark regarding agency actions. Further, the agencies fight to subvert the legal struggles of vulnerable populations to claim their rights as their own—creating a cloak of power that has allowed human service agencies to use children and the poor in revenue maximization strategies.

Cloak of Power

The unfortunate flip in agency priority occurs, in part, because we allow it to occur. And we allow it to occur because we don't know. Owing to the hidden nature in which human service agencies and courts have often operated, the public is often simply unaware of agency practices. Further, as discussed in sections to follow, the diverted focus toward revenue maximization has been heightened by the control of agencies by their parent states—that are also in search of funds—and by the private sector capitalizing on the conflicts.

Actions taken by agencies and courts are often clouded within confidential systems and by an absence of due process. Regarding maltreated children, the parens patriae doctrine developed in America alongside early failings of the child welfare system and juvenile courts, systems in which the benign doctrine was often turned on its head to rationalize the denial of rights to children. Further, a denial of rights to mentally ill adults was similarly rationalized under the duty to protect.

Historically, courts and agencies viewed children as needing protection but undeserving of rights of their own. The juvenile courts and agencies reasoned that because they were the protectors of children's interests, they should be left alone to do their jobs without interference—

and certainly without legal rights provided to children that might disrupt or complicate decisions regarding the children's needs.

Then, in the 1967 landmark *In re Gault* decision, the U.S. Supreme Court recognized that children do in fact have constitutional rights of their own. Supreme Court Justice Fortas noted how the parens patriae doctrine had been inappropriately used to deny children their rights rather than to protect them: "The Latin phrase proved to be a great help to those who sought to rationalize the exclusion of juveniles from the constitutional scheme. "[23]

After the *In re Gault* case, courts began recognizing other children's rights and also solidified the duty of states to protect the welfare of children. However, children's rights are still often short-changed because the child welfare system continues to operate in the dark. Most foster care tribunals enforce confidentiality over proceedings, and state agency actions and procedures are also hidden from public view. In addition, such confidential systems and the lack of procedural safeguards apply to other vulnerable populations as well, whether in overwhelmed courts, agency tribunals with authority over services and programs for the poor, or in treatment facilities for the mentally ill.

Because juvenile court proceedings are also usually confidential, only a small handful of the hundreds of thousands of cases make it out to see the light of day through published appeals. The cases are often heard in overcrowded court dockets where jaded apathy can flourish:

> Set in Chicago's Near West Side, the juvenile courts and detention center (known colloquially as the Audy Home) were filthy, overcrowded, secretive, a haven for burnt-out judges, unaccountable, without published data, and a magnet for impoverished families and youngsters of color, primarily African-American children. Crowds of anxious parents and children were made to throng in the hallways, doors and toilet paper were missing in the bathrooms, public officials—judges, defenders and prosecutors, probation officers and court clerks—seemed not to look up as multitudes of accused were called forth and adjudged.[24]

This picture of juvenile courts is not uncommon, and is repeated in other tribunals and programs for the poor and disabled.

Further, in addition to the confidential nature of overcrowded courts, the actions and policies of human service agencies serving the vulnerable are also hidden. Agency records are often confidential or buried within a bureaucratic fog. Despite state laws that require public formal agency rule-making procedures, agency policies and practices are often established through informal and internal agency directives.

Agencies frequently fight against public disclosure of their records and practices, contending that confidentiality must be provided to protect the populations they serve. Then, within the confidential structure, the agencies often seek unfettered discretion—asserting that unquestioned and unexposed circumstances allow the agencies to do their best work on the behalf of their beneficiaries, and that judicial interference would violate the doctrines of sovereign immunity and separation of powers. For example, the level to which some agencies are averse to judicial review of their discretion is evident in a legal brief filed by the Georgia Department of Human Resources. Rather than focusing on the interests of children served by the agency, the Georgia agency asserts that its own rights to possess and make decisions regarding children are primary:

> When a deprived child is placed in the Department's temporary legal custody by a juvenile court, the Department "has the right to physical custody of the child, the right to determine the nature of the care and treatment of the child, including ordinary medical care, and the right and duty to provide for the care, protection, training, and education and the physical, mental, and moral welfare of the child."[25]

And then, the Georgia agency describes its disdain for the juvenile court's authority to review the agency decisions:

> Yet, the Court of Appeals' decision in the instant case ignores the express authority referenced above and now permits juvenile courts to render decisions regarding placement of children in the Department's custody, decisions which heretofore were deemed to be solely within the province of the Department . . . The net effect of this portion of the Court of Appeals' decision in this case permits any party which might disagree with placement decisions made by the Department to have those decisions

re-evaluated by the courts, thereby allowing the courts to assume the role of a "super placement agency" and thus abrogate the State's sovereign immunity. Such a role is not only improper for the courts, but also is violative of both the doctrines of sovereign immunity and separation of powers inherent in Georgia's Constitution.[26]

Most of us assume that human service agencies are generally pure in their pursuit of the best interests of their beneficiaries. We want to believe that an agency serving an abused and neglected child or vulnerable adult will strictly serve the welfare of that child or individual and put any conflicting interests aside. But in confidential systems with unfettered discretion as sought by the agencies like in Georgia, the rights of the vulnerable often give way to the self-interests of the agencies. Usually, the front-line caseworkers—although overburdened by high caseloads—are genuine in their desire to serve the best interests of children. However, the agency leaders are too often focused more on the financial bottom line.

Within the confidential systems, constitutional due process protections are often weak. The Supreme Court's decision in *Gault* provided a notable step toward stopping the misuse of the parens patriae doctrine that long deprived children of rights, and the decision recognized children's rightful place under the constitution. But, similar to the lack of adequate due process rights for other vulnerable populations, the practical application of children's due process rights has fallen short.

The long history of the child welfare system's view and actions against children's rights has not been overcome quickly. For example, although *Gault* provided children with the right to counsel in juvenile delinquency proceedings, the right to counsel has not yet been fully afforded to all children in child protection (foster care) proceedings. Also, although an individual's right to provide his own lawyer is recognized in other tribunals and issues impacting vulnerable children and adults, a lawyer or other advocate is often not provided for free. Thus, the vast majority of the poor try to navigate the systems without an advocate.

Even when rights for vulnerable children and adults have been recognized, the application of those rights is often truncated. As Professor Barbara Bennett Woodhouse explains, "[l]awyers and judges often dismiss or overlook children's due process concerns in civil cases, because the law has for so long been accustomed to treating children as parental property, lacking not only 'capacity' but personhood."[27] Some judges who are overwhelmed with large caseloads and jaded by years of exposure to the chaos of the child welfare system often only go through the motions of civil procedure and due process, and sometimes barely so. Much of the legwork might be shuffled down to judicial masters, with dockets even larger than the judges, who then often retreat to forcing settlements rather than seeking to uncover the necessary details to protect the best interests of the children. When a child does have a lawyer, they may meet for the first time in court because of the lawyer's crushing caseload. And the same practical barriers and limitations to the actual application of rights can impact other vulnerable populations as well.

Guardians Subverting the Rights of Their Wards

Seeking to protect their unfettered discretion, human service agencies unfortunately often fight against the rights of their own beneficiaries. The agencies exist as guardians, with their agency interests and actions intended to align with the best interests of the individuals they serve. It is thus a bitter irony when these guardians turn against those whose rights they are supposed to champion.

In case after case, as children and vulnerable adults struggle to expand their rights, their agency guardians are frequently engaged in the legal struggle as well. But, rather than aiding their beneficiaries, the agencies have often lined up against them. For example, fighting against foster children's asserted rights to a minimum quality of care, the Maryland child welfare agency argued: "the Due Process Clause does not itself impose on the State a generalized duty of optimal care, protection, and treatment to foster children, nor does due process demand that a state's administration of a system of foster care meet statutorily-defined professional standards."[28] Similarly, when a mentally ill patient at an Indiana state-run psychiatric hospital alleged he had been beaten and assaulted by hospital staff, he simply asked for his records so that his patient advocate could investigate his care. The Indiana agencies created to serve the disabled individual's interests fought against his rights by arguing against his request for access to his own records.[29]

At times, human service agencies seem to long for the past, when they were free to act without interference from constitutional rights.

Strikingly, the juvenile court judges of Ohio—the intended arbiters and ultimate protectors of juveniles—similarly pointed to the past in their impassioned argument against children's rights as amicus curiae in *Gault*. The judges looked to an 1882 decision to warn against placing constitutional limitations upon agency actions:

> It is the unquestioned right and imperative duty of every enlightened government, in its character of *parens patriae*, to protect and provide for the comfort and well-being of such of its citizens as, by reason of infancy * * * are unable to take care of themselves. The performance of this duty is justly regarded as one of the most important of governmental functions, and all constitutional limitations must be so understood and construed as not to interfere with its proper and legitimate exercise.[30]

In the practices of our nations' human service agencies, much has not changed. And as the agencies sometimes turn against their beneficiaries' attempts to establish and enforce their own rights, the agencies have also turned inward. The often-confidential nature of human service agencies and tribunals has allowed the agencies to focus on their own fiscal bottom line rather than solely protecting the best interests of the individuals they serve.

The turn inward has also encompassed a look back, with human service agencies acting similar to their ancestral roots in feudal England when the parens patriae doctrine was used to bring riches to the crown. But where the historical financial interests were aimed at children of wealthy landed gentry as a source of funds, today's agency self-interests are directed toward children and adults living in poverty.

Layers to the Conflict

Little is known about the details of agency actions in confidential bureaucracies, and often even less is known or understood about agency budget and revenue practices. As human service agencies have continued to face stagnant or shrinking budgets, they have increasingly turned to revenue maximization strategies. Agency self-preservation in such a cash-deprived environment has often overcome the interests of those served. The agencies rationalize their efforts as a means of growing capacity to serve children and adults in their care, but the fiscal strategies often result in taking resources directly from the intended beneficiaries without any corresponding increase or improvement in agency services.

This conflict between human service agencies' service mission and their own fiscal interests is further complicated on multiple interrelationship levels. These layers to the conflict are briefly introduced here, and explored in more detail in the chapters that follow.

First, the conflict exists within the fiscal federalism arrangement that provides the funding structure for many of the largest aid programs. Fiscal federalism aims to create a partnership between the relative strengths of the federal and state governments. The federal government's centralized power to raise revenue and withstand economic downturns is paired with the view that states are better able to understand and serve the more localized needs of their citizens. But the asserted strengths of state agencies in addressing regional and individualized needs often give way to self-interested revenue strategies. Fiscal federalism structure can add to this conflict. The complexities of the eligibility and claiming process of federal aid programs and the billions in funds potentially available encourage the state agencies to increase their gamesmanship and focus on the fiscal pursuit.

Second, the conflict between agency purpose and self-interest is further heightened by a growing private sector seeking to profit from the aid funds. Many companies have grown from the flow of money in federal aid programs and the desire of state agencies to maximize the federal funds. A web of contracts exists between private industry and state and federal governments to provide services in all aspects of government aid. And while taking on more and more operational services of poverty programs, private contractors are also aiming directly at the source of federal funds. As state agencies seek every dollar they can find, consultants have capitalized on the search by developing strategies to claim additional federal funds. Moreover, as poverty industry companies encourage state agencies to claim more federal aid dollars, the companies are also contracting with the federal government to monitor and reduce the pay out of those same federal funds.

Third, an additional conflict exists between the agencies' interests and the interests of their parent states. Human service agencies are subject to state control. As the agencies are searching for additional funds, so are the states. As a result, the additional federal funds from revenue maximization contracts often do not result in additional fiscal capacity for the human service agencies, but rather states often divert the funds into general revenue. Thus, the parens patriae power that is housed within state human service agencies—already diverted toward agency self-interest—is often further manipulated by the broader state powers. The states aim to control their agency-parts in order to serve themselves, and the intended welfare maximization goals of government are overcome by revenue maximization strategies.

Thus, the agencies often use children and the poor as a source of funds, states in turn often use their agencies as a source of funds—and the best interests- of the agency beneficiaries are often lost in the competing fiscal shuffle. The result is a conflict between agency purpose and self-interest, between the agencies and their parent states, and between the states and their agencies with the federal government. Rather than promoting collaboration between the federal and state governments, the self-interested practice—spurred on by the revenue maximization consultants—pits the levels of government against each other. As explained in more detail in the next chapter, the ideals of fiscal federalism are undermined as a result, and the interests of children and other vulnerable populations are harmed.

2

Poverty's Iron Triangle

With a tagline of "Helping Government Serve the People," MAXIMUS, Inc., grew from the basement of its founder in 1975 to become one of the world's largest private contractors for government aid programs.[1] The company is now "a leading operator of government health and human service programs in the United States, United Kingdom, Canada, Australia and Saudi Arabia," and "has more than 13,000 employees worldwide."[2] MAXIMUS is an example of a growing private sector that is profiting from government funds for the vulnerable.

As billions in aid funds flow through a complex regulatory framework, and as states try to claim their share, private companies have taken notice. Vast contractual interconnections between government and private contractors—focused on revenue maximization strategies—are undermining the legal and economic structure of America's government assistance programs and siphoning billions in aid from those in need.[3]

This chapter first explains the concept of fiscal federalism, an intended collaboration between the federal government and states in funding and operating America's largest government aid programs. The private sector of the poverty industry is then described, and examples are provided of how the poverty industry often includes pay-to-play tactics, a revolving door of personnel, contractors performing inherently governmental functions, and potential organizational conflicts of interest. Further, this chapter sets out a theoretical construct, poverty's iron triangle, to help describe the consequences of the interrelationships between government and private companies.

Fiscal federalism relies on a partnership of strengths: the federal government's financial power is paired with an asserted ability of states to better understand the regional needs of their citizens. But unfortunately, fiscal federalism theory ignores the interconnections between government and private sector contractors.

The resulting poverty industry is expansive, to the point where private companies now provide services in almost every aspect of government aid programs. And, in addition to running entire agency offices, some poverty industry contractors have also tapped into the money at its source—developing strategies to help states claim every possible dime of federal aid.

Underfunded state agencies defend contracts with revenue maximization consultants as necessary to improve their ability to maximize federal funding. However, the contracts frequently lead to improper claims. Agencies often rely on consultant recommendations without sufficient oversight, which can result in inappropriate claims for federal funds. Further, the poverty industry often diverts the additional federal aid resulting from the revenue strategies. The consultants take their cut as a contingency or flat fee, and the remaining funds are often routed by states into their general coffers. Through such practices, the intended beneficiaries of government aid continue to go without much-needed services while states siphon billions in federal funds for other uses.

The scope and character of the poverty industry is undermining the structure of America's safety net programs. Fiscal federalism's belief that state and county governments will better serve the regional needs of their unique populations does not contemplate a private sector working to maximize profit rather than the social welfare, and also does not contemplate states and their agencies seeking to serve themselves over their constituents. The theory's hope for collaboration between the federal and state governments has become a culture of conflict.

Further, although fiscal federalism only applies to certain programs such as the matching grant programs of Medicaid and Title IV-E, the structure and its failings resulting from the poverty industry are also interlinked with the other aid programs discussed in this book. Although each of the programs is distinct, with different structures and purposes, the aid programs are all often viewed by states and human service agencies as simply funding sources—interconnected with different tricks and strategies for the states and agencies to maximize the funds.

Practices within the poverty industry can result in conflict with statutory purpose and regulatory requirements, sometimes to the point of illegality. But even when illegalities are uncovered, growth of the poverty industry has continued. For example, in 2007, MAXIMUS agreed to pay $30.5 million to resolve an investigation by the U.S. Department of Justice (DOJ) into False Claims Act allegations.[4] In a deferred prosecution agreement, MAXIMUS acknowledged causing knowingly incorrect Medicaid claims as a revenue maximization consultant for the District of Columbia in which foster children were used to claim federal Medicaid funds.[5] The DOJ described the settlement as demonstrating "strong commitment to vigorously pursuing those companies that defraud the Medicaid program."[6]

However, MAXIMUS was almost inextricably linked to government agencies through numerous contracts to provide services in Medicaid, Medicare, and other aid programs. And the available sanction of exclusion from continued participation in federal aid programs was not included in the settlement.[7]

Within months of the settlement regarding allegedly fraudulent Medicaid claims, MAXIMUS won a contract with the state of New York to help prevent Medicaid fraud.[8] The District of Columbia extended the same Medicaid revenue maximization contract with MAXIMUS that resulted in the allegations.[9] From the time of the settlement in 2007 through the end of 2008, MAXIMUS entered into or extended contracts related to Medicaid or Medicare worth well over $200 million, including contracts directly with the Centers for Medicare and Medicaid Services (CMS)—the federal agency to whom the allegedly fraudulent claims had been submitted.[10] Then, one year after the DOJ settled its claims against MAXIMUS, the company won a contract within the DOJ itself, to provide "investigative and analytical support, consulting, technical services, financial management, and case-related professional support during the investigation and prosecution of criminal cases."[11] As another example, WellCare Healthplans, Inc. had a busy year in 2009.

In 2009, WellCare agreed to pay a $10 million Securities and Exchange Commission fine related to allegations of defrauding Florida's Medicaid and Healthy Kids programs.[12] The U.S. Centers for Medicare and Medicaid Services (CMS) also sanctioned the company for allegedly misleading beneficiaries and forging applications.[13] WellCare also acknowledged illegal campaign contributions to the Attorney General and the head of the state's health care agency.[14] Also, the company agreed to pay $80 million and entered into a three year deferred prosecution agreement in order to avoid criminal prosecution for alleged conspiracy to commit health care fraud.[15]

Then, in 2010, a whistleblower lawsuit was made public, with allegations that WellCare schemed to save money by removing neonatal babies and the terminally ill from its insurance rolls.[16] According to the lawsuit, "the company threw a celebratory dinner for the 'neonatal babies disenrollment team' after the team successfully removed 425 babies from its membership rolls."[17] Five former WellCare executives were indicted, and evidence also included "taped conversations between executives discussing how they could duplicate their bills to the state."[18] The company reached a settlement agreement with the U.S. Department of Justice, paying $137.5 million to settle allegations of violations under the False Claims Act.[19]

WellCare barely skipped a beat in its business success despite the legal concerns. The year after the Department of Justice began its criminal and civil investigations in 2006, the company named former U.S. Senator for Florida Bob Graham as a paid board director. WellCare then won a contract with the federal government to continue providing Medicare Part D prescription drug plans in all fifty states plus the District of Columbia.[20]

One month after federal and state agents raided WellCare's headquarters on a search warrant regarding alleged health care fraud, the company was selected as a Senior Choice Gold Award recipient.[21] When a WellCare employee's guilty plea was unsealed, acknowledging an alleged scheme to inflate health care bills, the company's stock rose by 3 percent on a day when the global markets plummeted.[22] One year after the whistleblower lawsuit in Florida was made public, the company won a contract to help run the Medicaid program in Kentucky in 7 out of 8 of the state's regions.[23] And the next year in Florida, WellCare brought out former Senator Graham to help its efforts to seek a new contract to manage the state's Medicaid programs by touting the company's corporate integrity.[24]

As illustrated by the MAXIMUS and WellCare examples, legal concerns and even criminal investigations have not slowed the poverty industry. The industry continues to expand as states continue to seek out private contractors, both with operational needs and in the continuing effort to develop revenue maximization strategies.

The impact of the poverty industry has been little understood due to practices that are hidden from public view and difficult to decipher once exposed. This chapter provides essential background before the details of specific poverty industry revenue strategies are explained.

The Flow of Federal Aid

This section explains fiscal federalism theory and describes the framework of two of the larger federal aid programs structured under the theory, Medicaid and Title IV-E Foster Care. Understanding the structure of these programs helps to provide a basis for then analyzing how the poverty industry is undermining the intended federal-state partnership in providing the needed aid. Further, as discussed above, although fiscal federalism structure does not directly apply to all of the aid programs discussed in this book, the programs are interlinked as the poverty industry pursues each type of aid.

Federalism

Federalism provides the governmental structure on which the United States was founded, sharing responsibility and power in the country's governance between the states and the national government:

> The balance in this partnership has continuously shifted to reflect America's changing practical necessities and political culture: from the tug-of-war at our country's founding between the Federalists' hopes for a strong central government and the Anti-Federalists' opposition to centralization; through the clash between national government and the states in the Civil War; into the Progressive Era and the Depression leading up to the New Deal and its centralized social welfare programs; shifting back towards state autonomy with Ronald Reagan's "New Federalism"; and a reassertion of central power during the more recent financial crisis.[25]

As the balance in power between the federal government and states has shifted throughout the years, several benefits of federalism have been consistently expressed. For example, in addition to promoting democracy and protecting against tyranny, federalism is often praised for allowing more flexibility in meeting regional needs and for promoting local experimentation in how to best provide needed government services.

Fiscal Federalism

As an offshoot of the broader concept of federalism, fiscal federalism is an economic theory that seeks cooperation between states and the federal government in financing and administering government programs for the vulnerable. Under the theory, the central government should provide financial stability in paying a significant part of program costs, and the decentralized state and local governments should take more control of program operations so that local needs and preferences are addressed. More simply, the central government should provide most of the funds and the state and local governments should run the programs.

Fiscal federalism theory includes a purist's view of government functions: that government exists to maximize the social welfare.[26] Thus, the theory assumes that federal, state, and local governments will each seek to maximize the social welfare of their respective populations. According to the reasoning, the decentralized state and local governments will focus on the unique and local needs of their constituencies, while the centralized federal government will aim to deliver a more uniform approach to serving the combined needs of the populations across the country.

Seeking to balance the strengths between the different levels of government, fiscal federalism theory provides the basis for federal grant-in-aid programs. The partnership between the federal and state governments is often described in terms of cooperation, highlighting the hopeful benefits from two levels of government cooperating to provide needed services. As examples of applied fiscal federalism, the following sections describe the framework of two specific federal grant-in-aid programs that are structured as matching grants, Medicaid and Title IV-E Foster Care.

Fiscal Federalism and Federal Aid: Medicaid and Title IV-E Foster Care

Two of the larger aid programs applying fiscal federalism theory are Medicaid and Title IV-E Foster Care. They are frequently targeted for private contractual services and have been the subject of federal scrutiny into revenue maximization strategies.

MEDICAID

Medicaid is the largest federal grant-in-aid program, enacted in 1965 to provide needed healthcare to the poor. Medicaid is an example of a matching program through which states receive federal payments to match state spending on healthcare services for low-income residents. Following fiscal federalism structure, state agencies administer the program. A formula called the federal medical assistance percentage (FMAP) determines the amount of federal matching payments a state can receive. The FMAP is based primarily on each state's relative wealth—so that states with less wealth generally receive greater federal match percentages. The federal matching payments are also called federal financial participation (FFP), and the payments are usually provided without caps to encourage states to increase their own spending on healthcare services for the poor. If a state spends more money on Medicaid-eligible services, the state can claim more federal matching payments.

Individuals who are eligible for Medicaid do not receive any Medicaid payments. Rather, after providing services to eligible individuals, the healthcare providers make claims to the state Medicaid agencies for payment. Those state payments then entitle the states to federal matching funds at the relative FMAP. The state may claim federal matching funds for the medical services provided as well as reimbursement for certain administrative costs in operation of the state Medicaid program.

Private consultants often assist in every level of the claiming process. First, healthcare providers hire private consultants to help maximize claims for payments from the state agencies. States then hire private contractors to audit and reduce the payout of those same payments. Simultaneously, state agencies and their parent states often hire private consultants to maximize claims for Medicaid funds from the federal government. And, completing circle, the federal government also hires poverty industry contractors to help audit the federal Medicaid payments and to review state agency practices.[27]

TITLE IV-E FOSTER CARE

The Title IV-E Foster Care program is also a matching grant program, with federal payments intended to increase the ability of states to provide foster care services. Just like Medicaid, states are required to spend their own money on eligible services in order to receive the matching federal payments. The amount that a state receives from the federal government is based on the same match percentage as the state's Medicaid match rate. The amount of funding available is generally only limited by the number of eligible children (and the amount of state match payments).

Although Title IV-E funds are considered income to the individual children, the federal payments are directed to the states to help increase and improve foster care services. Children do not receive an actual cash payment. And, in addition to receiving federal funds for foster care services, states can also seek federal Title IV-E funds to reimburse state administrative costs.

As with Medicaid, the eligibility rules for Title IV-E can be complex and burdensome. The rules require states to meet several legal and administrative requirements, including a core requirement that the child must have been removed from a poor family to be eligible for the federal funds.

Because of the complexity of Title IV-E eligibility requirements along with the desire of states to increase the federal funds, many states contract with revenue consultants. The contractors can help the states develop strategies to maximize the federal Title IV-E payments with as little state spending as possible. For example, a contractor may help a state develop strategies to increase its claimed administrative costs for purposes of federal reimbursement, and to increase its "penetration rate"—the percentage of children in the state's foster care system who are eligible for Title IV-E funding.

Scope of the Poverty Industry

This section describes the extent to which states are contracting with private companies for services related to government aid programs. To help illustrate the scope, examples are provided regarding pay-to-play tactics, the revolving door of personnel between government agencies and private contractors, possible organizational conflicts of interest, and contractors performing inherently governmental functions. Revenue maximization contracts are also explained, along with strategies to divert aid into general state revenue. Then, poverty's iron triangle is described—explaining the resulting impact of the poverty industry on the structure and perceived benefits of fiscal federalism theory.

The private sector is profiting from contracts in virtually every aspect of government services for the poor, from running entire government programs to simply making copies of government documents. Even huge military contractors have recognized the money that can be made from poverty-related programs. In addition to building warfare machines, Northrop Grumman sets up state Medicaid eligibility systems,[28] and helps states "locate non-custodial parents, establish paternity and equitable orders, and collect, distribute and disburse child support payments."[29] Lockheed Martin has also provided contractual services to assist with child support enforcement, and the company was chosen for a $124 million contract when the Social Security Administration needed help in making digital copies.[30] Similarly, many companies that became profitable providing entirely different services or products have now entered the poverty business, such as IBM and Xerox contracting to provide services to state Medicaid programs.

It's possible to buy stock in companies profiting from the poor. And larger corporations are buying or merging with such companies as they develop. Private equity firms such as the Carlyle Group and Bain Capital have bought up large national corporations that provide services regarding vulnerable populations.

Also, many private companies like MAXIMUS have grown with a primary focus related to poverty programs. The Public Consulting Group (PCG) was founded approximately ten years after MAXIMUS and also provides services to health and human service agencies and programs. Although still a fraction of the size of MAXIMUS, PCG has grown to more than forty offices across the United States, Canada, and Europe.[31] Similarly, Health Management Systems (HMS) provides contractual services related to government healthcare programs. Clients of HMS "include health and human services programs in more than 40 states,

. . . over 135 Medicaid managed care plans, the Centers for Medicare and Medicaid Services (CMS), and Veterans Administration facilities."[32]

When times are bad, poverty industry companies often thrive. While many company stocks were declining during the financial crisis of 2007–2008, MAXIMUS provided increased cash dividends to its share-holders.[33] The company explained in a 2008 earnings call that there were "more unemployed people and they look for job opportunities, and that plays right into the sweet spot for our welfare to work programs."[34] Similarly, in the third quarter of 2008, the holding corporation for HMS announced strong earnings.[35] The company's earning call transcript explains how the company benefits from economic turmoil: "In general, the macroeconomic environment continues to play its fiscal duress on our government clients, which in turn generates opportunity for HMS."[36] And HMS further described how the company prefers high unemployment rates: "We believe the economic backdrop for the remainder of 2008 and for 2009 will support continued strong demand for HMS's services. [T]he unemployment rate is the most important leading indicator of growth in the Medicaid program and growth in the Medicaid program was one of the most important drivers of HMS's revenue."[37]

The scope of private sector involvement with government programs for vulnerable populations is seemingly endless. As the next sections explain, the poverty industry is often spurred on by lobbying efforts, campaign contributions, and a revolving door of personnel between the government agencies and private contractors. The poverty industry has expanded to a point where it seems that any government task can be contracted out.

Pay-to-Play

Concerns regarding possible pay-to-play tactics have long been associated with the defense industry, where military contractors may seek to increase their chances of winning government contracts through campaign donations and lobbyists with insider connections. Now, such concerns have also been expressed regarding poverty-related contracts, and the poverty industry is apparently beating the defense industry at the pay-to-play game.

In 2011, the defense industry spent in excess of $134 million on government lobbying efforts.[38] Impressive. But the healthcare industry spent almost four times that amount—more than half a billion dollars, including a significant focus on lobbying related to government healthcare programs for the poor.[39] The defense industry also spent almost $24 million in 2011 on campaign contributions,[40] but the healthcare industry multiplied that amount by almost eleven.[41] In fact, campaign contributions made only on behalf of hospitals and nursing homes were about equal to all the campaign contributions made on behalf of the entire defense industry.[42]

Numerous circumstances illustrate concerns regarding pay-to-play allegations in the poverty industry. For example, Illinois Governor "Rod" Blagojevich became infamous in 2008 for allegations of trying to sell a U.S. Senate seat, and a few years before that he faced scrutiny for contract dealings with MAXIMUS. Stories in the *Chicago Sun Times* reported on state contracts and possible links to campaign contributions to Governor Blagojevich.[43] MAXIMUS helped Illinois develop a revenue maximization plan to increase claims for federal Medicaid and other aid funds. Then, according to the paper, the company was "handed a waiver from state contracting rules by Blagojevich's administration so it [could] bid on the lucrative contract proposal it helped the state develop."[44] MAXIMUS reportedly gave more than $25,000 to Blagojevich's political fund, and the company's lobbying firm hired Blagojevich's former congressional chief of staff and donated more than $80,000 to the governor.[45] Blagojevich's predecessor, former Governor James R. Thompson, has been a member of MAXIMUS's board of directors since 2001, and he was also the co-chairman of Blagojevich's transition committee in 2003.

Further, when MAXIMUS faced the possibility of losing a $32 million welfare-to-work contract with Los Angeles County, the company reportedly increased its lobbying efforts.[46] The county's human service agency apparently chose another company's bid.[47] However, according to the *Los Angeles Times*, MAXIMUS then spent $200,000 in lobbying fees and thousands more in campaign contributions,[48] and the county supervisors voted to re-bid the contract so MAXIMUS could have another chance.[49]

Other private contractors have faced similar questions regarding alleged pay-to-play tactics. Centene Corporation contracts to run state

Medicaid managed-care plans and to provide other services related to healthcare programs for vulnerable populations. According to the *St. Louis News Dispatch*, the Missouri Medicaid agency terminated a contract with a subsidiary of Centene, SynCare LLC, in 2011 for failing to fulfill contractual obligations regarding eligibility services for elderly Medicaid patients.[50] But one year later, another subsidiary of Centene was chosen to help manage Missouri's statewide Medicaid managed-care program. According to news reports, Centene used a dozen lobbyists, including one of the closest advisors to Missouri Governor Jay Nixon, and the company and its executives gave more than $400,000 in campaign contributions to Missouri politicians.[51] Sitting on the board of directors of Centene is Richard Gephardt, former congressman from Missouri who served as U.S. House Majority Leader.[52] The chief executive officer of Centene, Michael Neidorff, was quoted by the *Wall Street Journal* as saying, "I call a governor, I usually get a call back within 24 to 48 hours."[53]

Deloitte Consulting has also been mentioned in pay-to-play allegations. A 2008 story in Pennsylvania's *Patriot-News* explained how Deloitte Consulting received more than $400 million in state contracts, primarily with the Department of Public Welfare.[54] The story described connections between Deloitte and Governor Rendell's administration, and that Deloitte employees made significant campaign contributions to Governor Rendell and other Pennsylvania elected officials.[55] In 2009, after extensive criticism, Rendell announced that he "would sign legislation to ban the practice of awarding state contracts to large political donors, maintaining that his administration hasn't engaged in so-called 'pay-to-play' activity."[56]

By 2011, under the new administration of Governor Tom Corbett, Deloitte received another contract with the Department of Public Welfare, worth a quarter of a billion dollars. According to the *Patriot-News*, the new contract was again the subject of allegations and concerns regarding the state's bidding process, but state representative Glen Grell explained there had been no favoritism for Deloitte.[57] Both Rep. Grell and Governor Corbett had worked under Pennsylvania governor Tom Ridge. Grell previously handled contract review and approval for the Ridge administration.[58] Corbett had also been appointed by Ridge as state attorney general. Ridge joined Deloitte as an advisor in 2006.[59]

Revolving Door

In addition to concerns regarding possible pay-to-play tactics, a revolving door of personnel exists between government agencies and private companies of the poverty industry. As Pennsylvania faced scrutiny regarding its contracts with Deloitte, discussed above, multiple personnel were changing hands. In addition to former governor Tom Ridge, other examples of the apparent revolving door between Deloitte and Pennsylvania state officials include:

- A former Deloitte partner served as the state's chief information officer and then became the governor's deputy chief.[60]
- The deputy chief information officer for health and human services was a Deloitte public sector consultant.[61]
- The state's deputy secretary for procurement for the Department of General Services was married to a Deloitte partner.[62]
- A senior manager for Deloitte became the state's chief information officer, and then returned to her same position at Deloitte after leaving public service.[63]

Also, former Wisconsin governor Tommy Thompson offered his services to Deloitte alongside former Pennsylvania governor Tom Ridge. While governor of Wisconsin, Thompson was nationally known for trying to privatize welfare and other poverty programs,[64] and former president George W. Bush named Thompson as his secretary of the U.S. Department of Health and Human Services.[65] When he left his federal post, Thompson received multiple positions in the private sector: he joined Deloitte Consulting as a chair of the Center for Health Care Management and Transformation;[66] he became a partner with Akin Gump Strauss Hauer & Feld LLP, where he focused on healthcare industry and public sector clients;[67] and he joined the boards of directors of multiple private companies in the healthcare field—including joining former U.S. House Majority Leader Richard Gephardt as a member of the board of directors for Centene Corporation.[68]

Other poverty industry companies also provide examples of the exchange of personnel. For example, the founder of the Public Consulting Group (PCG) was previously the assistant revenue director for the

Massachusetts Department of Mental Health and Mental Retardation.[69] And several other former government officials are part of the company's personnel roster:

- former eligibility director for Wisconsin Medicaid[70]
- a former Medicaid policy specialist with the U.S. Health Care Financing Administration (now Centers for Medicare & Medicaid Services)[71]
- former deputy budget director of the Executive Office of Health and Human Services, Commonwealth of Massachusetts[72]
- former deputy education advisor to the governor of Massachusetts[73]
- former CFO and budget director for the Massachusetts Medicaid Program[74]
- former acting Medicaid director and bureau chief, Medicaid Policy for the state of New Hampshire[75]
- former deputy director for the District of Columbia's Developmental Disabilities Administration[76]
- former director of IDEA Early Childhood Services in the Tennessee Department of Education[77]
- former Chief Counsel, Region I, for the U.S. Department of Health and Human Services[78]
- former presiding judge of the Marion Superior Court, Juvenile Division in Indiana[79]

Also, MAXIMUS has hired former government leaders. For example, the company's president, Human Services North America, was the chief legal counsel for the New Hampshire division of child support.[80] The company's Human Services president and general manager was deputy district director of the Los Angeles County Department of Public Social Services.[81] And the MAXIMUS board of directors includes the former deputy associate commissioner for the Massachusetts Department of Public Welfare, Russell A. Beliveau; the former mayor of Denver, Colorado, Wellington E. Webb; and the former governor of Illinois, James R. Thompson, Jr.[82]

Organizational Conflicts of Interest

Louisiana governor Bobby Jindal has been a proponent of privatizing government programs, including his state's Medicaid program. It was therefore no surprise that Jindal tapped someone from the private sector, Bruce Greenstein, to direct the Louisiana state healthcare agency. When scandals occurred, Jindal has blamed big government.[83] But it was Greenstein's private sector connections in his effort to increase privatization that brought contracting concerns to the Jindal administration.

When the Louisiana healthcare agency initially contracted with Deloitte to build a new eligibility determination system, the contract did not require any specific type of software. However, when Greenstein arrived, he reportedly added a contract requirement to use "Microsoft Dynamics"—a computer program sold by Microsoft Corporation.[84] Greenstein had been Microsoft's director of worldwide health that included increasing Microsoft's offerings for healthcare IT needs, so his push to add a requirement to use software of his former employer raised conflict of interest concerns.[85] One month later, Louisiana canceled the contract.

The cancelation also came shortly after Greenstein resigned his post because of another contract concern, involving another of his prior employers. Before leading Microsoft's healthcare offerings, Greenstein was a vice president of CNSI, Inc. According to the *Times-Picayune*, when Louisiana chose CNSI for a $200 million Medicaid contract, Greenstein denied any involvement in the contract decision and said he had no communications with CNSI related to the contract proposal.[86] But according to news reports, he admitted in his confirmation hearing that he pushed for changes in the bid solicitation that made his former employer eligible for the contract.[87] Further, later reports indicate he had "hundreds of telephone calls and thousands of text messages" with CNSI management during the bid and contract award process.[88] As a result of increasing press and a federal investigation into the contract process, Greenstein resigned his post and the contract with CNSI was canceled.[89]

Possible conflicts of interest such as those in Louisiana can be prohibited under state or federal contracting rules. For example, federal rules attempt to limit organizational conflicts of interest (OCIs) that may result when companies perform multiple types of government contract work that may be at odds with each other—and from the revolving door of personnel between government and private contractors.[90]

However, despite the federal and state rules, potential and actual conflicts of interest are commonplace. Ironically—and disturbingly—a July 2012 report by the U.S. Department of Health and Human Services Office of Inspector General (OIG) uncovered a vast number of such concerns: In contracts with private companies to improve the integrity of the Medicare program, rampant potential conflicts of interest were present that could undercut the integrity of the contractual work.

CMS sought offers from private companies to serve as "Zone Program Integrity Contractors" (ZPICs), who were to be tasked with fighting fraud and abuse in the Medicare program. The OIG report focused on conflicts of interest, because of concern that ZPICs with conflicts of interest may be "less vigilant in combating fraud" and "taxpayer dollars may be wasted on payments to unscrupulous providers." Despite the concern, the report uncovered the following:

- The eighteen offers from companies bidding on the contract resulted in almost 2,000 actual and potential conflicts of interest.
- The majority of the conflicts appeared with the five offerors who were ultimately chosen as the Medicaid "Zone Program Integrity Contractors."
- A single subcontractor associated with three offerors that were awarded ZPIC contracts accounted for 1,231 possible conflicts.
- Of the five successful offers, there were ten circumstances of "impaired objectivity," which means "the offeror or subcontractor could be in the position of evaluating work performed or associated with its own company."
- The contracting process required offerors to propose methods to mitigate conflicts of interest. The most common mitigation strategy proposed was simply to assert that information and resource sharing would be limited.
- Of the more than 2,500 mitigation strategies proposed by offerors, only three were to include later audits in order to actually follow up on the conflict concerns.[91]

At the time of the OIG report, CMS had no written policy for reviewing conflicts of interest information. Despite the almost 2,000 potential and actual conflicts of interest in these contracts that were intended to improve program integrity, CMS did not disqualify a single offeror.[92]

Possible conflicts of interest may also exist but have either gone un-noticed or do not fall within the technical reach of the OCI process. For instance, the Public Consulting Group (PCG) landed a contract in 2010 with North Carolina to be the "Medicaid Program Integrity" contractor in order to reduce inappropriate Medicaid claims by healthcare provid-ers.[93] Simultaneously, the company also had contracts to help hospitals in North Carolina to increase Medicaid claims: "We've helped public, state-operated hospitals in North Carolina to generate more than $200 million in additional non-state funds (Medicare, Medicaid, DSH and Commercial Insurance) in the last 10 years and continue to provide $7 million to $10 million annually for these providers."[94]

Also, a 2005 report by the U.S. General Accounting Office (GAO) highlighted conflicting contracts in Massachusetts.[95] The University of Massachusetts Medical School (UMMS) is a public entity, but includes a consulting division that contracts with state agencies to maximize claims for federal aid (and to provide other services).[96] UMMS was under a contingency fee contract to maximize school-based Medicaid claims in Massachusetts while simultaneously contracting with the state on a con-tingency fee basis to monitor the integrity and appropriateness of such school-based Medicaid claims. Thus, UMMS was apparently getting paid a percentage of increased Medicaid claims it prepared while also getting paid a percentage of the same types of Medicaid claims it decreased.[97] However, Massachusetts would not acknowledge the conflict: "Massa-chusetts disagreed with our view that UMMS's role as a contingency-fee consultant working for school districts to prepare their claims and as a contingency-fee consultant working for the state to monitor school dis-trict claims creates the appearance of a conflict of interest."[98]

Inherently Governmental Functions

Concerns also exist that contractors should not carry out certain types of government functions, because of the government authority and discretion required. Federal contracting policy prohibits private con-tractors from performing "inherently governmental functions," defined by the Office of Management and Budget as follows: "[A]n activity that is so intimately related to the public interest as to mandate perfor-mance by government personnel. These activities require the exercise of substantial discretion in applying government authority and/or in making decisions for the government."[99]

The limitation is interpreted as prohibiting private companies from making decisions regarding eligibility for government benefits.[100] However, when revenue maximization contractors help states to maximize their eligibility claims for federal aid, the companies often help with making eligibility determinations. Even if state government personnel make the final decisions whether to submit claims for federal aid by signing off on contractor recommendations, the role can be illusory. States often rely on the contractor recommendations without meaningful agency oversight.[101] For example, an audit by the U.S. Department of Health and Human Services, Office of Inspector General, examined school-based Medicaid claims in Washington State and found that the use of contingency-fee revenue maximization consultants "may increase the risk of claims being submitted that were not properly scrutinized for allowable costs."[102] The report concluded, "[t]he school district relied almost entirely on the consultant to calculate the claim and submit it to the State."[103] In such circumstances, even if the government personnel sign off on the final claims, the extent of reliance on the contractor for preparing the claims for federal aid can conflict with the spirit of the inherently governmental limitation.

The prohibition has been weakened by a countervailing effort to increase the privatization of government services. The very rule prohibiting private contractors from performing inherently governmental functions was amended in 2003 to expand the use of private contractors. The Federal Activities Inventory Reform (FAIR) Act requires government agencies to take inventories and determine every possible government activity that might be contracted out.

This pressure to increase privatization led to confusion over the limits on privatization, and the poverty industry has not shied away from the vagueness—often pushing the boundaries of acceptable contractor work. We have reached a point where private contractors are even reviewing private contracts. For example, in an announcement from the Substance Abuse and Mental Health Services Administration, the agency explained that it "does not maintain adequate resources to support the number of contract proposal reviews that require detailed cost and price analysis and financial audits" and therefore needed assistance from private contractors to help with the contract review process.[104]

Thus, regardless of limitations on companies performing inherently governmental functions, companies within the poverty industry are now performing virtually every function related to aid programs for vulnerable populations. And in addition to providing operational services related to government aid programs, the next section explains how the companies are profiting by helping states to increase the amount of federal aid.

Money Guides: Revenue Maximization Consultants

Companies within the poverty industry have inserted themselves directly into the flow of aid money, recognizing a profitable niche of developing revenue maximization expertise and helping states to increase claims for the federal funds. During lean economic times, as states seek revenue from almost any available source and as human service agencies look to offset budget cuts, such revenue maximization contracts have expanded as a way to bolster revenue.

Consultants help states to maximize federal funds in numerous ways, often targeting the Medicaid program or Title IV-E Foster Care program, and even helping foster care agencies take assets directly from foster children. In the Title IV-E foster care program, contractors encourage states to establish "penetration rate" strategies focused on increasing the percentage of foster children eligible for funding because they were removed from low-income families and meet the other eligibility requirements. The contractors also develop tactics to increase claims for federal funds for administrative and training costs—including such methodologies as Random Moment Time Studies (RMTS) that push the limit to increase claims for administrative costs.

Strategies to increase claims of federal Medicaid dollars are even more extensive. According to the U.S. General Accounting Office (GAO), most states were using contingency-fee contractors to increase Medicaid claims as of 2004, and the numbers were growing.[105] Chapter 4 provides a more detailed discussion of specific Medicaid maximization strategies. But to highlight the scope here, revenue strategies developed by private consultants in just two states from 2000 to 2004 resulted in increased claims for federal Medicaid funds of more than $2 billion—with the consultants taking more than $90 million of the funds as a contingency fee.[106] While chairman of the U.S. Senate Committee on Finance, Senator Charles Grassley communicated concerns to the secretary of the U.S. Department of Health and Human Services: "I am extremely disconcerted that Medicaid monies intended to benefit low-income Americans, pregnant women and poor children, may instead be lining the coffers of consulting firms."[107] A resulting 2005 report by the GAO expressed an urgency: "[t]he concerns we identified with the appropriateness of states' Medicaid claims stemming from contingency-fee projects illustrate the urgent need to address the issues we have identified with CMS's overall financial management of the Medicaid program."[108]

However, the use of private contractors to maximize state claims for federal aid continues to grow. Georgia provides a state view of the need for revenue maximization contractors:

> The Medicaid statute has been called "among the most completely impenetrable texts within human experience. . . . Congress also revisits the area frequently, generously cutting and pruning in the process and making any solid grasp of the matters addressed merely a passing phase." (citation omitted) It is nearly impossible for state Medicaid agency staff to keep abreast of the multitude of both new requirements and new opportunities that result from Congress' frequent amendments to the Medicaid law. [109]

The Georgia agency therefore explains that "[t]his complexity can and does compel states to turn to expert consultants for assistance."[110]

Thus, state use of revenue maximization consultants is not slowing. If the practice led to more efficient access and effective use of aid funds to best assist those in need, the revenue strategies should be applauded. But unfortunately, such is often not the case.

Maximizing and Diverting Federal Aid into State Revenue

As asserted by Georgia in the preceding text, states have struggled under complex rules and lack of sufficient capacity and expertise to maximize claims for federal aid. Such frustration, combined with an economic and political environment in which states are seeking non-tax revenue, provides rationale for states and human service agencies to use the revenue strategies discussed in this book. However, the moneys intended for the vulnerable are often diverted for other use.

Supplantation and General Revenue Enhancement

Rather than helping agencies leverage federal funds to provide increased services to those in need, the poverty industry revenue practices are often undermining the statutory purpose of the aid funds. The revenue strategies (also sometimes referred to as "refinancing") often result in the money being diverted into a state budget black hole. Mark Friedman, who worked for about twenty years with the Maryland Department of Human Resources, including six years as the agency's chief financial officer, should be aware of such concern.[111] And twenty years ago, he wrote just that:

> One of the great dangers of refinancing work is the risk that money produced by such efforts will not be used to advance the reform agenda for families and children. Refinancing proceeds usually take the form of state or local general fund revenue, which can be used for many different purposes, not necessarily those related to reform. . . . Without some way to protect the freed up money, it is likely that refinancing funds will return to the general treasury to be used for whatever priorities appear on the state or local political agenda at the time.[112]

The diversion of federal aid causes tension between the federal government and the states, and between states and their local human service agencies. The Urban Institute explains how the federal government's view of federal aid programs aligns with statutory purpose, to increase total funding for needed safety net services by providing federal funds along with incentives for states to simultaneously spend more on the programs themselves: "[T]he purpose of federal entitlement and block grant programs is to finance safety net provisions more adequately; the federal formulas are intended to give states incentives to spend more on necessary programs they would not otherwise (fully) fund because of prohibitive cost."[113] Unfortunately, however, states often view federal aid as simply a means of replenishing their general coffers. For example, congressional testimony by the GAO regarding revenue maximization schemes explains how Medicaid funds are often not used for Medicaid purposes:

> There is no assurance that these increased federal reimbursements are used for Medicaid services. . . . In examining how six states with large schemes used the federal funds they generated, we previously found that one state used the funds to help finance its education programs, and others deposited the funds into state general funds or other special state accounts that could be used for non-Medicaid purposes or to supplant the states' share of other Medicaid expenditures.[114]

A GAO report regarding school-based Medicaid claims found that the federal Medicaid funds often went to the respective states' general coffers, rather than to provide additional Medicaid services to children in the schools. In one of the states reviewed, schools received only $7.50 of every $100 in federal Medicaid funds claimed on behalf of Medicaid-eligible schoolchildren.[115]

In addition to increased tension between the federal government and states by the diversion of funds, human service agencies are also frustrated as funds intended for them to provide additional services are instead used by their parent states: "[f]rom a local perspective, any additional local or federal funds should be used to expand a program, not relieve the burden on state general revenue."[116]

Examples of supplantation (replacing required state spending with federal funds) and diverted federal aid are commonplace. Such diversion of federal aid occurs both with complex revenue maximization schemes and also with more direct grants of aid. For example, state and federal governments negotiated for billions in housing aid in 2012 through a nationwide legal settlement with large banks regarding their mortgage and foreclosure practices. But several states then took a significant part of the aid intended for assisting families with foreclosure prevention and simply directed the money into state general revenue.[117] Similarly, Louisiana governor Bobby Jindal took $666 million in federal stimulus funds and used the money to "replace general fund dollars" rather than to increase services for the vulnerable as intended.[118]

Former U.S. senator Judd Gregg was briefly named as a bipartisan pick for commerce secretary in the Obama administration before he became a critic of Obama's increased spending on federal aid pro-grams to address the economic downturn and budget difficulties faced by states.[119] However, as described in the introduction, when Senator Gregg was governor of New Hampshire and faced his own state budget deficit, he came up with a plan to claim additional federal Medicaid matching funds without spending state funds as the required matching payments. Then, he took all the federal Medicaid funds and diverted the money for general state purposes. He even established a general revenue line item in his state budget called "Medicaid Enhancement Revenue." In the first year of his scheme, Gregg's strategy of diverting federal aid accounted for 28 percent of New Hampshire's total general fund revenue. Gregg balanced the budget in New Hampshire by taking aid from the poor, and governors who succeeded Gregg continued his legacy.[120]

While not always as overt, and as described in more detail in the chapters that follow, countless examples exist of states maximizing and then diverting federal aid into general state coffers. For example:

- Maine introduced emergency legislation to address state budget concerns, including a provision to "[a]uthorize the Department of Behavioral and Developmental Services to credit Title IV-E [foster care] federal reimbursement to the General Fund as undedicated revenue."[121]
- An Arizona budget report regarding a "Federal Revenue Maximization Initiative" explained how the savings created by the initiative "were not allocated to specific agency budgets; rather they were assumed as part of the overall 'balance sheet.'"[122]
- Another Arizona report describes the revenue maximization initiative, contracting with Public Consulting Group (PCG) to review past foster care placements to increase claims for federal foster care funds. After PCG received its contingency fees, the remainder was used to offset "continuing budget shortfalls" as well as to cover state budget reductions. The report explains how two revenue maximization projects—one to increase the number of children receiving Title IV-E assistance and another to increase the amount of reimbursed Title IV-E administrative costs—were coordinated with state budget reductions of $500,000 and $900,000 made by the state legislature in anticipation of the increased federal revenue resulting from the projects.[123]

As efforts to maximize and divert aid funds have continued to grow, efforts to audit and clamp down on inappropriate claiming of federal aid have likewise increased. Poverty industry contractors are hired to help increase claims for aid funds. And then, as concern grows, contractors are also hired to audit and reduce payout of those same funds.

Poverty Industry Auditing the Poverty Industry

In the Medicaid program, healthcare providers make claims to state agencies for Medicaid payments to reimburse services provided to eligible individuals. Then, the states make claims for federal Medicaid matching funds to match payments the states give to the healthcare providers. Revenue maximization consultants are present at both levels: healthcare providers hire private companies to help them maximize Medicaid reimbursements from the state agencies, and the states hire companies to help claim more Medicaid funds from the federal government.

With so much money changing hands, concern regarding fraud and error is always present. Thus, in addition to maximizing Medicaid claims, poverty industry companies have also recognized money to be made by helping to audit and reduce Medicaid payments. Private consultants may be receiving contingency fees to maximize aid payments, while consultants are simultaneously receiving contingency fees to reduce the payments.

In the Medicare and Medicaid programs, examples of the poverty industry auditing the poverty industry are plentiful. Contractors are hired in numerous auditing and oversight functions, creating a growing list of acronyms:

- MACs (Medicare Administrative Contractors)
- Medicare RACs (Medicare Recovery Audit Contractors)
- Medicaid RACs (Medicaid Recovery Audit Contractors)
- MICs (Medicaid Integrity Contractors)
- ZPICs (Medicare Zone Program Integrity Contractors)
- PSCs (Program Safeguard Contractors)
- MEDICs (Medicare Part D Prescription Drug Integrity Contractors)
- QICs (Qualified Independent Contractors)

Some of the companies represented by the acronyms, all intended to reduce fraud and improve integrity within the Medicaid and Medicare programs, have been investigated for alleged fraudulent activities themselves. And some of the companies have competing interests, including being hired to audit the work of subsidiaries, business partners, or parent or sister companies.

Further, data have now shown that contracts with private companies to audit claims for federal aid are sometimes costing more money than the resulting savings from decreased federal aid payments. In 2012, the federal government audited the auditors and found that the cost of the Medicaid Integrity Program—implemented by the private contractors— was more than five times the resulting overpayments uncovered by the contractors.[124]

Cutting Services While Maximizing and Diverting Aid

While contractors profit from helping to both maximize and reduce payments of aid funds, and while states divert the federal aid from its intended purpose, the vulnerable receive no additional services and their prior existing services are often simultaneously cut. For example, as described in chapter 3, Kentucky hired private contractors to obtain foster children's Social Security benefits as agency revenue. Meanwhile, Kentucky froze the kinship care stipend program that would normally pay small amounts to help family members care for abused and neglected children.[125]

As another example, Montana legislation required a statewide "refinancing" effort by the state's human service agency to replace state spending with increased federal aid funds.[126] Budget documents related to the Child and Family Services Division noted a resulting state general fund savings from the refinancing effort of $3 million each year for fiscal years 2004 and 2005.[127] Then, while describing how $3 million in federal aid was diverted from services to the poor to state general savings, the budget document simultaneously lists millions in cuts to services: requests to cut the agency's funding for in-home services by more than $1.1 million, eliminate funding for the Big Brothers Big Sisters Program for savings of more than $183,000, eliminate the approximately $325,000 in funding for Child Protective Services Day Care, cut funding for the Domestic Violence Program by more than $77,000, and cut staff positions for savings exceeding $261,000.[128] Such practices of diverting federal aid while simultaneously cutting services cause even more harm to the vulnerable populations.

The Subversion of Fiscal Federalism in Federal Aid Programs

Fiscal federalism suggests that state and local governments should run government aid programs in order to better serve regional needs, but that goal is undermined when the goal of maximizing social welfare is replaced with strategies to maximize revenue. The hope for a collaborative partnership between the federal government and states has instead become a relationship of tension and distrust as states maximize and divert federal funds and the federal government struggles to stop the practices. Private contractors of the poverty industry benefit from the conflict—profiting from the flow of money both coming and going. Thus, the poverty industry is undermining the potential benefits of fiscal federalism and is subverting the structure and intended purpose of federal aid.

Poverty's Iron Triangle

The "iron triangle" is a political science model that describes the self-serving interrelationships between government and the private sector and their influence over government policy and funding. This section sets out a new variation of the traditional iron triangle in order to frame the discussion of the poverty industry's impact on fiscal federalism and federal aid programs.

Iron triangles illustrate how the intended purposes of government programs can be diverted to serve the self-interests of government and private actors—to the detriment of the public interest. In his farewell address, President Eisenhower warned against the growth of such an iron triangle within the "military-industrial complex" of defense contracting:

> Now this conjunction of an immense military establishment and a large arms industry is new in the American experience. The total influence— economic, political, even spiritual—is felt in every city, every Statehouse,

every office of the Federal government. We recognize the imperative need for this development. Yet, we must not fail to comprehend its grave implications. Our toil, resources, and livelihood are all involved. So is the very structure of our society. In the councils of government, we must guard against the acquisition of unwarranted influence, whether sought or unsought, by the military-industrial complex. The potential for the disastrous rise of misplaced power exists and will persist. We must never let the weight of this combination endanger our liberties or democratic processes.[129]

Unfortunately, President Eisenhower's warning was not heeded and the iron triangle of the military-industrial complex became an example of how funds intended to serve the public can be diverted to benefit the self-interests of government actors and private defense contractors.

The iron triangle construct is typically used to describe concerns at the federal government level, with the top corner of the triangle occupied by the U.S. Congress with control over legislation and funds. At another corner you find federal agencies, who are intended to serve a public function but are seeking to expand their power base. The private sector then lies at the third corner, hoping to influence and profit from the laws and government funds flowing from Congress to the federal bureaucracy.[130] Noticeably, the intended beneficiaries of the government services are not included in the triangle.

The Congressional Research Service (CRS) is the research division of the Library of Congress that provides nonpartisan reports and analysis to members of Congress. The CRS issued a report in 2006 with caution about privatization in the federal government: "[c]ontracting out can promote iron triangles and other corrupt relationships between the federal government and the private sector."[131]

A variation of the iron triangle provides a framework to consider the impact of the poverty industry. For poverty's iron triangle, the federal government is at the apex, and the state governments and private sector are at the other corners. The line between the federal and state governments represents the intended vertical fiscal federalism relationship, and the private contractors then hold the third corner with lines to both the federal and state governments. Further, through the revenue maximiza-

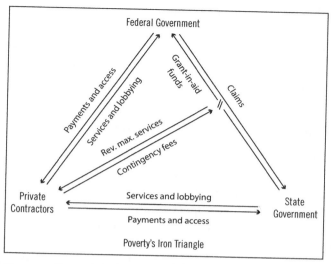

Figure 2.1. Poverty's iron triangle.

tion role, the private sector also cuts a line from its corner through the middle of the triangle to tap into the funds from the federal government to the states. And, like the result in traditional iron triangles, the intended consumers of the government aid services—children and the poor—are left out of the triangular relationship, as depicted in figure 2.1.

Poverty's iron triangle does not follow the traditional iron triangle norms, because it occurs across the levels of state and federal governments and the private sector has inserted itself through contractual relationships at all levels of government. Also, traditional iron triangles are described with a strong "cozy triangle" structure that is mutually beneficial to each corner. Poverty's iron triangle is instead a destabilized relationship, with the private sector targeting the interests of each level of government and adding to intergovernmental conflict.

However, while poverty's iron triangle does not follow traditional iron triangle theory, the variation is helpful: it illustrates the distortive effects of the poverty industry on the intended structure and benefits of fiscal federalism. Fiscal federalism only considers the relationship of funding and regulation between the federal government and state governments, only one side of the triangle. Poverty's iron triangle provides context to consider the impact of the other lines of the triangle, the relationships between the private sector and the federal and state governments, and the insertion of revenue maximization consultants cutting across the triangle. The additional lines comprise the poverty industry, and the impact is significant.

Social Welfare Maximization Yields to Revenue Maximization

Fiscal federalism is founded on idealism. The theory presumes that government is guided by the pure goal of maximizing the social welfare of its citizens. Because each level and location of government should be guided by the needs of its respective populations, each decentralized government is presumed to be better suited to maximize the welfare of its local constituencies.

Applied to federal aid programs, fiscal federalism's idealistic views come with an unstated but obvious assumption—that government functions in maximizing the welfare of vulnerable citizens will be carried out by government actors. Fiscal federalism theory fails to recognize the increasing role of the private sector in aid programs.

The perceived strength of local governments to better meet the needs of local constituencies is undermined when the government function is contracted out to private companies focused on maximizing profit rather than social welfare. Further, fiscal federalism theory also fails to account for the fiscal self-interests of states and their agencies. In the revenue maximization strategies developed with private contractors, states are focused on their own bottom line rather than on how to best use federal aid for the vulnerable. Under a welfare maximization strategy, states would only consider the specific needs of their impoverished citizens and the best means of meeting those needs. However, under the revenue maximization strategies of the poverty industry, states pursue the goal of increasing federal funds regardless of specific needs, often diverting the funds from their intended purpose while simultaneously supplanting state spending.

Undermining Intergovernmental Collaboration

The Medicaid program must be a Federal-State partnership,
not an exercise in financing gamesmanship.[132]

At the outset, when two different levels of government share the financing and administration of aid programs, tension will surely exist. This inherent tension can have a positive impact if the federal and state governments can work through their differing perspectives and reach agreement on the best means of serving those in need. But, unfortunately, the tension between the federal and state governments in the funding and operations of aid programs is turning toward unhealthy conflict as the poverty industry practices pit each level of government against the other.

Poverty industry revenue maximization strategies cause significant frustration to the federal government as the strategies undermine the purpose of the federal funds. Such frustration is evidenced by countless federal audits of state revenue strategies and also by policy reports condemning the revenue schemes. Then, as private companies increase the intergovernmental conflict by encouraging state revenue practices, the poverty industry contractors simultaneously profit by contracting with the federal government to reduce inappropriate claims for federal aid. As the tension builds, the poverty industry contractors just profit further. The cycle continues, fiscal federalism's idealistic hopes of intergovernmental collaboration are undermined, and harm results. And in addition to the harm, the next section describes how illegality can arguably result from poverty industry practices that subvert the purpose of federal aid programs.

Illegality: Conflict with Statutory Purpose and Policy

This section of the book sets out some overarching legal concerns resulting from the poverty industry practices, including conflict with the statutory purpose, the potential illegality of contingency-fee revenue maximization contracts, and False Claims Act liability that can occur as a result of the revenue practices. Then, additional legal concerns are presented regarding specific examples of the poverty industry practices that are discussed in more detail in some of the chapters that follow.

Converted Purpose of Federal Aid Funds

The statutory purpose of federal matching grant programs such as Medicaid and Title IV-E foster care is to increase the ability of states to provide services to children and the poor. The federal government provides aid payments to increase total funding available for the services when paired with state spending. However, the poverty industry is siphoning off a significant percentage of the aid into private profit and state general revenue. This diversion of the federal funds conflicts with statutory purpose.

When the Medicaid program was created as part of the Social Security Amendments of 1965, Congress sought to enhance state spending by providing additional federal matching funds "so as to make medical services for the needy more generally available."[133] The Medicaid program seeks to incentivize states to increase the provision of Medicaid services. The statutory intent was to increase overall Medicaid spending and services, not to just replace state spending with federal funds.

As part of statutorily required state plans, states must use federal Medicaid payments for "care and services available under the plan."[134] In other words, Medicaid funds are intended for Medicaid purposes.

Further, federal Medicaid match payments provided to states are considered federal financial participation, or FFP. Under this FFP structure, if a state with a 50 percent match rate spends $50 on qualifying services, the federal government will provide an additional $50 as FFP so there is $100 total for Medicaid services. If the federal Medicaid payments are used instead to supplant (replace) state spending or routed into state general revenue, the statutory purpose and intended structure of the federal payments as "participation" are thwarted. The poverty industry revenue strategies are therefore clearly at odds with the statutory purpose and structure of Medicaid.

Similar to Medicaid, the Title IV-E Foster Care program provides federal funds to increase the ability of states to provide foster care and related services. The funds are again provided as a match to state spending, and are supposed to increase the total amount of funds available for foster care services.[135] Thus, as with the Medicaid program, the use of the IV-E funds to supplant state spending or increase state general revenue conflicts with the statutory purpose.

Further, federal Title IV-E funds are considered income to eligible foster children. For example, if a state claims Title IV-E funds for a foster child who is disabled and also eligible to receive Social Security SSI benefits, the Title IV-E funds are considered income to the child and thus reduce the child's right to receive the SSI funds.[136] Therefore, when the Title IV-E funds are claimed by a state but then redirected from the provision of foster care services to state general revenue or private profits, the state is not only undermining the purpose of the federal aid but is taking income belonging to the children—causing additional possible legal and constitutional claims.

Illegality of Contingency-Fee Structure

The nature of contingency-fee revenue maximization contracts also raises legal concerns. The contracts can encourage inappropriate claiming practices, and the contingency-fee structure itself is also inconsistent with the statutory framework.

In a 2005 report, the GAO described significant legal problems with states' use of contingency-fee consultants to maximize federal aid: "[w]e identified claims from projects developed by contingency-fee consultants that appeared to be inconsistent with current CMS policy, claims that were inconsistent with federal law, and claims from projects that undermined the fiscal integrity of the Medicaid program."[137] For example, two Georgia agencies were placing children in privately run facilities that provide rehabilitative services. On the advice of its contingency-fee consultant, Georgia decided to increase the amount of Medicaid payments to the state agencies for the rehabilitation services, but then the agencies did not correspondingly increase the payments to the facilities that actually provided the services. The strategy resulted in increased claims for federal Medicaid funds, but did not result in increased payments to the facilities serving the children. The state netted $58 million in federal Medicaid funds from the strategy.[138]

In addition to incentivizing inappropriate claiming practices, the use of contingency fee contracts to increase federal aid is arguably inconsistent with the legal structure of the federal aid funds. Under a contingency-fee structure, fees paid to revenue maximization consultants come directly from federal aid funds and are therefore subject to statutory limitations.[139] One such limitation requires that Medicaid funds can only be claimed by states to help pay administrative, training, and other related operational costs if determined by the federal government to be necessary "for the proper and efficient administration of the State plan."[140] Thus, it follows that for contingency fees paid to revenue maximization consultants to be an allowable use of the federal funds, such fees must be considered necessary for "proper and efficient administration." However, federal policy already prohibits the use of Medicaid funds to reimburse states for contingency fees as administrative costs.[141] And as such, the federal government has already concluded that contingency-fee payments do not meet the statutory requirement of being necessary for proper and efficient administration.

False Claims Act Liability

Legal concerns also arise due to possible false claims. If the boundaries are pushed too far with inappropriate claiming practices, violations of the civil or criminal false claims acts can result.[142]

The federal government uses the civil False Claims Act (FCA) to combat Medicaid and Medicare fraud, and the Act's "qui tam" provision allows private individuals with inside information to file claims on behalf of the federal government.[143] The FCA is often used to address fraudulent Medicaid and Medicare claims filed by healthcare providers, but the law can also be implicated when states hire revenue maximization consultants. A revenue maximization contractor can be liable under the FCA for knowingly causing a state agency to present false or fraudulent information in claims for federal aid funds. The law does not require the specific intent to defraud, but rather a contractor can be liable if it "(i) has actual knowledge of the information; (ii) acts in deliberate ignorance of the truth or falsity of the information; or (iii) acts in reckless disregard of the truth or falsity of the information."[144]

In addition to FCA cases involving known false or fraudulent claims, a revenue maximization consultant can also violate the FCA when the asserted facts are true but a claim is ineligible for federal reimbursement based upon known federal policies. For example, as noted above, federal policy has long prohibited contingency fees paid to revenue maximization consultants as administrative costs eligible for federal reimbursement. Nonetheless, despite the prohibition, contingency fees paid to revenue maximization contractors have often been included in claims for Medicaid and Title IV-E administrative cost reimbursement. Some state agencies hire revenue maximization contractors to help increase claims for federal aid, and then seek reimbursement from the federal government for the cost of using the revenue maximization contractor. If a consultant assists in preparing such claims for administrative cost reimbursement, and knows or should have known the claims for contingency fees are not allowed, then arguably the FCA may be implicated.

Moreover, in addition to the potential FCA liability of revenue maximization contractors, some local governments and agencies could be subject to the Act as well. The Supreme Court ruled in 2000 that a state is not a "person" for purposes of qui tam actions under the FCA,[145] but the Court then concluded in a 2003 decision that local governments (municipal corporations) can be subject to FCA qui tam actions.[146]

Thus, the poverty industry revenue maximization strategies undermine the structure and purpose of government aid funds and can implicate multiple legal concerns. In the chapters that follow, specific examples are explored of how the poverty industry is using the vulnerable to maximize revenue. The revenue practices are exposed, policy implications considered, and some additional legal concerns are explored. The examples illustrate the lengths to which states and human service agencies will go to use children and the poor as a source of funds, the extent to which the poverty industry contractors are encouraging and profiting from the practices, and the extent of the resulting harm.

PART II

Examples of Using the Vulnerable as a Revenue Source

3

Mining Foster Children for Revenue

If there are human service agencies that are the most symbolic for serving our most vulnerable populations, it's foster care agencies. These agencies (often also called child welfare agencies) exist to serve and protect the interests of abused and neglected children, who almost always come from impoverished families and who face traumatic experiences both before and sometimes during foster care. In fact, foster children suffer from post-traumatic stress disorder (PTSD) at almost twice the level of U.S. war veterans.[1] Children in foster care, and children aging out of foster care, desperately need services targeted to meet their best interests.

Unfortunately, the leaders of these agencies are increasingly viewing the children as a revenue source. As introduced in chapter 1, child welfare agencies have developed a revenue strategy, often aided by consultants, to obtain foster children's Social Security benefits for state use. The agencies target the most vulnerable of the vulnerable, abused and neglected children who may be eligible for Social Security benefits either because they are disabled or their parents have died—and then take their money. And this is just one of the ways in which foster care agencies and their parent states use foster children as a source of funds.

Foster children serve as a focal point resource for intersecting revenue maximization tactics in which each child is analyzed and mined for multiple types of aid funds. A child may be determined a candidate by the poverty industry to obtain her Social Security disability or survivor benefits, to maximize federal payments under the Title IV-E foster care program on her behalf, to seek out various types of federal Medicaid funds, to take Veteran's Assistance benefits from her if her parents died in the military, and even to take her child support payments. As the money starts to flow, the poverty industry seeks to claim it—often diverting the funds from much needed assistance for the child into government coffers and company profits.

This chapter first outlines how states use foster children in multiple revenue strategies, to show the scope of how children are targeted for funds and how the multiple strategies can intersect. Then, the scheme of maximizing foster children's Social Security benefits is set out in detail. This takes the reader from the big-picture view of the multiple revenue streams involving foster children into the intricacies of one of the disturbing tactics. Additional details regarding the Medicaid maximization practices and efforts to obtain child support from children are then included in chapters 4 and 5, respectively, within the broader discussions in those chapters of how the practices also impact other vulnerable populations.

Foster Children as a Resource for Multiple Revenue Strategies

The dollar sign under a statehouse dome depicted in figure 3.1 is the graphic used by the Georgia Department of Human Resources at the beginning of every chapter of a training manual for social services case managers regarding the IV-E foster care program.[2] The graphic is perfectly symbolic: rather than portraying needed services to children, it illustrates the state's focus on maximizing funds from foster children to help prop up state finances.

Even before a child is taken into foster care, revenue goals and funding streams incentivize child welfare agency decisions about whether to provide assistance to keep a struggling family intact, or whether the child should be removed. Then, once a child becomes a ward of the state, numerous additional and overlapping revenue strategies come to life. The child is engulfed by revenue maximization efforts that all too often are not aimed at determining how to best meet the child's needs, but rather at how to best use the child to meet the fiscal needs of the agency and the state. Tracking how funds are actually used can be incredibly difficult. Consider the following.

Alabama Funding Example
- *In 2004, Alabama "spent" $278 million on child welfare.[3]*
- *There were about 5,900 children in foster care in Alabama in 2004,[4] so divided out, Alabama reported about $47,000 in funding per child. If IV-B*

Figure 3.1. Graphic used by the Georgia Department of Human Resources at the beginning of every chapter of a training manual for social services case managers regarding the IV-E foster care program.

funds are subtracted (which can be used to prevent the need for foster care,) the amount is still about $45,000 per foster child.

- *$45,000 annual funding per foster child = $3,750 per month per child.*
- *Alabama only paid its regular foster care providers between about $400–450 per month in 2004 to care for the children.[5]*

The Alabama example does not imply that none of the additional funding is used to provide needed services beyond the regular rate paid to foster care providers, but the numbers should certainly raise questions.

To illustrate the extent to which agencies and revenue contractors strategize to use foster children to maximize funds, a hypothetical child

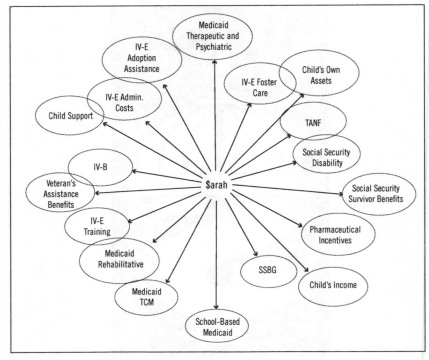

Figure 3.2. The revenue stream surrounding "$arah."

named Sarah is presented here. Sarah—who like most foster children comes from a poor family—becomes "$arah" as she is mined for potential funds. The chart in figure 3.2 shows a sampling of many of the potential revenue streams surrounding the child, along with a description of the haphazard interaction of the funding sources and resulting fiscal motives.

Title IV-B Child Welfare Services and Promoting Safe and Stable Families Programs

Nationally, the troubling policy issue arising with use of revenue maximization practices for these types of services is that an agency may have a greater financial interest in re-

moving a child from a home if the child is eligible for federal
foster care funds.[6]
—Report to the Mississippi Legislature on The Department of Human Services' Use of Revenue Maximization
Contracts

Before the child welfare agency removes $arah from her family into
foster care, the agency can first decide whether to provide assistance
to her family to help overcome hardships—such as lack of housing or
food insecurity or addiction—so that $arah's family can stay intact and
improve together. The majority of children determined maltreated are
due to neglect rather than abuse, and the circumstances described as
neglect are almost always a result of poverty.

The child welfare agency could seek federal funds to help $arah's fam-
ily in order to prevent the need for foster care. But such funds under the
Title IV-B Child Welfare Services and Promoting Safe and Stable Families program are capped at a low amount and thus more state spending
would be required to provide needed services to the family. As a result,
rather than electing IV-B funds and family preservation services, the
agency is incentivized to seek non-capped federal Title IV-E funds by
placing $arah into foster care. If the state receives more federal money,
less state spending is required.

IV-E Foster Care

All children entering foster care must be referred to Revenue
Maximization for a IV-E eligibility determination regardless
of length of stay in care.[7]
—Georgia Medicaid Manual, funding sources for children
in foster care

In contrast to the sparse federal IV-B funds that states can seek for
providing family preservation services, federal funds available when
children are taken into foster care are not capped. Title IV-E foster care
program funds are available for every eligible child an agency places in
foster care.

In addition to this funding discrepancy, a key eligibility requirement of Title IV-E payments results in another incentive: to favor taking poor children into foster care. Children are only eligible for IV-E funds if the children are removed from low-income families who would have been eligible for welfare assistance. Thus, if $arah comes from a poor family, the state agency is even more likely to target her for resulting IV-E funds.

Child welfare agencies hire private consultants to develop strategies to increase their "penetration rate"—the percentage of foster children who come from poor families and are thus eligible for the IV-E funds. Children in low-income families, already at increased risk of being assessed for child maltreatment, are further targeted because they are viewed as coming with money attached.

A national organization of family and juvenile court judges who preside over of the hundreds of thousands of foster care hearings across the country describe the concern:

> The chance of negative unintended consequences under this financing structure is enormous and potentially devastating for children and families. Limiting the lion's share of federal financing available to the dependency system to the support of children in foster care financially encourages placement of children in foster care. Limiting the eligibility of support for children in foster care to those who meet 15-year-old poverty level limits financially encourages children from the poorest of the poor families to be placed in foster care.[8]

The judges also express concern with resulting racial disparities: "as many racial and ethnic minority families live in poverty, the dependency system is financially encouraged to place racial and ethnic minority children in foster care."[9] Further, the judges explain how the lack of funding and services provided to help families stay intact, paired with uncapped funding to place low-income children in foster care—results in government fiscal interests trumping the interests of children and families: "With limited funding supporting service provision side by side with extensive funding supporting foster care placement, the reasonableness of efforts to prevent removal and to reunify the child with his or her family may be defined by financial considerations rather than by the needs of the child and family."[10]

IV-E Administrative Costs

Once $arah is taken into foster care and is processed through the revenue maximization unit, the state not only seeks federal Title IV-E funds for foster care services but can use $arah to maximize federal funds for a wide variety of administrative costs. The state can use $arah to claim federal funds to pay salaries, for costs of case planning and management activities, for other overhead expenses, to pay for a statewide automated computer system, and to pay for the expense of determining if $arah is eligible for IV-E benefits in the first place.

Such administrative cost claiming has been a boon for revenue maximization strategies employed by private contractors. The companies contract with states to maximize every federal dollar possible out of a child, through strategies ranging from "random moment time studies" to "cost allocation plans"—and even selling software to manage the claiming process in addition to consulting services.

Again, the incentives are concerning. The higher the state's "penetration rate" (the percentage of children in foster care taken from low-income families and eligible for IV-E), and the more days the child is in foster care, the more federal dollars the state can claim for asserted administrative costs: "The IV-E penetration rate is applied to the total allowable administrative cost to determine the IV-E reimbursable administrative cost. The IV-E reimbursable administrative cost is divided by the IV-E Child Care Days to determine the Per Diem for the allowable Administration cost."[11]

The potential for using foster children to claim federal funds for administrative costs is so high that some states are essentially trying to be as inefficient as possible in order to claim more administrative dollars. For example, a Texas financial report complained about how the state should be doing better in *increasing* administrative costs—by comparing to other states with greater reported administrative costs: "In other states, Title IV-E administrative costs typically equal the cost of the actual services provided. In fact, IV-E administrative costs exceeded IV-E maintenance costs in 22 of the 50 states."[12] The report complained that Texas' administrative costs were only at 20 percent of the cost of services, so should be increased.

So the goal in Texas? The report apparently seeks to increase foster care administrative costs as equaling or exceeding the costs of actually providing foster care services—so more federal dollars can be claimed through foster children. And who should help with that goal? The Texas Comptroller's office—the agency completing the report—proposed it could help local governments increase such funds, including increasing administrative costs. The Comptroller's office also proposed it should reap up to 20 percent of the additional federal aid for itself, in return for its administrative services aimed at increasing administrative costs in order to maximize revenue from foster children.[13]

IV-E Training Costs

In addition to using $arah to claim federal funds for foster care services and administrative costs, the state can also use $arah to claim federal funds to reimburse agency training–related costs. Like with administrative costs, the greater the percentage of poor children the state takes into foster care (penetration rate), the more federal reimbursement for training costs the state can claim. Also, the federal funds can be claimed at a higher rate for training costs than with administrative costs (75 percent for training and 50 percent for administrative costs).

IV-E Adoption Assistance

Child welfare agencies are financially incentivized to terminate parental rights within fifteen months after a child is taken into care in order to continue to receive maximum federal funds. States often rush forward regardless of the children's best interests in order to maximize funds, often resulting in the termination of parental rights when no adoptive resources are available.

Then, if an adoptive resource is in fact available, and if $arah is adopted rather than reunified with her family, the state can receive adoption incentive payments. Further, after changing an agency plan for a child from reunification to adoption, the agency can claim federal funds for administrative and training costs related to adoption. And after adoption, the agency can claim federal funds for adoption subsidy payments if the child is determined by the state to be a special needs child or is eligible for SSI benefits due to a disability.

Social Security Disability Benefits (SSI)

As described in more detail in the next section of this chapter, when $arah enters foster care the agency has a fiscal incentive to have her determined to be disabled. Likely with the assistance of a revenue contractor, $arah may be assessed and processed for an application to the Social Security Administration to have her considered disabled and thus eligible to receive SSI benefits. The agency will then apply to become her payee, without telling $arah, and will keep all of her resulting disability payments for itself or route the money to state general funds.

Social Security Survivor Benefits (OASDI)

Also as described in the next section, the child welfare agency will also screen $arah's background to determine if she has a parent who died. If so, the agency will apply for survivor benefits, again without telling $arah, and to become the payee for her survivor payments so the agency can keep the money for itself or state general funds rather than use it to help $arah.

Veteran's Benefits

One of $arah's parents may have fought and died in the military. If so, she may be eligible for Veteran's Assistance benefits. In such a situation, the child welfare agency may help determine if $arah is eligible and will likely take control of such benefit payments to keep them for the agency's own fiscal needs or state general funds rather than to help $arah.

Medicaid Claiming (TCM)

In addition to using $arah as a means of maximizing federal Title IV-E foster care funds, the state may simultaneously use $arah to maximize Medicaid funds, often for overlapping claimed services. In addition to the claims for federal Medicaid funds related to health services and administrative costs that are available for eligible adults or children, more Medicaid claiming can occur with foster children. The state agency may use $arah to seek out federal Medicaid funds for transportation costs, rehabilitation services, and therapeutic and psychiatric services. Also, the agency may employ $arah in revenue strategies for claiming Medicaid funds for "targeted case management" (TCM) services related to medical, social, educational, and other claimed services.

As will be explained in chapter 4, Medicaid is a key target of revenue maximization consultants hired to help human service agencies and their parent states claim more federal aid. The revenue strategies often do not actually result in more direct Medicaid services but rather can result in a general revenue stream for the agency or state or both.

School-based Medicaid

In addition to the several types of state claims for federal Medicaid funds that $arah can provide, she can also trigger additional claims for school-based Medicaid funds. For Medicaid-eligible children (all foster children are eligible for Medicaid), states can seek federal Medicaid matching funds when schools provide certain types of eligible health services for the children and also for school administrative costs related to Medicaid services. Even if a school does not provide direct health services to an eligible child, the school system and state can still use the child to claim school-based Medicaid administrative costs. In some states, as with the other revenue strategies, much of the resulting school-based Medicaid funds are routed to general state funds or general revenue for a school district—rather than targeted services for the child.

Prescription Medications

$arah may also be medicated. A lot. Prescription medications can be linked to revenue strategies involving foster children. In the effort to increase the number of foster children determined disabled so the poverty industry can obtain their Social Security disability (SSI) benefits, states and their contractors might assert the use of prescription drugs as evidence that a condition is severe enough to warrant a disability finding. For example, the Public Consulting Group's proposal to help Kentucky obtain foster children's Social Security benefits explains how the company will handle appealing decisions after denials of applications for SSI benefits: "[w]e also will request the most up to date prescription drug information, and other treatments. This information is extremely important to the appeal because it provides the evidence of severity and duration on a claim as well as new and material evidence that can be used to overturn a prior denial decision."[14] Also, the use of prescription drugs can be linked to additional Medicaid-related services such as rehabilitation, and therapeutic and psychiatric services.

Further, as explained in more detail in chapter 6, both the child welfare system and juvenile justice system have used prescription medications to sedate child behavior in order to reduce staffing costs. According to the *Palm Beach Post*: "[T]he Florida Department of Juvenile Justice has been buying twice as many doses of the powerful anti-psychotic Seroquel as it does ibuprofen. As if the state anticipated more outbreaks of schizophrenia than headaches or minor muscle pain."[15]

In Texas, a 2004 study "revealed that 34.7 percent of Texas foster children were prescribed at least one anti-psychotic drug—and 174 children aged 6–12 in the care of the state were taking five or more psychotropic medications at once."[16] Also, "[a]n investigation by the *Atlanta Journal-Constitution* exposed several companies operating foster care homes in Georgia repeatedly used anti-psychotic medications to "subdue" children in their care."[17]

Temporary Aid to Needy Families (TANF)

Federal aid is also provided to states for the welfare program, called Temporary Aid for Needy Families program (TANF). The funds are generally available for cash assistance to low-income parents. However, states can also use TANF federal aid for claimed child welfare activities, including educational services for parents, family reunification, crisis intervention, and relative or kinship care. Such claims can easily overlap with other funding sources.[18] And, like with other federal aid, supplantation and other budget practices can often lead to diversion of funds.

Social Services Block Grant (SSBG)

$arah can also provide states with a source of federal funds under the Social Services Block Grant (SSBG). The SSBG funds are available for states related to a wide variety of services, including for foster care children. Again, use of the funds for such services can overlap with other available funds and can be subject to diversion strategies.[19]

Child Support

As described in chapter 5, states pursue child support obligations against the parents of children in foster care but then take any resulting payments from the children and their families. Child support owed to foster children is diverted to replenish government revenue.

Child's Assets and Income

In addition to all the revenue sources described above, several states will also take other assets belonging to foster children, and even take the child's own income. The Nebraska human service agency wrote a regulation that allows it to take almost all of a child's resources to pay foster care costs. In addition to Social Security and VA benefits, the regulation provides the following nonexclusive list as example resources the Nebraska agency can take from a child—even burial spaces:

1. Cash on hand;
2. Cash in savings or checking accounts;
3. Stocks;
4. Bonds;
5. Certificates of deposit;
6. Investments;
7. Collectable unpaid notes or loans;
8. Promissory notes;
9. Mortgages;
10. Land contracts;
11. Land leases;
12. Revocable burial funds;
13. Trust or guardianship funds;
14. Cash value of insurance policies;
15. Real estate;
16. Trailer houses;

17. Burial spaces;
18. Life estates;
19. Farm and business equipment;
20. Livestock;
21. Poultry and crops;
22. Household goods and other personal effects; and
23. Federal and state tax refunds.[20]

Thus, the list of potential revenue streams for which a state uses $arah is long, and often overlapping. In the next section, one of the revenue strategies, maximizing and taking foster children's Social Security benefits, is discussed in more detail.

Converting Foster Children's Social Security Benefits into State Revenue

The practice of foster care agencies taking children's Social Security benefits is an alarming example of subverted agency purpose.[21] Agencies created to serve abused and neglected children are using the children to serve the agencies' own fiscal self-interests. With the assistance of private contractors, the revenue strategy is growing.

First, before turning to the state-sponsored practices occurring across the country, consider the story of a foster child in Westchester, New York, in which the social worker responsible for the child's best interests took more than $16,000 of the child's Social Security survivor benefits for her own use. It's hard to imagine a greater breach of trust than a social worker stealing from an abused and neglected child after his adoptive mother just died of cancer. The social worker was "accused of making numerous withdrawals from a Social Security Death Benefit fund account that was set up for the 16-year-old boy last year by his foster mother."[22] According to the report, "the foster mother had adopted the boy and was dying of cancer when she started the account and gave [the social worker] access to it."[23] The report continues that:

Following the adoptive mother's death, the boy was sent to another foster home and his new foster parent reported in November that money was missing from the account. An investigation by the DA's office revealed

that [the social worker] allegedly withdrew money several times last year
between April and November.[24]

Now, compare the social worker's theft from a sixteen-year-old foster
child to the practices of state foster care agencies in which agency personnel responsible for the children's best interests are again taking foster
children's Social Security survivor benefits. A local paper in Greensboro,
North Carolina published the following story about a fifteen-year-old
boy in foster care named John:

> [A] story of uncommon cruelty, compounded by layer upon layer of bu-
> reaucratic incompetence. And finally, no remorse from the only parent
> the boy, at age 15, has left—the Department of Social Services. . . . In a
> case that illustrates the daunting odds that face teens aging out of foster
> care, the story began when the boy was a baby and his father, soon after
> adopting him, died of cancer. In his will, [the] church custodian . . . left
> young John a savings account, a monthly survivor benefit and a Habitat
> for Humanity house with a small monthly mortgage [of $221 per month].
> But the boy was also left with a stepmother who subjected him to daily
> abuse for his first seven years—whippings with belt buckles and Venetian
> blinds, the judge recounted. To the doctor at UNC who noted broken
> bones and cigarette burns on the child, John had confided that the step-
> mother "would become mean when she smoked the rock." Enter an aunt,
> who next adopted John and moved into the little house. . . . What social
> workers didn't know—for another six years—was that the [stepmother]
> enlisted the child to sell drugs for her. . . . Meanwhile, according to court
> testimony, [the aunt] was cashing his $538 monthly benefit, neglecting
> to make his $221 a month house payment . . . With the boy now left in
> foster care and the custody of the DSS, what at last forced the case into
> public view was that Habitat was about to foreclose on the vacant house,
> having received no payments in a year. The DSS, it turned out, was using
> the child's survivor benefit to reimburse itself for his support. Though the
> child's lawyers pleaded that protecting the child's inheritance was "the fair
> and decent thing to do," an attorney for DSS argued that the agency had
> no obligation to use the boy's money to pay his mortgage. "What if he had
> a $2,000 monthly mortgage? What if every kid (in foster care) wanted

a car?" argued [the] DSS attorney. . . . "It would be wonderful if all this court had to do was what's 'fair and decent.'"[25]

In John's case, the foster care agency applied to become his representative payee after several relatives had first misappropriated his Social Security funds.[26] But then the agency began taking his benefits as well, using the funds to replenish state coffers rather than to benefit John by paying his small mortgage payments to keep the Habitat for Humanity home left by his deceased stepfather.

The social worker in New York faced felony charges and up to seven years in prison for taking a foster child's benefits, but not the North Carolina agency. Rather, foster care agencies across the country continue to use the practice of taking money from foster children without their knowledge as part of state-sanctioned revenue strategies. In fact, in the very county of Westchester, New York in which the county district attorney charged the social worker with grand larceny for taking resources from a foster child, the county foster care agency has contracted with private companies since 2007 to maximize and take foster children's Social Security benefits for county use.[27]

In the court hearing for John, the lawyer for the agency argued against any obligation of the agency to do what was best for the children, or even to do what was "fair and decent." However, because John's guardian *ad litem* intervened by filing a motion to protect John's interests, the trial court concluded, "DSS's use of J.G.'s Social Security benefits to reimburse itself, rather than make the $221.00 monthly Habitat mortgage payment, had not been reasonable."[28] The North Carolina Court of Appeals upheld the trial court's decision: "Here, both the guardian *ad litem* and the trial court acted consistently with their supervisory roles in seeing to J.G.'s best interests, and J.G.'s best interests were central to the court's order, which noted that if Habitat for Humanity foreclosed on the Habitat home, J.G. would receive very little money from the sale and would be homeless when he aged out of foster care."[29]

Luckily for John, the court required that the agency use his Social Security funds to serve his needs. But unluckily for the rest of the foster children in North Carolina, the state has not slowed in its process of taking Social Security benefits from abused and neglected children.[30] And most—if not all—other states are similarly ramping up their revenue practices of obtaining foster children's benefits, as set out in more detail below.

How States Take Foster Children's Benefits

Foster care agencies are taking more than $250 million in assets each year from children in their care. The agencies develop strategies to identify foster children who may be eligible for Social Security benefits, either because the children have potential to be labeled with a qualifying disability or because the children's parents have died or are disabled. The agencies apply for the benefits on the children's behalf, and if the children are determined eligible, the agencies apply to become the children's representative payee to gain control over the money. After becoming payee, the agencies use the money as government revenue rather than for the children's individualized needs and best interests. All of this is done without informing the children or the children's legal advocates. Often, private contractors carry out the entire process.

Children can receive two types of Social Security benefits—Old-Age, Survivors, and Disability Insurance (OASDI) and Supplemental Security Income (SSI). OASDI benefits are intended to help eligible children after a parent has died or become disabled. Such "survivor benefits" are almost like life insurance, with a child's eligibility dependent on whether parents worked and paid sufficient contributions for the insurance benefit through payroll taxes. SSI is intended to benefit low-income disabled individuals, including disabled children. Both types of benefits and resulting payments are considered property belonging to the children.

When a child receives Social Security benefits, the payments must be directed to a representative payee. The law presumes that children do not have the ability to manage their own money, so payees are selected to protect the children's interests in the funds and to ensure the money is used to benefit the children. Representative payees are similarly appointed for adults who receive Social Security benefits when the adults are determined unable to manage their own money, again for the purpose of protecting the interests of the disabled adults.

A foster child's representative payee assumes a fiduciary relationship to the child, with a directive to manage and use the child's money only in the child's best interests. Federal regulation explains that a representative payee must use the child's funds "only for the use and benefit" of the child beneficiary and in a manner that the payee determines "to be in the best interests of the beneficiary." The fiduciary role is clear: Representative payees should assess the various options for how to use the child's money and decide what is best for the child based on the child's individualized circumstances.

However, despite the clear mandate, foster care agencies developed a work-around and a rationale to ignore their fiduciary obligations. After setting out the over-arching requirement that representative payees may only use a child's funds in a manner that best helps the child, another federal regulation gives an example of what might meet the needs of a beneficiary: using the funds for the child's "current maintenance" needs. According to the regulation, current maintenance can include costs "incurred in obtaining food, shelter, clothing, medical care, and personal comfort items." So if a child has unmet needs for food or housing or other basic needs, common sense would dictate that using the child's money to meet those needs is surely in the child's best interests.

Foster care agencies have relied on the current maintenance clause as green-light for them to barrel forward in large-scale revenue maximization schemes, using children's Social Security benefits for the fiscal interests of the agencies and states rather than for the best interests of the children. Because agencies spend state money to care for foster children, the rationale goes, the agencies should be able to reimburse themselves for those costs by taking the children's resources.

But in relying on the current maintenance clause, state agencies ignore the intent that the children's funds are supposed to be used for *unmet* needs in the best way to help the children—not the states—and that a representative payee should consider and weigh various choices and decide what's best for each child. If states are already legally required to provide and pay for foster care services for abused and neglected children, which they are, then taking foster children's resources to pay the costs of their own care cannot possibly be in the children's best interests. Rather, a whole host of other specialized current or foreseeable needs of the children that are not already paid by the government are likely present, or the money can be saved for the children to help them when they leave foster care. In fact, the federal regulations make this clear: If the benefits are not needed for the children's "current maintenance or reasonably foreseeable needs," representative payees are directed that the benefits "shall be conserved or invested on behalf of the beneficiary."

Because state agencies have engaged in this practice without sufficient public awareness, the scheme has continued. In the following sections, details are exposed regarding use of private contractors to help grow this revenue strategy. Policy debates regarding the state practices are then discussed, and analysis is provided regarding how the state practices are illegal and unconstitutional.

Revenue Maximization Contractors

States and foster care agencies are becoming increasingly sophisticated in their efforts to maximize and divert children's Social Security benefits into government revenue, including hiring private contractors to either assist or take full control of the process. Recognizing the amount of money available, private revenue maximization consultants have developed expertise in helping the foster care agencies obtain the children's funds. MAXIMUS explains the results in Iowa: "MAXIMUS saves states money . . . Looking closer, our Iowa [Social Security] SSI Advocacy project has generated in excess of $16.2 million in revenue for the state."[31]

Similarly, the Public Consulting Group claims to be the largest vendor for seeking out foster children's Social Security benefits through its "Social Security Advocacy Management Services—SSAMS™."[32] The company's website explains that it has "filed and represented over 30,000 applications, generating over $250 million in additional revenue" for its foster care agency clients.[33]

While conducting research for this book, I sent several state freedom of information act requests and secured contracts, proposals, communications, and other records regarding efforts to maximize revenue involving children's funds. The following examples of documents and information obtained from various states provide a window into how children are viewed and treated almost like components of a factory process in which children's hardships are converted into government revenue.

MARYLAND
Going after any possible disability, and taking all the funds. The Maryland human service agency hired MAXIMUS to perform an assessment

of how to increase efforts to obtain foster children's Social Security benefits. The agency provided internal emails and other documents, including an email explaining that MAXIMUS looks for children with any possible disability in order to obtain the children's funds:

> We will be looking for children with identifiable physical or mental disabilities. Generally, we encourage caseworkers to refer any child suspected from suffering from any illness—from a quadriplegic to ADHA [sic]—to be referred to us for evaluation.[34]

MAXIMUS explains its recommendations are "designed to promote the identification of and subsequent acquisition of all SSI/SSDI benefits for all qualifying foster care children."[35] The report describes foster children as a "revenue generating mechanism."[36]

Goal to increase percentage of disabled children from 2 percent to up to 20 percent and take up to $6 million of the children's funds. The MAXIMUS assessment indicates a suggested goal to increase the number of Maryland foster children determined disabled for Social Security benefits from the current 2 percent to 15–20 percent, and plans to obtain up to $6 million or more annually in resulting children's benefits for the state.[37]

Double dipping. The MAXIMUS report included a warning that Maryland might be double dipping by obtaining foster children's assets and other funds to reimburse itself for state costs more than once. Under a section titled "Fiscal Management," the report explained: "While all counties interviewed identified a solid process for accounting for and applying SSI revenue to individual foster care maintenance costs, few were able to identify sufficient protocols to avoid double dipping."[38] Further, the report highlighted that Maryland was not tracking foster children who are receiving child support payments. For children in foster care, such child support payments go to the state to pay back the cost of care. So again, Maryland could be double dipping.[39]

A warning that Maryland is losing a half million dollars a month by not taking more children's disability benefits. In an internal email provided by the state agency, a MAXIMUS representative urges:

> I'd like to move forward with finalizing the report and scheduling an opportunity for formal presentation with stakeholders . . . By our rev-

enue estimates and projections, Maryland stands to lose approximately a half million dollars each month the state goes without implementing a comprehensive SSI advocacy solution. As belt tightening has become the norm for social service agencies, new revenue opportunities such as this are a welcomed change.[40]

A pilot project work plan. For just twenty foster children applications, the MAXIMUS pilot project work plan estimated 50 percent approval rate. The estimate explained for just those ten children, "we project the Department will realize $6,980 in additional monthly revenue and $83,760 in annual revenue . . . ," and that "[t]he pilot project stands to yield the Department a 16.75:1 ratio in income versus costs."[41]

MAXIMUS explains how it helps obtain foster children's resources to achieve "maximum revenue impact." The assessment report explains:

> As SSI/SSDI initiatives, both in-sourced and outsourced, have become a vital, continuous, and reliable funding source for social service agencies across the nation, the development of best practices that promote revenue enhancement, regulatory compliance, and operational efficiency have been developed and implemented as the result of decades of trial and error. Experience has taught us exactly what this process should look like, what gains should be obtained and resources are necessary for maximum revenue impact.[42]

KENTUCKY
Taking 6.4 million annually from foster children, and seeking to increase that by 1.7 million. A proposal to the Kentucky human service agency from F.M. Blake, A Division of Public Consulting Group, explains the success of the past contract to maximize children's Social Security benefits: "Based off of the Cabinet's own report, this project is hugely successful for the State, with annual federal revenue exceeding $6,391,980."[43] However, a 2008 proposal from a competitor, McDowell, Stromatt & Associates, asserts that the state could obtain more resources from children: "The numbers provided in the RFP, that there are 855 children in the care of the Cabinet resulting in nearly 6.4 million in revenue . . . you may be missing out on an additional 277 claims providing

SSI benefits resulting in an additional $1.7 million annually in revenue to the State."[44]

Contractors fight it out to use foster children as revenue. After several years of using F.M. Blake/PCG, in 2008 Kentucky changed contractors to McDowell, apparently won over by McDowell's assertion that it could obtain more children's SSI funds. Then in 2010, F.M. Blake/PCG fought to take the contract back—explaining how it's all about the money:

> In 2007 . . . while we were serving as the vendor, the number of foster children receiving SSI totaled 855. . . . as of January 2010 there were only 642 children receiving SSI, a decrease of 25% or 213 children. In 2007 the amount of revenue received by Kentucky for children eligible for SSI totaled $6,390,000 annually as a result of PCG's efforts. By 2010 this revenue stream had dropped to $5,143,968, a 19% decrease for an annual loss of $1,246,032.[45]

"Insider's view"—Hiring Social Security Administration district manager and staff to obtain children's funds from the Social Security Administration. The 2008 proposal submitted by F.M. Blake/PCG explains how the company division specializing in obtaining children's social security benefits was "[f]ounded by former SSA district manager Fred Blake."[46] Further, the proposal notes that:

> Many of our key staff are former Social Security employees who have hundreds of years of combined experience working within SSA . . . Our "insider's" view of the Social Security process, coupled with our comprehensive knowledge of the Social Security rules and regulations, allows us to work closely with all levels of SSA.[47]

"Special operating procedure." F.M. Blake/PCG also explained that because of its insider connections, the company arranged its own special procedures with the SSA in order to obtain children's funds in a shorter time frame: "Our experience and relationship with them has permitted us to establish special operating procedures that win more cases in the shortest possible time frames."[48]

Targeting mentally disabled children. To help Kentucky increase its revenue, F.M. Blake/PCG explains how the company increased the targeting of disabled children to include those with mental and behavioral disabilities:

> Many firms maintain a focus on children who suffer from physical dis-
> abilities because they are easier to document and submit. However, we
> have an extensive background dealing with diverse disabled populations,
> including those with mental and behavioral disabilities. This allows us to
> significantly widen the breadth and potential for disability determination
> and enrollment.[49]

Data analytics, algorithms, prioritization, and dissection. F.M. Blake/PCG sets out a complex strategy to maximize state revenue via disabled foster children: "We use predictive analytics—statistical/ mathematical methods and data mining techniques to uncover in- teresting patterns and relationships within data—to help us identify foster children who are likely to be eligible for SSI."[50] The proposal further explains:

> Our automated system applies SSA eligibility policy rules to the resulting
> data set and analyzes the results (potentially qualifying disabilities) to
> discover patterns and predict likely SSI eligibility. All likely foster care
> candidates are scored and triaged for SSI application. We then track the
> results of these applications (who did/didn't receive SSI) and incorporate
> this information back into our system to modify our analyses and better
> target potentially eligible children.[51]

In a description of "Data Acquisition and Mining," PCG explains that it "administers a dimensional database architecture to ensure optimal performance for users . . . PCG's [sic] uses this platform to conduct a proprietary analysis that employs a complex set of algorithms and pre- dictive models to target foster children with a high probability for SSI entitlement."[52] Then, the company describes its system of "Identification and Prioritization of Likely Eligibles" in terms of dissecting the foster care population:

> PCG prioritizes members for outreach on the bases of probability of en-
> titlement and expediency of enrollment . . .

Based on the data analysis, PCG will assign each identified foster child with a risk score, a key facet of prioritizing the targeted applicants . . . Implementation of the data analytics involves an initial dissection of the foster care population according to disabling condition. We categorize each member in terms of likelihood of enrollment (High, Moderate, Low) based on the output of the predictive modeling analysis.[53]

NEBRASKA

Nebraska law to take foster children's assets. Nebraska provided text of a statute as grounds for taking children's benefits. The Nebraska legislature enacted a statute requiring that the "Department of Health and Human Services shall take custody of and exercise general control over assets owned by children under the charge of the department."[54]

Nebraska even takes foster children's burial spaces. Regulatory language provided by Nebraska indicates the state will take almost everything from a child, even including burial spaces. 479 NAC 2-001.08. There are only a few things the state won't take—luckily including the child's clothing.[55]

Nebraska took $9.5 million from children. Records show that Nebraska obtained about $9.5 million in Social Security benefits from foster children from 2008 to 2013.[56]

Targeting children in juvenile detention. MAXIMUS provided an SSI Advocacy Project presentation for the director of the Nebraska's Children and Family Services agency. The slides explain the benefit of maximizing foster children's social security benefits as "Enhanced revenue for the state."[57] The presentation also suggests targeting children in juvenile detention to make them eligible for SSI so their funds can be obtained quickly if the children end up in foster care. The presentation explains that because many children leaving juvenile detention do end up in foster care, if SSI eligibility is established when the children are in detention, then the state "may immediately begin to receive the SSI dollars" when they enter the foster care system.[58]

Increasing children determined disabled to increase state revenue. MAXIMUS submitted a proposal to the Nebraska agency to help increase the state's use of foster children's Social Security benefits. The company explains its "goal of increasing the number of title II [OASDI survivor benefits] and Title XVI [SSI disability benefits] eligibility approvals and thereby increasing revenue for Nebraska."[59]

GEORGIA

SMILE Accounting System. Georgia has a sophisticated accounting system for using children's resources as government revenue. Apparently telling children to grin and bear it, the state named this accounting system "SMILE"—a "Payment system that produces and receives payments from funding streams for children."[60] SMILE is linked with "SHINES," an automated statewide child welfare information system that was developed by Accenture.[61] A state manual explains how the SMILE system is used to methodically apply children's Social Security benefits to replenish state funds.[62]

Using foster children to "leverage" $13 million in revenue. Georgia hired the Public Consulting Group for an assessment of how to increase claiming of foster children's Social Security benefits. The resulting PCG assessment explains how foster children can be used to leverage their funds for state use:

> SSI and SSDI are Federal funds that can be used by the Department to offset the cost of care and maintenance. DFCS can leverage over $8,000 in federal funds (with no state match) for every eligible child that is enrolled onto SSI benefits. DFCS can expect to enroll over 1,200 foster children onto SSI benefits and over 700 children onto SSDI benefits upon the implementation of a comprehensive SSI/SSDI Advocacy Program. This should result in over $13 million in annual federal benefits.[63]

Children plugged into "data match algorithms." The Public Consulting Group assessment discussed using children in "data mining" and algorithms to best identify children who might be eligible for Social Security benefits, and then to prioritize the children who are most likely to bring in revenue for the state. "States can use a variety of available medical and clinical data files to design a series of data match algorithms to identify foster children with a qualifying disability . . . Once identified, states can prioritize these children's SSI/SSDI applications."[64]

IOWA

Charging children a fee after already taking their money. The Iowa human service agency provided a spreadsheet and explains how it shows the amount of Social Security benefits obtained from foster children. The agency explains that after taking the children's resources to pay the state cost of care, the state charges those children who still have resources an additional $250 per month administrative fee: "a column showing the administrative fee retained by the department for those clients in family foster care in which income exceeded cost of care. In each of these cases, the department is allowed to retain up to $250.00 per month as an administrative fee."[65]

Children as "units." A cost proposal was submitted by MAXIMUS to the Iowa Department of Human Services regarding a proposal to help the state obtain more foster children's Social Security benefits. The pricing structure treats children as "units" with associated unit costs to be charged by MAXIMUS for services rendered in helping Iowa obtain the children's resources.[66]

Converting foster children's assets into $16.2 million in state revenue. The opening letter of the technical proposal from MAXIMUS explains how in the previous four years of the MAXIMUS contract to obtain foster children's Social Security benefits, "approximately $16.2 million has been generated for the State of Iowa."[67]

FLORIDA

"Load the cannon" strategy. Florida also hired the Public Consulting Group to complete an assessment of how the state can increase efforts to obtain foster children's Social Security benefits. The report describes a "load the cannon" strategy for applications for children's Social Security benefits—to load the cannon "with all available information (e.g., medical and psychological records, education records, function reports, and case manager interviews)" so the state can obtain the revenue as soon as possible.[68]

"Predictive analytics" to "score" and "triage" foster children as revenue source. The PCG Florida assessment describes how states should use children in "predictive analytics" to obtain funds from the children:

> Predictive analytics—statistical/mathematical methods and data mining techniques to uncover interesting patterns and relationships within data—can be used to help identify foster children who are likely to be eligible for SSI . . . The system applies SSA eligibility policy rules to the resulting data set and analyzes the results (potentially qualifying disabili-

ties) to discover patterns and predict likely SSI eligibility. All likely foster care candidates are scored and triaged for SSI application.[69]

Increase "penetration rate" of disabled children to convert their benefits into $21 million annual government revenue. In its assessment of Florida's practices, the PCG report is critical of the fact that only 6 percent of children in Florida's foster care system were receiving SSI benefits: "In comparison to other states where PCG performs SSI/RSDI foster care advocacy, typically 10% to 20% of the total foster care population is eligible to receive SSI benefits."[70] The report further explains the increased benefit to Florida of obtaining the children's SSI benefits:

> Because Florida operates under a Title IV-E waiver all children in CDF care can be considered state-funded for purposes of income calculation by SSA. This was approved by SSA in 2009 and allows Florida to pursue SSI for any child or youth that meets medical criteria, regardless of foster care funding type. We believe that this unique set of circumstances will yield a larger SSI eligible population that is not possible in other states.[71]

Further, the report explains: "PCG has estimated that increasing the SSI penetration rate to meet the national best practice of 20% would produce approximately 2,538 children newly eligible for SSI benefits," which the report explains would result in $21 million annually in new government revenue.[72] The report also indicates the current "RSDI" (survivor benefits) penetration rate of 2% could be increased to 8% resulting in another $8.9 million in annual revenue.[73]

In the next section, the tactics described above are considered in a policy context, focusing on a key question: Are the revenue strategies using foster children to maximize their Social Security funds actually beneficial to children and society—or harmful?

The Policy Debate: Legitimate State Revenue Practice or Stealing from Children?

The poverty industry's use of foster children's Social Security benefits goes to the heart of the tension between the purpose of government and the self-interests of government. Human service agencies—and their parent states and counties—rationalize their diversion of children's assets due to agency financial distress. This section of the book explores such reasoning. Further, additional policy concerns and rationales regarding the practice are addressed: states' assertions that they will stop screening children for disabilities and stop serving as representative payees if they can't take the children's money; whether allowing the children to benefit from their own funds would cause problems with SSI resource limits; and questions regarding the interaction of Social Security benefits with federal Title IV-E foster care funds.

Foster care agencies rationalize taking resources from children because of finances. In a political and economic climate in which states are unwilling to raise sufficient government revenue through general taxation, the agencies serving vulnerable populations are underfunded. In times when states cut spending, funding for human service agencies is often the first to be cut—even though needs are greater in times of economic stress. MAXIMUS highlights this reasoning in its proposal to help Iowa obtain foster children's Social Security benefits: "In today's environment, as government agencies struggle to balance a rising demand for services with unchanged or declining budgets, seeking innovative ways to manage increasingly complex programs, control costs, and uncover new revenue sources has become the norm."[74]

On September 11, 2012, the executive director of the Maryland Social Services Administration wrote a memo asking leaders of the state's local foster care agencies to work with MAXIMUS to determine how to obtain more foster children's Social Security benefits for government revenue. The memo explains how the revenue strategy is particularly important when children are ineligible for federal IV-E foster funds and thus are a greater drain on the state general fund. By taking foster children's federally funded SSI benefits, less state general fund dollars are required:

> Maximum attainment of SSI funds is important, particularly, for children who are determined to be ineligible for Title IV-E funding. The services provided to ineligible IV-E children are currently being paid for from

the state general fund. Our state general funds, as is the situation in most other states, are experiencing great pressure to fund all of the services our clients require. Therefore, it is critical that we do everything we can to ensure we are appropriately maximizing every federal dollar possible.[75]

Next, North Carolina provides an example where the onus of human service agency operations falls to county governments. In the case of John G., described earlier, the counties of North Carolina wrote an amicus brief to support the foster care agency's argument for taking John's Social Security benefits rather than using the funds to preserve his Habitat for Humanity house. Because of financial distress, the counties argue that they need to take money from foster children in order to help foster children:

> Presently, few county resources remain to support critical public services such as foster care. By allowing district courts across the state to prevent county DSS departments from using a juvenile's social security benefits to pay for the cost of feeding and sheltering the juvenile, counties across the state will suffer dire financial consequences.[76]

The counties express frustration about the difficulty of locating funding for social services agencies if they can't take the funds from foster children:

> If district courts across the state are allowed to prevent county departments of social services from using these funds to offset the costs of care, where will the additional money needed to provide for the current maintenance expenses of these juveniles come from? It will not come from the state and federal governments, and counties have already been forced to raise taxes and slash expenditures to fund their current budgets. In the case of Guilford County alone, even if district court judges only prohibited the Guilford County Department of Social Services from using a fourth of the juvenile's SSS benefits to pay for their cost of care, Guilford County would still have to find an additional $100,000 in its budget to feed and house these juveniles.[77]

Thus, state and local governments seek to take foster children's Social Security benefits in order to avoid the need to raise revenue through taxes or other means. The practice of using a foster child's resources to repay foster care costs does not result in more funds available to help foster children, but rather results in revenue savings to state and local governments. The children's benefits are paid fully by the federal government and are either routed directly into general government coffers or are used to replace state spending for child welfare programs, thus saving state funds for other purposes.

TAKING RESOURCES FROM FOSTER CHILDREN TO HELP FOSTER CHILDREN?

States and their agencies argue that it is beneficial for all foster children to take Social Security benefits from those who are eligible. Although individual children are deprived of their resources, the states argue that more resources are available for all foster children if children's benefits are used to reimburse foster care costs.

The argument raises a policy question: does the fact that foster care agencies are underfunded rationalize a policy of taking Social Security benefits from children who are disabled or whose parents are deceased in order to increase foster care agency revenue? More simply, should agencies fund foster care services by taking money from the foster children the agencies are supposed to serve?

Considering the question, there is little support for the states' rationale. First, the revenue strategy often does not result in more revenue for foster care agencies but rather in savings or general fund revenue to the states. The children's Social Security benefits are often routed directly to state (or county) general coffers, or to agency general revenue while state funding is simultaneously reduced for the agency. By using foster children's Social Security benefits to reimburse state costs, state legislatures can reduce the amount they would otherwise need to appropriate to foster care agencies.

Further, when foster care agencies take children's funds, they are forcing children to pay for their own foster care costs when states are already legally obligated to pay those costs. As explained in more detail below, federal and state laws require that states provide and pay for foster care services. For example, a 2008 contract in Kentucky for a company to help obtain foster children's Social Security benefits first explains how the state law requires the agency "to provide safety, permanency and well being to abused/neglected children."[78] However, because "[t]he cost of services to support these efforts is extraordinary," the state takes funds from the foster children to pay for the cost of care: "To control the cost to the State, the Cabinet seeks every opportunity to offset the use of state general dollars by drawing federal monies," including the contract's purpose to obtain foster children's Social Security benefits.[79]

Also, even if the Social Security benefits were actually used to increase foster care agency revenue, foster children as a class would receive little benefit. The Social Security benefits taken from foster children amount to less than 1 percent of the total funds reported by states for foster care agency costs, and much of the money would simply be absorbed and lost into agency administrative costs. And while foster children as a class would receive little benefit, individual foster children are severely harmed when their Social Security benefits are diverted from their use. Countless uses for the funds exist that could provide significant benefit to these children, whether current specialized unmet needs while in foster care (and not already required to be paid for by the state) or in plans to strategically conserve and use the funds as the children age out of foster care and struggle for economic independence.

REPRESENTATIVE PAYEE OF LAST RESORT?

Foster care agencies also assert a rationale that if they can no longer take children's Social Security benefits, then the loss of financial incentive will cause them to stop serving as representative payees. Stated another way, the agencies will not take on the duty of protecting the children's money if the agencies are not allowed to take the children's money.

Nonsensical? Yes. And the reasoning is also entirely inaccurate because foster care agencies are not the representative payee of last resort, and children would be better off with anyone else serving as their payee, or even with no payee at all.

The Social Security Administration is required to conduct an investigation to find the most preferred person or organization as representative payee. Federal regulations provide a ranking of possible payees, and state agencies are the least preferred. However, although the SSA is required to try to find someone more preferred, the agencies are chosen as the payees for foster children by an almost automatic process.

Although foster care agencies are often in the best position to know if other, more preferred individuals or organizations exist in a child's life to serve as representative payee, the agencies do not suggest other possibilities. Rather, many agencies ask their revenue contractors to help the agency become representative payee for every child in foster care—so the agencies can start taking the children's funds as quickly as possible. For example, documents from Iowa explain that the agency "workers need to inform MAXIMUS of a payee change for every youth receiving SSI or SSDI Benefits when they enter care so we can make DHS the payee."[80] In its proposal to the Iowa human service agency, MAXIMUS explains the importance of making sure the agency is made the payee for foster children: "MAXIMUS is prepared to process [social security] Change of Payee Request forms for the State of Iowa . . . Representative Payee changes are given a high priority to ensure that DHS and the State of Iowa begin receiving the benefits for children coming into care."[81]

Similarly, a Public Consulting Group assessment report in Georgia explained, "DFCS should be made rep payee for any child in custody who is eligible to receive SSI/SSDI benefits."[82] On a list of action items, the company notes a problem that the agency is not yet the representative payee for all foster children. The corrective action suggested by PCG is to "[c]orrect rep payee status for all [foster children] for whom DFCS should be receiving SSI payments."[83] And despite state agencies being the least preferred choice for becoming representative payees—meaning it should not be easy for an agency to become representative payee—PCG describes the "Implementation Difficulty" of its task of ensuring the agency as representative payee for all foster children as "low."[84]

In Nebraska, MAXIMUS proposed automating the process for the state agency to become representative payee to such an extent that the applications would be completed, signed, and submitted by the company—along with any needed discussion with the Social Security Administration—so that the foster care agency was not even part of the process. In an internal email, a unit administrator at the Nebraska Department of Health and Human Services (DHHS) explains:

> I am getting information from Travis [at the Social Security Administration] about what has to happen so that Social Security will accept the rep payee applications directly from Maximus, without them coming to

DHHS. Maximus will send us a list, so we can monitor if we need to, but we don't need the step of our signing . . . When Maximus has had a question on why an application remained pending, [Maximus] has had to contact DHHS . . . who then looked on SDX for information or contacted Social Security. Maximus would welcome being able to talk directly with Social Security to get these questions answered, contacting us only when there are issues.[85]

Further, as the agencies seek to become the representative payee for all foster children even though they are the least preferred choice, the Social Security Administration is also ignoring its requirement to conduct an investigation to look for more suitable payees. Instead of individualized investigations, the SSA created a computer programing tool it calls the "kiddie loop" that allows it to process in batches agency applications to become the children's representative payees.[86]

So, rather than only serving as payee for children when no other choice exists, foster care agencies are pushing to the head of the line in the hopes of becoming representative payee for every foster child receiving Social Security benefits. In most cases, there are likely more preferred choices that already exist at the time of application, and more options that could easily be developed to better serve the children's best interests and truly protect their funds.

Federal regulations explain that the list of possible representative payees is flexible and that the primary concern is "to select the payee who will best serve the beneficiary's interest."[87] Further, the SSA's internal guidelines suggest that it should consider other possible payees not explicitly listed in the regulation preferences. In addition to relatives and family friends, several other possibilities exist. Some government agencies and non-profit organizations have already created volunteer representative payee programs, recruiting volunteers to serve as representative payees for adult beneficiaries. Such volunteer programs could also be created for foster children, such as encouraging retired individuals to serve as representative payees for the children—thereby providing a needed service to help children manage and benefit from their own money, and to establish mentoring relationships between the retired individuals and foster children. Similarly, accountants and lawyers might be interested in providing the service as a way of providing pro bono help to vulnerable children. Many organizations already provide representative payee services for a small fee.

From the view of foster children, any other person or organization would likely be preferable to foster care agencies. The agencies are taking the children's funds, whereas non-agency representative payees cannot be forced to spend the money to repay the foster care costs. In fact, even having no payee would be better for foster children. Agencies have argued that since foster care agencies are the representative payee of last resort, if the agencies refuse to serve in the role then children will lose their Social Security benefits. Again, the assertion is not correct. The SSA is obligated to find suitable representative payees, and that duty does not end if a state agency declines the responsibility.[88] In fact, even if there is no other representative payee available, the child's eligibility does not end. Rather, the Social Security payments would be conserved and then paid out once a suitable representative payee is chosen—or to the child directly once the child reaches adulthood. In such a scenario, the conserved benefits would then be available to assist the child rather than being taken by the foster care agency.

Further, in addition to the concern that agencies are becoming representative payees to divert foster children's Social Security benefits, there are concerns that the agencies are not even managing that revenue effort well. When the SSA's Office of Inspector General audited social service agencies serving as representative payees, the results were not good. For example, the Baltimore City Department of Social Services (BCDSS) had almost nonexistent record keeping and accounting practices. BCDSS either failed to record—or recorded incorrectly—the agency's receipt and use of children's Social Security benefits in 82 percent of the cases. In more than 25 percent of the cases reviewed, the children were no longer in agency care, but BCDSS continued to take the children's benefits.[89] The audit concerns of BCDSS were not isolated, as the OIG uncovered many similar concerns with several other agencies serving as representative payee for foster children. In fact, an audit of the SSA itself found that it is doing a very poor job overall of monitoring representative payees.[90]

Finally, even if foster care agencies were the representative payee of last resort, should we really conclude that agencies should take children's resources because such financial incentive encourages them to take on the role of managing the children's resources—that if bribery works, it must be ok? In addition to obvious concerns with such a conclusion, the reasoning would lead to nonsensical results: that in order to protect against the concern that children may not receive any Social Security benefits, we should let foster care agencies take all of the children's Social Security benefits. Further, the reasoning ignores the fiduciary responsibilities of foster care agencies and their very reason for existence—to help and protect the best interests of foster children. As a comparison, several state and county agencies already act as representative payees for disabled adults, and without financial motivation of taking money from those served. Rather, these human agencies have provided the services solely because of their governmental purpose in helping their client population. Foster care agencies should do the same for children.

MAXIMIZING CHILDREN DETERMINED DISABLED TO
INCREASE STATE REVENUE

The ability to take children's disability benefits is a strong incentive for foster care agencies to maximize the number of children who are classified as disabled. Agencies have indicated that if they can no longer take the children's SSI benefits, then the agencies will not care about helping the children become eligible for SSI in the first place. Then, the agencies argue, if fewer foster children are screened for potential eligibility for SSI benefits, it's possible that fewer children's disabilities will be recognized.

However, the strength of the financial incentive does not lead to the conclusion that taking assets from foster children is good public policy. Without the incentive, multiple federal laws already require health screening and treatment services for foster children. For example, foster children must be provided with Early and Periodic Screening, Diagnosis and Treatment (EPSDT) services under Medicaid, which include comprehensive medical screenings and necessary treatment for physical and mental health conditions. Also, the Individuals with Disabilities Education Act (IDEA) requires the identification and treatment of children's disabilities for educational purposes.

Rather than helping foster children receive disability benefits in order to best meet the children's needs, foster care agencies are trying to maximize the number of foster children determined disabled in order to maximize agency and state revenue. The children, regardless of age, are not even informed about the application for disability benefits on their behalf or how the money is used. Agencies and their revenue contractors are literally processing and ranking children based on how much money they can bring in to the state, rather than on their disabilities and needs. Even if a foster child is the most disabled and in need of services, the agency will not prioritize seeking disability benefits for the child if doing so does not bring in more state revenue.

For example, when a child is not eligible for federal IV-E funds, states must use more state funds to pay the foster care costs. Revenue maximization contractors therefore suggest ranking foster children to seek disability benefits, first targeting children who are not IV-E eligible. Moreover, SSI benefits and IV-E benefits count each other—meaning if a state elects to receive Title IV-E benefits in the name of a particular child, the child's SSI benefits (if eligible) will be reduced dollar for dollar. So states and their private revenue contractors develop detailed strategies to determine which funding stream to choose when children are eligible for both programs.

In a proposal obtained from the Maryland public records request, MAXIMUS explains how every decision should be about what brings in more government revenue—and suggests the following ranking of foster children:

> The MAXIMUS strategy is simple [sic] maximize revenue to the Department by identifying the greatest stream in each case . . . To ensure the Department gets the greatest positive financial impact from the SSI advocacy operations, the MAXIMUS team evaluates all foster children who are ineligible for Title IV-E benefits first. . . . After reviewing children who are ineligible for Title IV-E benefits, children who are eligible for Title IV-E benefits are reviewed . . . Again, to maximize revenue gain, children are reviewed in order of receiving the least Title IV-E revenue to the greatest.[91]

The strategy is alarming because disabled foster children may be passed over in having their disabilities recognized simply because they do not bring in more money to the state.

In its proposal to provide Social Security claiming services in Kentucky, F.M. Blake/PCG similarly explains:

The relationship between various federal and state programs and SSI/RSDI is critical to a successful project. Misunderstanding of this relationship can actually result in a net loss to the agency. Failure to understand the importance of this could result in the filing of cases, which would actually cause the Cabinet to lose revenue.[92]

The proposal suggests that the "filling of cases" (filing applications for SSI benefits for children) could cause the foster care agency to lose revenue if the SSI funding stream results in less money taken by the state than IV-E benefits would provide. Further, another contract for such services in Kentucky demands the following:

> For children committed to CHFS, the Vendor, while reviewing the files for possible initial application, will first determine if the child is Title IV-E Foster Care and Adoption Assistance Program eligible reimbursable. If the determination is that the child is IV-E eligible reimbursable, the Vendor must make a correct determination whether the IV-E monthly benefits or the SSI monthly benefits would be the most beneficial in the interest of the Cabinet.[93]

Thus, the state contract demands that agency revenue take priority—that the decision of seeking SSI or IV-E benefits should be controlled by what is the best for the foster care agency, not the child.

CHILDREN'S RESOURCE LIMIT

Yet another state policy argument is that foster children have a $2,000 asset limit for SSI eligibility, meaning that if more than $2,000 is conserved, their eligibility for benefits could end. Thus, by foster care agencies diverting the children's money to state revenue, the children's funds are not saved and the asset limit is avoided.

Concern about the asset limit is real, but numerous options exist to address the limitation while still using the children's money as intended—to help the children. In fact, this is exactly why a representative payee is appointed—to manage the children's funds in a fiduciary manner, including keeping an eye on resource limitations and making decisions in the children's best interests.

If a representative payee exercises true fiduciary discretion, a virtually unending list of uses for the money could provide real benefit to the disabled foster children. In addition to spending the funds on current unmet needs of the children, several exceptions exist to the resource limitation. For example, exceptions to the resource limitation include a special needs trust, ownership interest in a home, purchasing an automobile, and buying household items and personal effects. Also, a 2014 federal law called the Achieving a Better Life Experience Act (or "Able Act") created a new 529A plan similar to the existing 529 plans for college savings, but much more expansive and specifically for disabled individuals (including children) receiving SSI benefits. SSI funds can be deposited into the 529A plan and are exempt from the asset/resource limit. Then, in addition to education, the funds can be used in numerous ways to help a disabled child/young adult—including housing, transportation, employment training and support, assistive technology and personal support services, health, prevention and wellness, and financial management and administrative services. Further, the SSA even has a specific program called the Plan for Achieving Self Support (PASS) in which the funds can be conserved under a plan that is exempted from the resource limitations. The PASS program could be used as a wonderful planning and resource tool, using the children's benefit payments to develop a resource savings plan that includes participation from the children—and thus could also help encourage financial literacy and inspire the children to be engaged in the process of planning for their future.

Legal Concerns with Foster Care Agencies Using Foster Children as Revenue Source

The revenue strategy of agencies taking foster children's Social Security benefits also raises many legal concerns. This section describes those legal issues, and includes discussion of specific court cases challenging the practice.[94]

When children are placed in foster care, states pay a monthly rate to the foster care providers. States are legally obligated to pay this cost of foster care, and the Supreme Court has recognized that children are not obligated to pay for their own care—that the foster care payments are made "without strings attached," in that children do not owe a debt to repay the state.[95] Nonetheless, a rationale used by states to take children's Social Security benefits is that the state should be able to pay itself back for its costs of providing foster care to the children.

The issue of a foster care agency taking a child's Social Security benefits was addressed by the U.S. Supreme Court in 2003 in *Washington State Dep't of Social & Health Services v. Guardianship Estate of Keffeler*. However, the Court only addressed whether a federal law that prohibits creditors from attaching benefits (the anti-attachment provision of the Social Security Act) applies to the practice used by foster care agencies. The Court ruled that the provision did not apply to the agencies because they were not creditors of foster children, because no law "provides that [children] are liable to repay the department for the costs of their care."[96] The Supreme Court also recognized that the several other legal questions regarding the practice remained undecided, including the issues discussed below.

FOSTER CARE AGENCIES SUBVERTING THE CONSTITUTIONAL RIGHTS OF CHILDREN

Several constitutional concerns arise—not surprisingly—when foster care agencies take foster children's assets, including equal protection violations and unconstitutional appropriation of children's property. But perhaps the most striking constitutional concern stems from states disavowing foster children's due process rights.

Agencies hire private contractors to help develop statewide efforts to obtain foster children's funds. The children are plugged into complex strategies of data analytics, algorithms, prioritization, and dissection—as described above—and then those children who are ranked as the best prospects of providing income to the state are used to apply for Social Security benefits. No one tells the children or their advocates. Then, the foster care agencies use the same private contractors to facilitate a process of becoming representative payee for every foster child. Again, no one tells the children, so they are denied the ability to suggest someone else to manage their money. Then, month after month the agencies route the children's benefits into state coffers. The children receive no notice or opportunity to suggest how they would like to use their funds for current unmet needs or to plan for their future.

Agencies defend keeping children in the dark, arguing the children do not deserve due process rights. In Alex's court case, mentioned in chapter 1, the Maryland foster care agency went even further than arguing Alex was not entitled to due process rights, but also argued his lawsuit was time-barred. Although Alex had no notice whatsoever of the agencies actions, the agency argued he had to file his claim within one year of when the agency became his representative payee and started taking his funds—while Alex was still a child in foster care.

In fact, federal law does require notice to be sent from the Social Security Administration when someone applies to become representative payee for an individual's benefits, so the individual has an opportunity to object or suggest someone else. However, for notices regarding state foster care agencies applying to become representative payees for children, the notices of the agencies' applications are sent back to the agencies themselves since they are the children's legal guardians. Amazingly, the state agencies have argued that notifying themselves when they apply to become the children's representative payees is sufficient to protect the children's interests.

So in Alex's case, similar to other cases across the country, the foster care agency created a circumstance where Alex and his lawyer had no knowledge of the agency's actions. Then, the agency, whose sole duty is to protect the interests of foster children, argued that children who can't comply with a statute of limitations due to circumstances beyond their control (such as infancy or disability), or having no knowledge of the agency actions, should nonetheless be barred from filing claims to protect their own interests.

This agency argument to extinguish children's rights compares disturbingly to the rationalizations used to deny constitutional rights for children before the Supreme Court's ruling in In Re Gault—that because the children already had the state acting in their best interests under the power of parens patriae, they needed no rights of their own. The actions of foster care agencies seeking to subvert children's rights is precisely why the Supreme Court ruled in Gault that children's due process rights must be preserved: at times the courts must step in to protect children from the very agencies entrusted to act in their best interests.

However, although the importance of protecting children's due process rights is clear, especially when children are in the custody of a state agency, only one state court has acted to protect children's due process rights as foster care agencies seek to take their Social Security funds. In Ryan's case, also mentioned in chapter 1, the Maryland Court of Appeals concluded that the foster care agency violated his due process rights. The court ruled that the agency must begin providing notice to foster children and their lawyers when the agencies apply to take control over the foster children's funds, and when the agencies become payee they must provide regular accountings to the children and their lawyers of how the money is used.[97] With such notice, foster children in Maryland might be able to challenge the appointment of the foster care agency as their representative payees, and request a payee that will truly protect their interests.

The hope is that other state courts will follow the lead of the Maryland Court of Appeals. But unfortunately, foster care agencies will likely continue to fight foster children's rights because the denial of children's due process rights lies at the foundation of the states' revenue strategies. Agencies depend on the automatic process established with their revenue maximization contractors of establishing the foster care agencies as representative payees, so they can then take the children's money. The recognition of children's constitutional rights could thus throw a wrench into the process states have established with their private contractors—the complex but efficient assembly line process, augmented by algorithms and data analytics, using vulnerable children as a revenue source. If children are allowed to exercise their due process rights in order to suggest another person or organization to manage their money, then the state will no longer be able to take the children's funds.

FOSTER CARE AGENCIES SHIRKING THEIR DUTY TO PAY, BY FORCING CHILDREN TO PAY

States rely on a simple argument to take children's resources: The agencies should be able to use the foster children's Social Security benefits to repay the "current maintenance" costs of children's care. However, the argument ignores the equally simple legal and moral fact that states—not children—are obligated to provide and pay for foster care. Every state in the United States participates in the Title IV-E federal foster care assistance program, which provides federal matching grants to improve states' ability to provide foster care services. A state's matching share of the costs for children's care must be paid using *state funds*, and the state payments cannot be made up of other federal funds such as Social Security benefits. However, foster care agencies are ignoring this requirement, and courts have yet to adequately address the legal concern.

More specifically, federal law requires that states participating under Title IV-E "shall make foster care maintenance payments on behalf of each child."[98] And the foster care maintenance payments must include "payments to cover the cost of (and the cost of providing) food, clothing, shelter, daily supervision, school supplies, a child's personal incidentals, liability insurance with respect to a child, and reasonable travel to the child's home for visitation."[99] Thus, states are legally required to pay the current maintenance costs that they claim children must pay.

In fact, courts have even ruled that foster children—as the beneficiaries of this federal mandate—have privately enforceable rights to force states to pay the foster care maintenance payments on their behalf. A federal court in Massachusetts explains:

> Each of the cited provisions similarly discusses how the state must distribute benefits to *each child* . . . . 42 U.S.C. § 672(a)(1) (requiring that "each State with a plan approved under this part shall make foster care maintenance payments *on behalf of each child*") (emphasis added). Plainly, these directives are both couched in mandatory terms and are unmistakably focused on the benefitted class, *i.e.*, foster children.[100]

If foster children have rights to force states to pay their foster care maintenance payments, it would be nonsensical for the state to have the countervailing ability to force children to repay those same costs of care.

Further, the Social Security Administration's Office of Inspector General (OIG) has explained how states receiving federal Title IV-E foster care payments are explicitly prohibited from applying children's Social Security benefits to the cost of foster care. The Title IV-E payments are intended to match states' own spending on children's foster care, so states cannot use other federal funds like Social Security survivor benefits to pay or repay the state share of costs. An audit by the OIG of the Hawaii foster care agency explains:

Contrary to Federal regulations, HI-DHS [Hawaii Department of Human Services] used OASDI benefits to partially reimburse itself for the foster care payments it disbursed to the children's providers. HI-DHS was unaware that it could not reimburse itself for the State's share of Title IV-E costs from a child's OASDI benefits. . . . Federal regulations prohibit HI-DHS from using a child's OASDI benefits to reimburse itself for the State's share of Title IV-E costs. To receive Federal Title IV-E benefits, HI-DHS must pay its share of the foster care costs with State funds. *Therefore, the OASDI benefits for a child who also receives Title IV-E benefits must be saved or used for a child's other needs.*[101]

But despite the mandate, states continue to require children to reimburse foster care costs that states are obligated to pay. And unfortunately, courts have thus far failed to address the fact that foster care agencies have a legal obligation to pay foster care costs, and children do not.

FOSTER CARE AGENCIES BREACHING THEIR FIDUCIARY OBLIGATIONS

It is striking—and not in a good way—that child welfare agencies are engaged in this practice. These agencies are guardians of our nation's most vulnerable children. But rather than using their guardianship power to best serve each child's individualized needs, the agencies are hiring revenue maximization consultants to sort out the children by revenue potential, maximizing the number of children determined disabled in order to take their disability benefits, and taking the last remaining assets left to children from their deceased parents. The practices conflict with fiduciary obligations the foster care agencies owe to children, under federal law and state law.

First, foster care agencies are created under state laws to protect the interests of abused and neglected children. This duty creates a fiduciary obligation owed by state foster care agencies to the children. As a fiduciary, an agency must act in the children's best interests and cannot use its fiduciary power to serve itself over the children. Thus, when a foster care agency takes a child's property for a self-serving purpose, the agency's fiduciary obligation under state law is violated.

Second, when foster care agencies become representative payees for children's Social Security benefits, the agencies take on an additional fiduciary obligation under federal law. The Social Security Act requires representative payees to use Social Security benefits in a manner that they determine is in the beneficiary's best interest.

Foster care agencies ignore this fiduciary obligation and claim they have no duty to exercise any discretion as representative payee to decide how Social Security benefits can best be used for the children's interests. The agencies rely on a federal regulation that indicates using the funds for current maintenance needs can be in the beneficiaries' best interests: "We will consider that payments we certify to a representative payee have been used for the use and benefit of the beneficiary if they are used for the beneficiary's current maintenance. Current maintenance includes cost incurred in obtaining food, shelter, clothing, medical care, and personal comfort items."[102]

Thus, foster care agencies argue that because this regulation recognizes the use of Social Security benefits for current maintenance needs, the agencies should be able to take foster children's benefits to pay back the costs of foster care. However, the agency argument ignores the fact that states are already legally required to provide and pay for those current maintenance costs for foster children, as discussed above. Another federal regulation clarifies that if the current maintenance needs are already met, the children's Social Security benefits should be conserved.

The agencies ignore the core concept of fiduciary discretion. The exercise of discretion in the interests of the beneficiary lies at the heart of any fiduciary relationship. When promulgating the federal regulations relied on by the foster care agencies, the SSA recognized this principle: "[a]lthough we provide guidelines as to what is in the beneficiary's best interests, there is a considerable amount of discretion provided to the payee."[103] Also, additional SSA guidance encourages representative payees to consider both "current needs and reasonably foreseeable needs," and to specifically consider conserving the benefits for children who may need assistance with the transition to independence.[104] The SSA also directs its staff to ensure that "the payee understands the fiduciary nature of the relationship, and that benefits belong to the beneficiary and are not the property of the payee."[105]

Further, the SSA explains that organizational representative payees (like foster care agencies) serving as fiduciaries for multiple beneficiaries must consider the best interests of each individual beneficiary. An SSA training manual for organizational representative payees directs that "[t] he most important duty of all payees is to know the needs of each beneficiary and to use the benefits in the best interest of the beneficiary."[106] The guidance directs that organizational representative payees should collaborate with each beneficiary to decide how to best use the beneficiary's funds. The guidance even provides examples of how a payee should involve each beneficiary in making individualized decisions:

- Meet regularly with the beneficiary (preferably face-to-face);
- Establish a budget, discuss it with the beneficiary, and involve him/her as much as possible in financial decisions;
- Explain Social Security and/or SSI [Supplemental Security Income] payments and the beneficiary's expenses to him or her;
- Ensure that the beneficiary is aware of current and large retroactive payments.[107]

In addition to the direction from the SSA, the federal Consumer Financial Protection Bureau (CFPB) also provides commonsense direction to representative payees. Using a hypothetical individual named Roberto who is receiving Social Security benefits but needs a representative payee, the guidance explains: "Since you have been named to manage money or property for someone else, you are a fiduciary. The law requires you to manage Roberto's money for HIS benefit, not yours."[108] The CFPB guidance also explains how the first duty of Roberto's representative payees is to act only in Roberto's best interests: "Because you are dealing with Roberto's money, your duty is to make decisions that are best for him. This means you must ignore your own interests and needs."[109]

Thus, the fiduciary principles are clear. An individual or organization appointed as fiduciary over a foster child's funds must exercise discretion to determine how to best use the child's funds in the child's best interests. Because states are already required to pay for foster care costs, the child's own funds should not be used for that purpose. The fiduciary should make reasonable efforts to engage the child in deciding how to best use the child's funds. The decision includes countless options to meet the individualized needs of each child, including: (1) possibly applying the benefits toward current needs (if not already provided for); (2) considering how to allocate the funds among the different categories of possible unmet current maintenance needs; (3) deciding whether to apply the money toward other foreseeable or special needs; or (4) deciding to conserve the benefits for future needs if current needs are already met.

The many possibilities and changing circumstances are precisely why a representative payee is appointed, to weigh all the options and make individualized decisions to best meet the child's evolving needs. Managing Social Security benefits for the individualized best interests of abused and neglected children is difficult, but such difficulty is precisely why a fiduciary is appointed. As the SSA explains:

> Organizations really do make a difference when they act as payees . . . because they provide a critical service to one of the most vulnerable segments of our population. Being a representative payee can be very demanding, but it can also be very rewarding. Representative payees can make a difference.[110]

However, contrary to the federal guidance, foster care agencies suggest a representative payee system that amounts to automatic cost reimbursement—where the agencies do not apply fiduciary discretion but automatically apply the children's funds to repay the state for the costs of their own care. Consider the following example of a foster care agency arguing against its fiduciary obligations:

Foster Care Agency Arguing against Its Fiduciary Obligations to Children

In 2014, legislation was introduced in Maryland with a purpose that should not have been controversial: "[f]or the purpose of requiring the Department of Human Resources to serve in a fiduciary capacity for children in its custody; requiring the Department, in any action, service, or decision on behalf of a child in its custody, to protect and serve the best interest of the child . . ."[111]

The bill would have required the agency to do what it was created to do, serve the best interests of children. And within that requirement, the bill would have prohibited the agency from forcing foster children to pay for their own care—so the agency could no longer use foster children's own resources as a revenue source.

The Secretary of the Maryland agency stood before the Maryland Senate and testified against the requirement to act as a fiduciary for foster children's resources. The Secretary asserted that prohibiting the agency from using children's resources to pay state costs amounted to an unfunded mandate, and threatened that if the legislature stopped him from taking the children's Social Security benefits and other resources to use towards state costs, then he would impose cuts to services for other children in the agency's care: "The bill is an unfunded mandate that will require cuts to services for other children in DHR's care."[112]

So we return to core the conflict discussed in chapter 1, an agency created to serve the vulnerable using its power to take from the vulnerable. The Maryland agency asserts it must take assets from children in order to help children, creating a form of foster care that is self-funded by abused and neglected children. The secretary's argument against its fiduciary obligation in protecting children's resources is legally incorrect. As explained earlier, the state is already required to provide foster care services for all children under both federal and state law. Thus, the secretary's threat that he will cut foster care services in reply to a bill prohibiting the agency from taking children's resources is not legally permissible.

Moreover, the simple conclusion is inescapable that it is not good public policy to fund an agency created to help foster children by taking assets from foster children. Despite the anti-tax climate among state governments, there must be a better way to fund the agencies than by taking money from children. The Supreme Court has explained that the government should not force "some people alone to bear public burdens which, in all fairness and justice, should be borne by the public as a whole."[113] If any class of persons should not bear public costs of child abuse and neglect, it's the children.

4

Medicaid Money Laundering

The poverty industry's efforts to mine foster children's Social Security benefits are widespread and growing, stripping millions each year from vulnerable children. But as stark as the practice is, it pales in comparison to the scope of revenue strategies involving Medicaid. Through numerous and evolving Medicaid maximization strategies, again often developed with private contractors, the poverty industry is siphoning not millions, but billions in federal Medicaid funds into state revenue and private profit.

To begin uncovering these revenue strategies, it is helpful to first revisit how Medicaid is supposed to work. Medicaid is a matching grant program. If a state spends its own funds on eligible healthcare services for needy populations, the state can receive a federal match to increase the total funds available for such Medicaid purposes. So if a state has a 50 percent match percentage like Massachusetts and spends $50 on qualifying services, the federal government will provide an additional $50—resulting in $100 total for needed healthcare services. In other states, the federal match percentage is higher, such as in Alabama where the federal government pays almost 70 percent and in Mississippi almost 75 percent.

The intended match, however, is often not a match. Rather, states and revenue maximization contractors have developed several financing schemes to claim additional federal matching funds with no additional state spending. Under such strategies, the intended match structure is subverted. Using the Massachusetts example, rather than adding $50 state spending with $50 federal spending for $100 total for Medicaid services, the schemes result in only $50 in federal funds with no corresponding state match. But the strategies often do not end there. Many states further the subversion by routing some or all of the federal matching funds to general state coffers—leaving nothing targeted to Medicaid services. In such instances, healthcare funds intended for the poor are

diverted to general state coffers after the revenue contractors first take
their fee.

Mediscam

The federal Medicaid program provides matching funds for hospitals that
serve a disproportionate share of the poor ("disproportionate share hospitals" or DSH). Under the direction of then Governor Judd Gregg, New
Hampshire discovered it could turn this money intended for the poor into
a general revenue source. The state created a "Medicaid Enhancement Tax"
(MET) to tax the DSH hospitals based on their patient revenues, put the
money temporarily into an "uncompensated care fund" and then the federal government would provide Medicaid matching funds. The state would
give the original MET tax amount back to the hospitals, so there was no
actual additional state spending for the poor, but the state would still keep
the federal matching funds.

Then, New Hampshire pocketed the additional payments in its general funds. Over time, New Hampshire claimed over $2 billion in Medicaid
funds intended to help hospitals serve the poor that were instead diverted
into general state revenue.[1]

These are bipartisan practices. With an anti-tax climate in both red
states and blue states, state and local governments are increasingly
turning to such revenue schemes. When the federal government has
attempted to clamp down on illusory Medicaid maximization practices, governors from both sides of the political aisle have been up in
arms. The governors argue any restrictions on the revenue practices
are "cuts" to Medicaid rather than acknowledging the reality that the
federal government wants to ensure that federal Medicaid funds are
used as intended.

Although a specific total figure is unknown, the scope of these
practices is enormous. And it's alarming that we don't know how
much of what we call Medicaid funding is actually used by states
for Medicaid services, compared to how much is diverted from services to the vulnerable to state general revenue. A 2007 GAO report
explains:

GAO has reported for more than a decade on varied financing arrangements that inappropriately increase federal Medicaid matching payments. In reports issued from 1994 through 2005, GAO found that some states had received federal matching funds by paying certain government providers, such as county operated nursing homes, amounts that greatly exceeded established Medicaid rates. States would then bill CMS for the federal share of the payment. However, these large payments were often temporary, since some states required the providers to return most or all of the amount. States used the federal matching funds obtained in making these payments as they wished. Such financing arrangements had significant fiscal implications for the federal government and states. *The exact amount of additional federal Medicaid funds generated through these arrangements is unknown, but was in the billions of dollars.*[2]

Ironically, while states engage in revenue schemes to maximize and divert federal Medicaid funds, the states are also ramping up efforts to deter Medicaid fraud. States are tracking down and prosecuting bad actors, including doctors, dentists and other health care providers who falsely claim reimbursement of Medicaid funds from the states through illusory practices for their own self-interests. But as states take on a public image almost like an old-time western sheriff trying to stop bandits, behind the scenes the states are bilking the federal Medicaid program for billions—using their own illusory practices to divert funds intended for the vulnerable to general state use. As the GAO explains, *"we designated Medicaid to be a program at high risk of mismanagement, waste, and abuse, in part due to concerns about states' use of inappropriate financing arrangements."*[3]

This chapter explains some of the various and evolving Medicaid maximization schemes used by states, often under the direction of their private consultants. Further, after practices are exposed and described, explanation is provided of how the federal government has tried but has not done enough to reduce use of the schemes.

Intergovernmental Transfers and Upper Payment Limits

For well over two decades, states have used variations of financing mechanisms to leverage increased federal Medicaid funds—often using a form of "intergovernmental transfers" or IGTs. Under typical IGT financing schemes, a state would make a large payment to a healthcare provider, triggering the ability of the state to claim federal Medicaid matching funds. But then the healthcare provider would immediately return the initial payment back to the state through an IGT (so no state spending actually occurs, and the state retains the federal funds). In addition to other types of healthcare providers, states have often used Disproportionate Share Hospitals (DSH) that serve a larger share of the poor for the schemes. The U.S. General Accounting Office explains the illusory practice:

> In particular, these arrangements create the illusion that a state has made a large Medicaid payment . . . which enables the state to obtain a federal matching payment. In reality, the large payment is temporary, since the funds essentially make a round-trip from the state to the Medicaid providers and back to the state. As a result of such round-trip arrangements, states obtain excessive federal Medicaid matching funds while their own state expenditures remain unchanged or even decrease.[4]

Figure 4.1 illustrates how such a practice was used in Michigan. Michigan made Medicaid payments of $122 million to county health facilities, which were then combined with $155 million in federal Medicaid matching funds for $277 million total paid to the county facilities. But then, on the very same day of the payments, the county health facilities only kept $6 million and transferred $271 million back to the state. Thus, through the sleight of hand and round-trip of funds, the state cleared $149 million. The GAO also noted how some states have engaged in a variation of the practice, forcing counties to carry out the transactions using bank loans. The states would require the counties to take out bank loans for an amount the states could use to claim federal Medicaid funds. After the counties wired the bank loan money to the states, the states would send the money right back to the counties as "Medicaid payments." The counties then repaid the bank loans with the

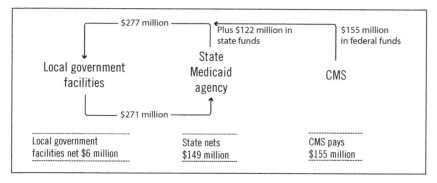

Figure 4.1. Michigan's IGT Financing Scheme. Source: U.S. GAO.

Medicaid payments, and the states would claim and keep the federal Medicaid matching funds.[5]

The federal government has made some effort to reduce such illusory practices, but states and their contractors continuously find new methods. The GAO explains: "As various schemes involving IGTs have come to light, Congress and CMS have taken actions to curtail them, but as one approach has been restricted, others have often emerged."[6]

For example, IGTs have been used along with another device that states and their revenue contractors have honed in on, Upper Payment Limits (UPLs). The UPLs are limits placed on how much the federal government will pay to match state Medicaid spending on certain healthcare facilities. Although intended to reduce excessive and illusory claiming of federal funds by states, the limits have been turned into a key part of such illusory practices.[7] For example, the federal UPL on a day of nursing home care might be $150. But often the established state payment rates to the facilities are substantially lower than the UPL limit. A state might only pay $100 per day to nursing homes—$50 per day less than the UPL. The state then exploits that gap between the UPL and actual state payments in revenue schemes. Figure 4.2 illustrates how the UPL structure works: States make additional supplemental payments above their normal payment rate up to the UPL, claim federal Medicaid matching funds for those payments, and then require the facilities to return the supplemental payments

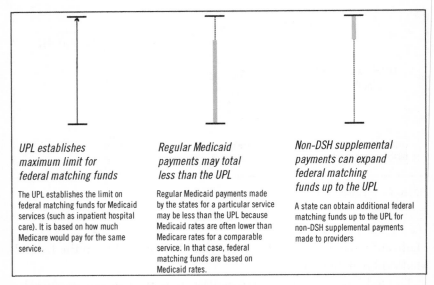

UPL establishes maximum limit for federal matching funds

The UPL establishes the limit on federal matching funds for Medicaid services (such as inpatient hospital care). It is based on how much Medicare would pay for the same service.

Regular Medicaid payments may total less than the UPL

Regular Medicaid payments made by the states for a particular service may be less than the UPL because Medicaid rates are often lower than Medicare rates for a comparable service. In that case, federal matching funds are based on Medicaid rates.

Non-DSH supplemental payments can expand federal matching funds up to the UPL

A state can obtain additional federal matching funds up to the UPL for non-DSH supplemental payments made to providers

Figure 4.2. The UPL Structure. Source: U.S. GAO.

back to the state as an IGT—and the states pocket the additional federal funds.[8]

Oregon's MUPL Program

As a result of such practices, states claim huge amounts of federal Medicaid matching funds without any additional state spending, and then often either use the money for other specified non-Medicaid purposes or just route the funds into state general revenue. For example, Oregon established a strategy of claiming the federal Medicaid funds in order to finance state education programs. A document from Oregon's Legislative Fiscal Office explains the plan:

> The federal Medicaid Upper Payment Limit (MUPL) program allows states to pay publicly affiliated nursing facilities a rate equal to the maximum Medicare rate for all Medicaid nursing facility clients in the state when the Medicare rate exceeds the rate the state would otherwise pay for Medicaid clients. This lets Oregon claim additional federal revenue at no added General Fund cost. The Department of Human Services

(DHS) implements the plan by making payments of General Fund and Federal Medicaid Funds to nine public health districts that operate nursing facilities. The health districts immediately give all or most of the payment to the state through an intergovernmental transfer. After the health districts transfer the payment back to DHS, DHS deposits the Federal Funds portion of the original payment into a special MUPL account as Other Funds. These funds can be used to finance legislatively approved programs.[9]

Here is how the three-step dance works:

1. DHS calculates payment amount; uses budgeted General Fund money to match Federal Funds for payment to health districts
2. Health districts pay back General and Federal Funds as Other Funds
3. Additional Federal Funds (now Other Funds) deposited into MUPL account for other approved state uses.

Oregon initially deposited all the resulting federal Medicaid funds into the state's general revenue. Then in 2001, the state started routing the federal funds into a "Medicaid Upper Payment Limit" (MUPL) account. For the biennial budget beginning in 2001, Oregon estimated the revenue strategy would net $227.3 million in federal Medicaid funds, with the state diverting about 90 percent of those funds to education programs rather than for Medicaid purposes (thus freeing up state general funds that would have been spent on education for other purposes).[10]

As Oregon used the scheme to claim and divert federal Medicaid funds to the state's education programs, other states have simply recycled the federal aid into claiming yet more federal aid—almost like a "pyramid" or "ponzi" scheme similar to that infamously used by Bernie Madoff. In fact, in New York, the state where Madoff was prosecuted, the GAO explains that "[f]unds generated by the state's UPL arrangement were deposited into its Medical Assistance Account. Proceeds from this account were used to pay for the state share of the cost of Medicaid payments, effectively recycling federal funds to generate additional federal Medicaid matching funds."[11]

Texas Diverts $1.7 Billion in Medicaid Funds to General Revenue

Texas is a state where many of its politicians, like former governor Rick Perry, routinely express their disdain for federal aid. But using IGT and UPL strategies like those described above, Governor Perry sought to maximize his state's claims for federal Medicaid funds. From 2008 to 2013, Perry used such illusory schemes to divert more than $1.7 billion in federal Medicaid matching funds to his general coffers.[12] Although the intent of Medicaid programs is for states and the federal government to share in the cost of Medicaid services, "Texas contributes no money and instead forces the state hospitals to provide the state's contribution, then takes the federal contribution for the general fund."[13]

The funds that Texas is diverting are intended to help the poor, and the poor are suffering as a result: "The practice discourages state hospitals from treating the poorest Texans."[14] Because Texas has diverted the federal Medicaid funds away from hospitals serving the poor to its general funds, state hospitals have been forced to cut back severely on providing health to the poor. For example, the University of Texas Medical Branch "dramatically reduced the number of uninsured patients it cared for . . . dropping from 3,182 in 2008 to 233 in 2011."[15]

The GAO, the federal government watchdog organization, explains that practices like that used in Texas are illusory. To put it simply, Medicaid funds should be used for Medicaid purposes:

> The U.S. Government Accountability Office, however, believes the money should be used for its intended purpose. "Our position is that Medicaid payments should be made for Medicaid services made to Medicaid patients," said Katherine Iritani, GAO director for health care issues.[16]

Although concern has been expressed regarding the revenue strategies for well over twenty years, the practices continue. The numbers are staggering, and increasing. States reported in fiscal year 2011 making at least $43 billion in supplemental payments ($26 billion of which were UPL payments), a more than 34 percent increase in just one year, up from $32 billion in 2010[17]—and such supplemental payments are of the type that states have used in the illusory revenue strategies discussed in this chapter.

The federal government has not sufficiently monitored how states have employed such revenue maximization mechanisms, or how additional federal Medicaid funds obtained through the strategies are ultimately used by the states. As the GAO explained in 2012: "We and others have raised concerns about the need for improved transparency regarding the size of the payments and who receives them, as well as the need for improved accountability regarding how the funds are related to Medicaid services."[18]

Moreover, as states are expanding their Medicaid maximization efforts, an alarming incentive is apparent. *If states pay healthcare providers less and thus reduce the quality of care to vulnerable populations, the states can actually route more federal Medicaid funds to their general coffers.* As explained earlier, states have exploited the UPLs by making supplemental payments to healthcare providers at the amount between the state payment amounts actually given to the providers and the UPL, using such payments to claim federal Medicaid matching funds and then requiring the providers to return the original state supplemental payments. If the regular Medicaid payment rate that states pay to health facilities for providing care to vulnerable populations is lowered, then the gap between that rate and the UPL increases and allows states to potentially increase the exploitation. *And, in fact, the GAO notes that states have significantly increased amounts of such UPL payment strategies in recent years, and "[a]t the same time, we have reported that many states have reduced regular Medicaid payment rates in response to budgetary pressures."[19]*

"Bed Taxes"

In addition to intergovernmental transfers and upper payment limits (IGTs and UPLs), states also use tax schemes as another Medicaid revenue maximization mechanism. Commonly referred to as "bed taxes," states often label such tax strategies in more positive and nuanced terms, such as "provider assessments," "federal reimbursement allowances," "Medicaid enhancement," and "quality assessment fees" to name just a few.

Bed taxes work similarly to IGT strategies, but somewhat reversed. Rather than states providing large illusory payments to healthcare providers as the source of state "spending" used to claim federal funds, bed taxes provide the state money used for revenue strategies by taxing the healthcare providers. For example, a state may implement a new tax on daily services of healthcare facilities such as a hospitals, nursing homes, or psychiatric institutions (referred to as a bed tax because the tax may be based on the number of beds used for patients by the healthcare facility). The money from the tax is used to claim federal Medicaid matching funds, and then the healthcare providers are paid back for the tax through either direct payments or increased state Medicaid payment rates to the facilities. The state does not actually use any general fund spending to match the federal Medicaid funds as intended. Bed tax strategies are similar to the IGT and UPL 3-step dance described above, but slightly more complicated:

1. State initiates a tax on healthcare providers such as hospitals and nursing homes based on the number of beds or patients served.
2. Money from the tax is put into some sort of state trust fund such as an uncompensated care fund and then used to claim federal Medicaid matching funds.
3. The healthcare providers are often reimbursed for the total cost of the bed tax.
4. The increased federal Medicaid matching funds are then available for state use.

Although illusory because no state Medicaid matching payments actually occur, some states do use the additional federal Medicaid funds resulting from bed tax revenue strategies to (at least in part) increase payments to the healthcare providers, fund broad categories of state healthcare programs, and to free up state general revenue for other purposes. Other states have more blatantly used the federal aid simply as a source of general state revenue. For example, Wisconsin has diverted $13.8 million annually in bed tax scheme revenue from nursing homes into general revenue.[20] Below, Massachusetts and Missouri provide detailed examples.

Massachusetts: Romney's "Medicaid Money Laundering"

In his campaign for the presidency, Mitt Romney denounced federal aid—including his infamous "47 percent" comments against those who receive government assistance. But during his tenure as governor of Massachusetts, Romney aggressively pursued federal aid funds that he then converted to general state revenue.[21] The first year Romney served as governor, he touted in his summary of his proposed 2004 budget that he was balancing the state budget without increasing taxes, without tapping reserves, and "without the use of fiscal gimmicks."[22] However, tucked into the hundreds of sections of his budget proposal, Romney included fiscal gimmicks in the form of bed tax schemes to maximize claiming of federal aid and to divert the funds from services for the poor to his state coffers.

The *Wall Street Journal* labeled these practices "Medicaid Money Laundering" and a "swindle."[23] As the *WSJ* explained, plans such as Romney's attempt to "dupe Washington" by using illusory financing arrangements to claim federal Medicaid matching funds without actually spending the required state match.

Romney's budget shell games were similar to that created by Judd Gregg, the former governor of Romney's neighboring state of New Hampshire. As described earlier in the book, Gregg taxed state hospitals serving the poor, routed the resulting tax funds into an "uncompensated care fund," which he then sent right back to the hospitals. Although no additional state spending occurred, he used the round trip of hospital tax money to claim additional federal Medicaid matching funds that he then directed to his state's general revenue rather than using them to provide Medicaid services for the state's vulnerable citizens as intended.[24]

Romney's versions of the schemes are laid out in the "outside sections" of his 2004 budget details. For example, his strategies included taxing public hospitals and shifting money in and out of an uncompensated care trust fund, back to hospitals as adjustment payments. And he proposed diverting all resulting federal Medicaid funds from Medicaid services into the state general funds. Here is one example of how he proposed maximizing federal Medicaid matching funds (or "federal financial participation"):

SECTION 280. . . . the division of medical assistance . . . shall *take any appropriate action to obtain the maximum amount of federal financial participation available for amounts paid to hospitals,* determined by the division to be disproportionate share hospitals . . . . Such appropriate action may include, but shall not be limited to, the *assessment on hospitals for their liability to the uncompensated care pool* . . . . Such appropriate action shall include the establishment or renewal of an interdepartmental services agreement between the division and the division of health care finance and policy which may authorize the division to make deposits into and payments from an account established for the purposes of this section within the Uncompensated Care Trust Fund, . . . or authorize the division of health care finance and policy to *transfer uncompensated care fee revenue collected from hospitals. . . . to the division for the purposes of making disproportionate share adjustment payments to hospitals* qualifying for such payments. . . . In no event shall the amount of money assessed upon each hospital exceed the hospital's gross liability to the uncompensated care trust fund. . . . *Any federal funds obtained as a result of said actions shall be deposited in the General Fund.*[25]

And another example:

SECTION 281 . . . the department of mental health, the department of public health, the division of medical assistance and the division of health care finance and policy *shall take any appropriate action to obtain the maximum amount of federal financial participation available for amounts paid for low-income care costs at those mental health and public health facilities determined to be disproportionate share hospitals* . . . . Such appropriate action may include, but shall not be limited to, the establishment of a separate account within the Uncompensated Care Trust Fund, . . . for the purpose of making disproportionate share payment adjustments to such qualifying mental health and public health facilities . . . *Any federal funds obtained as a result of actions taken pursuant to this section shall be deposited in the General Fund.*[26]

Romney also suggested similar strategies to maximize federal funds using mental health facilities, and he proposed using taxes on nursing homes and pharmacies as another means to increase claims for federal

Medicaid funds. Resulting federal Medicaid matching funds had been credited to the Health Care Security Trust Fund. But Romney's 2004 budget proposals suggested diverting all of the resulting tax revenue and federal Medicaid funds into his general coffers.[27]

In such strategies, healthcare facilities serving vulnerable populations are used to claim federal funds. But the healthcare facilities and the poor may get little or nothing, as the state diverts the federal aid and revenue maximization contractors reap millions in contingency fees. Romney used such private companies to help carry out his strategies, including contracts with the Public Consulting Group. In fact, Romney's CFO and budget director for the Massachusetts Medicaid program later joined PCG as a senior consultant working on issues including Medicaid finance and revenue enhancement.[28]

The GAO issued a 2005 report due to concerns with states' use of contingency-fee revenue maximization consultants in revenue strategies such as those used by Massachusetts. A letter from the Romney administration vigorously defended the use of consultants and revenue maximization practices that the GAO labeled as illusory. But the GAO maintained its concerns:

> We did not question the state's authority to make supplemental DSH payments . . . Rather, *our concern was that hospitals should benefit from increased federal reimbursements and Massachusetts's arrangement appeared to result in lower payments to hospitals, despite increased claims for federal reimbursement.*[29]

Similarly, when the Romney administration disagreed that "certain aspects of its upper payment limit (UPL) arrangement . . . were inappropriate," the GAO responded: "[W]e maintain our view that illusory supplemental payments in which providers net only a small portion of the supplemental payments—such as those made in Massachusetts—are inconsistent with Medicaid's federal-state partnership."[30]

Missouri's "Federal Reimbursement Allowance" Program

Former governor John Ashcroft (who became Attorney General under George W. Bush) initiated Missouri's "Hospital Federal Reimbursement

Allowance" (FRA) program. The FRA is a bed tax that has resulted in federal Medicaid funds used as a state revenue source larger than Missouri's corporate income tax, inheritance/estate tax, and county foreign income tax—combined.[31] Legislation signed by Ashcroft in 1992 illustrates the sleight of hand, how money taxed from the hospitals and used to claim federal Medicaid funds can be returned (or offset) right back to the hospitals (thus claiming federal matching funds with no state match):

> 208.420. 1. The director of the department of social services shall make a determination as to the amount of federal reimbursement allowance due from the various hospitals . . .
>
> 3. The department of social services is authorized to offset the federal reimbursement allowance owed by a hospital against any Missouri Medicaid payment due that hospital, if the hospital requests such an offset. *The amounts to be offset shall result, so far as practicable, in withholding from the hospital an amount substantially equivalent to the assessment to be due from the hospital.* The office of administration and state treasurer are authorized to make any fund transfers necessary to execute the offset.[32]

The legislation further shows how any tax revenue payments made from the bed taxes on hospitals are then placed into a fund with the payments made by hospitals tagged for payments back to the hospitals:

> 208.435. 1. The federal reimbursement allowance owed or, if an offset has been requested, the balance, if any, after such offset, shall be remitted by the hospital to the department of social services. The remittance shall be made payable to the director of the department of revenue. *The amount remitted shall be deposited in the state treasury to the credit of the Federal Reimbursement Allowance Fund, which is hereby created for the purpose of providing payments to hospitals.*[33]

And the whole point? To claim more federal Medicaid matching payments: "The requirements of sections 208.400 to 208.470, RSMo, *shall apply only as long as the revenues generated under section 208.405, RSMo, are eligible for federal financial participation . . ."*[34]

In fiscal year 2009, eighteen years after Ashcroft initiated the effort, the practice netted a total of $2.4 billion, including $847.2 million in the initial "federal reimbursement allowance" tax against the hospitals and $1.522 billion in federal funds.[35] The resulting additional federal Medicaid matching funds are not limited to use on Medicaid services as intended, and were claimed without the intended state spending match (due to the illusory bed tax practice), but Missouri has apparently applied the funds at least in large part toward healthcare-related issues. However, the core of the revenue practice in Missouri is still driven by a desire to replace state spending with federal spending:

> Throughout the highs and lows of the state's financial condition, the program has evolved to maximize federal matching dollars and reduce the burden of [the state Medicaid program] on state general revenue . . . [T]he FRA is a major source of revenue to the state, surpassing all but the two largest sources of general revenue . . . This releases traditional general revenue to be used for other state priorities.[36]

Such revenue strategies as that used in Missouri undermine the partnership between states and the federal government in providing Medicaid services to those in need. To start with, Missouri's normal match rate to receive federal Medicaid payments is already generous—only about 37 percent (with some variations) to receive a 63 percent federal match (compared to the 50 percent match rate in Massachusetts). However, "[b]ecause Missouri has pursued provider taxes aggressively to fund its program costs, nearly half of the state's share of the cost of the Medicaid program comes from these provider taxes."[37] Because no state spending occurs in such provider tax structures, "[o]nly 21 percent of the cost of the Medicaid program comes from general revenue funds" rather than the intended 37 percent—which means Missouri's illusory practice has caused the federal government to pay almost 80 percent of Medicaid as opposed to the intended 63 percent.[38]

As a result of Missouri's Medicaid bed tax strategy, "vast amounts of general revenue have been made available over the years to be spent on other state priorities."[39] This effect is felt elsewhere. For example, Alabama bested Missouri in the use of various illusory Medicaid maximization schemes, converting the state's intended 2:1 match into a 9:1 match ($9 in federal Medicaid funds for every $1 dollar of state spending).[40]

School-Based Claiming

An increasing amount of state claims for federal Medicaid funds is not occurring through healthcare-related facilities at all, but through schools—further using children as a resource for maximizing revenue. When children are eligible for Medicaid, states can seek federal Medicaid matching funds under two categories of costs: when schools provide certain types of eligible health services for the children and also for school administrative costs related to Medicaid services.

The federal Medicaid funds are available to help schools provide various covered direct health services through school staff or health practitioners. Such services include health services in relation to special education and the Individuals with Disabilities Education Act (IDEA), services under Medicaid's Early and Periodic Screening, Diagnostic, and Treatment (EPSDT) program, physical and speech therapy, and rehabilitative services. Also, even if a school does not provide direct health services eligible for Medicaid, the school may still be eligible for federal Medicaid funds for administrative costs. For example, federal Medicaid funds are available to help schools pay for administrative costs related to outreach and education regarding the Medicaid program, assistance with Medicaid enrollment activities, referrals to healthcare providers, and coordinating services.

Just as states have turned to revenue maximization consultants to develop the financing strategies such as the IGT, UPL, and bed tax schemes described previously, states have also employed private contractors to help increase claims for school-based federal Medicaid funds. Some states direct all the resulting federal aid to the school districts. But as with the other revenue strategies, several states route the funds intended to help the vulnerable—in this case low-income schoolchildren with learning disabilities or other needs—to general state coffers.

The GAO explained in its 2000 audit report that Arizona, Missouri, and Rhode Island were examples of states that were providing all federal school-based Medicaid funds to the schools at that time. However, other states were routing significant amounts of the federal aid to general coffers. Eighteen states diverted part of the federal Medicaid payments away from schools to state general revenue. Of those identified, ten states diverted between 40 percent to 85 percent of the Medicaid funds to state coffers, and several states used revenue maximization contractors to claim the funds.[41] Further, some states have tried to cash in with the school-based Medicaid funds by not only looking forward but by looking back. For example, in addition to those eighteen states identified in the GAO report, the Office of Inspector General audited Maine for its retroactive claims for school-based Medicaid services. The state retroactively claimed $8.8 million in federal Medicaid funds for services for schoolchildren, but then routed all of the retroactive payments to the state's general fund to help balance the state budget rather than provide the funds to the schools for the Medicaid services.[42] Below are some additional examples of states using poor and disabled schoolchildren in revenue strategies.

Michigan: Contractor Gifts and Diverting Schoolchildren's Funds

Over a three-year period beginning in 1996, Michigan diverted $106 million in federal Medicaid funds intended for schoolchildren. The state used a revenue maximization contractor to help increase the school-based Medicaid claims, and even required the school districts to pay for the service. With 20 percent of resulting federal Medicaid funds paid to the consultant, Michigan school districts only received $4 out of every $10 in federal aid intended to help the schools provide needed Medicaid-related services to children.[43] Here is how the approach worked (using a hypothetical $200 claim):

1. School district expends resources on administrative activities related to Medicaid and submits claim to state for $200.
2. State submits claim to federal government.
3. Federal government provides $100 in federal Medicaid matching funds.
4. State keeps $40 and provides $60 to the school district.
5. School district pays $20 to the revenue maximization consultant.

While Michigan was maximizing and diverting school-based Medicaid funds, the amount of money at stake led to pay-to-play concerns. Another 2000 GAO report found that while Michigan was contracting with Deloitte for school-based Medicaid claiming services, Deloitte was providing gratuities and gifts to government officials responsible for the contracts:

> In our April 2000 report, we discussed the circumstances surrounding the process used by a consortium of eight Michigan intermediate school districts to contract with Deloitte Consulting LLC for consulting and billing services. . . .
>
> We conducted an investigation and determined that Deloitte had provided gratuities, including meals and tickets to professional sporting and theater events, to the school district officials responsible for awarding the contract for consulting services. Records provided to us by Deloitte show that it spent over $170,000 for the gratuities from 1997 through 1999. Officials receiving the gratuities included members of the school district consortium's Medicaid Program Steering Committee and Contract Negotiation Committee.[44]

Federal law prohibits providing such large gifts or gratuities in order to influence contract decisions and business transactions with government agencies, so the GAO referred the matter to the U.S. Attorney's Office for the Western District of Michigan.[45]

New York: A Hypocritical State of Mind

In 2012, the New York State Comptroller discovered that private companies hired to provide special education services for pre-K students were misusing public funds intended to help the children. The Comptroller called the schemes "unconscionable":

> This money was intended to give our most vulnerable children the services they needed, instead the money was used for contractors to landscape their second homes or for no-show jobs. Special needs kids were shortchanged by contractors that had figured out how to game the system.[46]

Similarly, the State Education Commissioner minced no words in saying that "[s]tealing from children with special needs is reprehensible."[47] The Manhattan District Attorney explained: "Through the work of the Office of New York State Comptroller Thomas DiNapoli, who discovered this fraud, and the Public Integrity Unit of my office, we were able to investigate and uncover a scheme that took thousands of dollars away from our city's already strapped education budget."[48]

Then, in 2013, fraud regarding misuse of special education funds was again uncovered in New York and the state again rightfully denounced the practice and prosecuted the perpetrator. The complaint alleged that a man who ran New York preschool programs was diverting aid funds for schoolchildren to himself. According to allegations that are strikingly similar to the various state illusory Medicaid maximization and diversion strategies, the defendant "intentionally inflated the amount of money paid to some employees and contractors" in order to "increase the amount of public money the company received, and much of that money was kicked back to [the defendant]."[49] The U.S. Attorney for Manhattan reportedly explained:

> [The defendant] allegedly orchestrated multiple schemes to enrich himself by taking funds intended for special needs children and diverting them into his own coffers, . . . As today's arrest makes clear, we will not tolerate individuals who cheat local, state and federal government under the guise of helping children, and will do everything in our power to hold them accountable.[50]

However, as the state has condemned and prosecuted individuals who have diverted thousands of dollars in government funds intended for schoolchildren to their own self-interested use, New York itself has diverted not thousands but hundreds of millions of dollars annually in federal funds intended to help schoolchildren to its own self-interested use. As of 2000, New York was using a revenue maximization scheme to claim school-based federal Medicaid funds intended to help provide services to schoolchildren, including special education–related services. Then, rather than using all of the funds as intended, the state would divert half of the aid funds—more than $170 million annually—to general state coffers rather than to help the children.[51]

New Jersey: The Leader in Taking Medicaid Funds from Schoolchildren

New Jersey has been diverting up to 85 percent of school-based federal Medicaid funds to state coffers, compared to 50 percent in New York. And it's worse than that, because not only is New Jersey diverting the funds from its schools, but the school districts must often spend their own money in order to trigger the claims for federal aid (most of which is then taken from the schools). As a result, New Jersey schools have only retained as little as $7.50 for every $100 in Medicaid funds intended for schoolchildren. The GAO explains:

> [S]chool districts' funds often are used to supply the state's share of Medicaid funding for school-based claims. In these cases, the maximum additional funding that a school district can receive is what the federal government contributes. This is substantially less than what a private sector Medicaid provider would receive for delivering similar services. For example, a physician who submits a claim with an allowable amount of $100 will receive $100: $50 in state funds and $50 in federal funds in those states with equal matching between federal and state sources. Given the source of the states' share of funding, states' policies to retain portions of the federal reimbursement, and schools' contingency fee arrangements with private firms, the net amount of federal funds returned to a school district varies considerably . . . as little as $7.50 in New Jersey in federal Medicaid reimbursement for every $100 spent to pay for services and activities performed in support of Medicaid-eligible children.[52]

New Jersey's governor Chris Christie aggressively continued the practice of maximizing and diverting school-based federal Medicaid funds into his general state coffers. The state hired a private revenue maximization contractor, the Public Consulting Group, to run the "Special Education Medicaid Initiative" or SEMI.[53] Under the initiative, local school districts in New Jersey are required to maximize their participation in the SEMI program in order to maximize federal Medicaid funds. Documents from the state show the SEMI revenue projections for the 2013–14 school year, and illustrate the target revenue projections by using schoolchildren in equations.[54] The contractor, the Public Consulting Group, determines the number of Medicaid eligible children who are then included in a target goal for revenue maximization of at least eighteen services eligible for federal Medicaid funds. The simplified revenue equation is described as follows:

Claimable Student Population x Annual Revenue per Student = District SEMI Revenue Projection[55]

New Jersey punishes schools through penalties of a reduction in school funding if they don't meet target goals of using schoolchildren to maximize revenue.[56] As part of the requirements to maximize federal revenue, parental consent is necessary for schoolchildren to be used in the process. The state therefore requires schools to obtain at least a 90 percent return rate on parental consents,[57] and the revenue maximization contractor advises the schools how to do so. The company explains that after working with more than 150 school districts in New Jersey for the SEMI program, "PCG has encountered several districts who have successfully managed the Parental Consent process."[58] Putting together best practices for maximizing parental consent, the company highlights that multiple methods will likely be necessary and that "[w]hen it comes to obtaining Parental Consent, districts sometimes need to be creative in their methods."[59]

Christie's FY 2013–14 budget explains how, after schools are required to maximize participation in the SEMI program, he diverts 82.5 percent of the resulting federal aid intended for special education related services for schoolchildren to his general coffers. The special needs schoolchildren are used as a revenue generator for the state, as the school districts only receive 17.5 percent of the federal funds intended to help them serve the children. The following is the relevant portion from Christie's budget:

39. Notwithstanding the provisions of any law or regulation to the contrary, each local school district that participates in the Special Education Medicaid Initiative (SEMI) shall receive a percentage of the federal revenue realized for current year claims. The percentage share shall be 17.5% of claims approved by the State by June 30.[60]

The diversion does not end there. The state also employs the use of the revenue maximization contractor for the "MAC" initiative to increase claims for federal Medicaid funds for school administrative costs related to Medicaid services—again diverting 82.5 percent of the federal aid to New Jersey's general coffers:

> 40. Notwithstanding the provisions of any law or regulation to the contrary, each local school district that participates in the Medicaid Administrative Claiming (MAC) initiative shall receive a percentage of the federal revenue realized for current year claims. The percentage share shall be 17.5% of claims approved by the State by June 30.[61]

Further, not only is New Jersey diverting funds intended to help schoolchildren, but the state's use of revenue maximization contractors to maximize the claims for school-based Medicaid funds has resulted in multiple audits. For example, a 2010 audit by the federal Office of Inspector General looked into New Jersey's claims for school-based Medicaid funds using MAXIMUS as its consultant. The audit found that over half of the claims sampled were "noncompliant."[62] The state was asked to refund more than $8 million in inappropriately claimed federal Medicaid funds, but the Christie administration refused the request.[63] Similarly, another audit of New Jersey's school-based Medicaid claims using the Public Consulting Group as its revenue maximization contractor found that 36 percent of the claims were noncompliant. Again, the Office of Inspector General requested that the state return more than $5.6 million in inappropriately claimed federal Medicaid funds, and again the Christie administration refused.[64]

As New Jersey has diverted millions in funds intended for special education services to general state coffers, the schools have had to resort to putting billboard type advertisements on its buses—such as using schoolchildren to raise revenue by advertising for Comcast.[65] Mike Yaple, a New Jersey School Boards Association public affairs officer, explains how schools would rather not resort to such advertising, but the underfunded school system is desperate for funds: "In a perfect world, schools would be fully funded and school boards wouldn't even have to think about programs like this . . . But, these are difficult times for many school districts and sometimes a community expects their school board to look at all different options."⁶⁶

Blame for the diversion of school-based Medicaid funds to state general revenue does not lie solely with the states. The GAO noted that federal oversight has been weak and federal guidance has been vague: "[t]hese weak controls permit an environment for opportunism in which inappropriate claims could generate excessive Medicaid payments."⁶⁷ Further, because the school districts and states often turn to private revenue maximization consultants, "[t]his places these firms 'in the driver's seat,' where they design the methods to claim administrative costs, train school personnel to apply these methods, and submit administrative claims to the state Medicaid agencies to obtain the federal reimbursement that provides the basis for their fees."⁶⁸ Both states and their private revenue contractors are incentivized to maximize school-based Medicaid claims: "[b]y being able to capture a share of the school district's federal payments, states and private firms are motivated to experiment with 'creative' billing practices."⁶⁹

Using Elderly Nursing Home Residents as Revenue

In addition to state revenue maximization schemes using schoolchildren and impoverished individuals and families in need of healthcare, the poverty industry strategies also target another vulnerable population—the elderly. The mechanics of the strategies are often similar to those discussed above, including using intergovernmental transfers (IGTs), upper payment limits (UPLs), and bed taxes as illusory schemes to maximize and divert federal Medicaid funds intended for nursing home facilities serving the elderly. State schemes using nursing homes have occurred under the radar of public knowledge for years. As a result, the elderly poor often languish in substandard care as states route their aid funds to private profit and state coffers.

The U.S. Department of Health and Human Services' Office of Inspector General (OIG) issued multiple reports considering the impact of state revenue strategies that use nursing homes, examining individual nursing homes as examples. In congressional testimony, the OIG first explained general concerns with Medicaid revenue maximization strategies such as those explained earlier using IGTs and UPLs:

This is the most common method we have noted by which States divert funds from an intended purpose after drawing down the Federal share of the benefit . . .

States' use of IGTs to divert funds has the following consequences: a State's share of its Medicaid program inappropriately declines; Federal taxpayers pay more than their statutory share; and the increased Federal Medicaid funding derived from those financing mechanisms becomes comingled in general revenue accounts, where it can be used for purposes unrelated to Medicaid, including as the State's match to draw down more Federal dollars for Medicaid and other federally matched grant programs.[70]

Then, the OIG explained how nursing facilities were inadequately funded due to Medicaid maximization and diversion strategies: "Some of our recent audits have explored States' use of IGTs in which some or all of the Medicaid funds that were directed to local public nursing facilities as enhanced payments made under UPL rules were returned to the States instead of being retained at the facilities for the care of patients."[71] The impact of the revenue tactics was not good:

In every case, we found that the gross Medicaid per diem and enhanced payments were sufficient to cover operating costs, but the net payments were not. The nursing facilities were required to return substantial portions of their enhanced payments to the States to be used for other purposes. As a result, the facilities were underfunded. We believe this underfunding had a negative impact on quality of care.[72]

Thus, although total Medicaid funds would have been sufficient to help the nursing homes achieve sufficient operational funding, the state diversion of substantial amounts of the Medicaid funds from the nursing homes to other state purposes resulted in underfunded nursing homes and poor quality care.

The impact of such revenue schemes in New York is described next—emblematic of the effect when aid funds are diverted from intended purpose. Then, the example is carried forward to a look at revenue maximization strategies using nursing homes in two other example states, Maryland and Indiana.

New York: An "F" Grade on Nursing Home Quality

In a 2013 national review of nursing home quality, New York received an "F" letter grade and is ranked forty-fifth in the country in terms of overall nursing home quality of care. The state also received multiple "F" grades in specific categories regarding staffing levels at nursing facilities: *"Professional nursing services were almost nonexistent in New York's nursing homes"*[73]

Despite the reported poor quality of nursing home care in New York, the state has been using its nursing homes in revenue schemes like those described above. The state set its regular daily Medicaid payments to nursing homes at a low rate, lower than the amount needed by the nursing homes. Then, New York has made enhanced UPL payments to the nursing homes above the regular daily rate in order to increase claims for federal Medicaid funds intended for the nursing homes, but the nursing homes have been forced to return up to 90 percent of the upper-payment limit funds to the counties and the state. Below, two county nursing homes in New York illustrate the harm caused by the state's use of UPL revenue strategies.

ALBANY COUNTY NURSING HOME (NEW YORK)
In an audit of the Medicaid payments for the nursing home over a three-year period, the Office of Inspector General uncovered that New York State and Albany County acted as co-conspirators to use the county nursing home in their revenue scheme. Figure 4.3 illustrates the steps of the shifting funds, resulting in more than $82 million in Medicaid funds intended to serve the nursing home residents instead diverted to the county and state general treasuries. Following the steps in the diagram:

1. State used $45.5 million in county funds for supplemental UPL nursing home Medicaid payments, resulting in $45.5 million federal Medicaid matching payments, and the state placed the combined $91 million in a holding account.
2. State paid the $91 million to the county nursing home operating bank account.
3. County took the $91 million out of the nursing home operating account and transferred all the money to the county general fund.

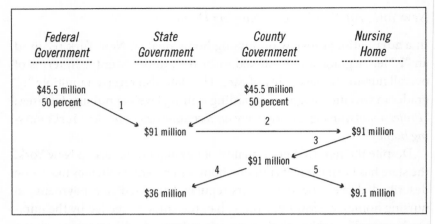

Figure 4.3. The shifting funds of Albany County's nursing home. Source: U.S. Department of Health and Human Services, Office of Inspector General.

4. Without spending a dime, the state took $36 million of the $91 million in Medicaid funds for state general revenue.
5. County took a little more than its original investment in the scheme, only giving $9.1 million to the nursing home.

After New York forced the nursing home to return 90 percent of the supplemental Medicaid payments to the state and county treasuries, the Medicaid funds for the nursing facility were $22 million less than its needed operating budget for the three-year period. The state's diversion of Medicaid funds from the nursing home took place despite the facility receiving an "immediate jeopardy" rating, the worst rating possible by the state Department of Health. Because of its lack of necessary funding, the nursing home could only fill 153 nursing positions although the nursing home's operational plan required 243 nursing positions, and the lack of nursing staff likely contributed to poor-quality care.[74]

A. HOLLY PATTERSON EXTENDED CARE FACILITY (NEW YORK)

During a three-year audit period, the A. Holly Paterson Extended Care Facility received $144 million in regular Medicaid per diem payments. The Medicaid operating costs for that time period were $190 million, far more than the regular payments. The state also provided $203 million in enhanced upper payment limit funding (UPL) but then required the nursing home to return 90 percent of the payments back to the state and county. Thus, the Patterson facility operated at a $25 million deficit. Figure 4.4 illustrates the scheme. Following the steps in the diagram:

1. State used $101.4 million in county funds for supplemental UPL nursing home Medicaid payments, resulting in $101.4 million federal Medicaid matching payments, and the state placed the combined $202.8 million in a holding account.
2. State paid the $202.8 million to the county nursing home operating bank account.
3. County took $182.5 million out of the nursing home operating account and transferred all the money to the county general fund.
4. State took $81.1 million from the county general fund.
5. Nursing home only allowed to keep 10 percent of the Medicaid funds intended to help nursing home residents.[75]

By keeping its regular daily state Medicaid payments to nursing homes low, New York could make greater enhanced UPL payments (the difference between the daily Medicaid rate paid to nursing homes and the limit on UPL payments) to claim more federal Medicaid funds that the state could convert into state and county general revenue. While the

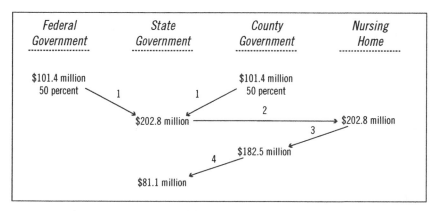

Figure 4.4. The Patterson facility Medicaid scheme. Source: U.S. Department of Health and Human Services, Office of Inspector General.

Holly Patterson nursing home was used in the revenue scheme, the facility received an "immediate jeopardy" rating by the state Department of Health, and nursing home deficiencies resulting from the lack of funding caused harm to residents—including the death of a resident. During the audit period, the nursing home could not afford to hire sufficient nursing staff and almost one hundred needed positions were not filled.[76]

Like the nursing homes in New York, other state nursing facilities reviewed by the OIG revealed similar results. The OIG also examined the impact of state revenue maximization strategies diverting Medicaid funds from the Newport Community Hospital, Long Term Care Unit (nursing facility) in Washington State, and the Nashville Metropolitan Bordeaux Hospital, Long Term Care Unit (nursing facility) in Tennessee. For each nursing facility, because the states diverted Medicaid funds to other state purposes, the nursing facilities were significantly underfunded and thus unable to hire sufficient staff—therefore likely reducing quality of care.[77]

Indiana: An "F" Grade on Nursing Home Quality and Greatest Number of the "Most Poorly Performing" Nursing Homes of Any State in the Country

Indiana nursing homes have not been receiving good marks for quality. A 2009 GAO report concluded that Indiana has the greatest number of the "most poorly performing" nursing homes of any state in the country.[78] Further, an *Indianapolis Star* investigation of nursing homes in 2010 found that one of the causes of the poor quality was that "the most critical caregivers are more scarce in Indiana nursing homes than anywhere else."[79] As the *Star* explains, "Indiana ranks 51st—lower than every other state and the District of Columbia—in the amount of time certified nursing assistants spend with residents."[80] Moreover, in a 2013 report, Indiana received an "F" grade and was ranked 49th out of all states and the District of Columbia in terms of overall quality of nursing home care. The report also uncovered that almost 94 percent of Indiana nursing homes had deficiencies, with more than one out of four nursing facilities cited with severe deficiencies.[81]

But despite concerns regarding quality of care in Indiana nursing homes, the state has diverted tens of millions of dollars annually in federal Medicaid funds intended for nursing home care to its general funds. Many states have created "bed taxes"—such as described earlier—that tax nursing homes for each occupied bed. The money assessed in bed taxes is usually given back to the nursing homes, but the transaction provides an illusory basis for the state to claim additional federal Medicaid funds (in this case intended to increase funding for services to low-income nursing home residents).

Then, states like Indiana have routed significant amounts (if not all) of the resulting Medicaid funds to other state uses. Poverty industry contractors often assist with the practices. For example, Indiana contracted with Myers and Stauffer, LC, to help set the state's Medicaid payment rates (including for nursing homes) and also to help administer the state's version of the bed tax (called the "quality assessment fee" or QAF), and Indiana has pocketed much of the resulting federal Medicaid funds into its general funds.[82] As a result of its revenue strategy, Indiana used the "quality assessment fee" to divert $59.2 million in Medicaid funds from nursing homes to state general funds in 2013,[83] $36.6 million in 2012,[84] $39.6 million in 2011,[85] and Indiana similarly diverted tens of millions annually for many years prior.

Further, the QAF is not the only strategy in Indiana using the elderly in poor-quality nursing homes as a source of funds. In addition to the QAF bed tax scheme, Indiana has been even more ingenious in its use of nursing homes to maximize and divert Medicaid funds—with its largest public hospital system leading the charge. As recognized by the *Indianapolis Star*, Indiana is filled with for-profit nursing homes that have been recognized for providing poor-quality care: "Indiana has among the highest percentages in the nation of for-profit chain nursing homes. And they also dominate the ranks of the state's most poorly performing homes."[86]

Recognizing opportunity, Indiana and the state's largest public hospital system conspired to gain control over many of those poorly performing for-profit nursing homes—but not to improve quality of care. As explained in more detail in chapter 6, the Indiana municipal corporation that runs the Marion County Health Department and hospital system (which includes Indianapolis) has been buying up for-profit nursing homes all across the state, using the nursing homes to claim higher federal Medicaid payments, and then routing the Medicaid funds to other purposes.

Maryland: One of the Richest States in the Country Gets a "D"
Grade in Nursing Home Quality of Care

Maryland is one of the richest states in the country, and Mississippi is
the poorest state. But in terms of quality of nursing home care, the states
are virtually tied—both receiving D grades and coming in 34th and 35th
in the national rankings respectively. According to a 2014 report, "Maryland is the worst nursing home state in the Mid-Atlantic Region."[87] More
than 95 percent of nursing facilities in Maryland have deficiencies, giving the state an F grade for that category. And the state also received D
grades in direct staffing hours and RN hours.[88]

Nonetheless, while Maryland has received such poor marks in terms
of nursing home quality, the state has used its nursing homes to maximize federal Medicaid funds and then has diverted a significant amount
of the money to other state uses.

Maryland has long used a bed tax on nursing homes to increase
claims for federal Medicaid funds, such as the strategies noted previously. In 2010, the administration of Governor Martin O'Malley doubled
the bed tax from 2 percent to 4 percent and simultaneously routed up to
35 percent of the Medicaid funds generated through the revenue scheme
to state general funds.[89] And then the administration increased the tax
again in 2011 to 5.5 percent, and up to 6 percent in 2012.[90]

Prior to the 2010 legislation, Maryland law required that funds generated through the bed tax scheme be used "only to fund reimbursements
to nursing facilities under the Medicaid program" and that "the funds allocated by the Department as reimbursements to nursing facilities under
this section shall be in addition to and may not supplant funds already
appropriated for this purpose."[91] Thus, the law required that additional
Medicaid funds claimed for nursing homes could only be used for the
nursing homes and could not cause a decrease in state appropriations
for nursing home care. But the 2010 legislation changed the requirement
so that only *"[a]t least 65% of the funds* allocated by the Department
as reimbursements to nursing facilities under this section shall be in
addition to and may not supplant funds already appropriated for this
purpose."[92] The legislation thus freed up to 35 percent of the funds generated through the revenue strategy using Maryland's poor performing
nursing homes to be used for other general fund purposes.[93]

Catch Me If You Can Game, and Federal Auditors Are Losing

The federal government has continuously struggled to stop or at least reduce the revenue schemes described above, but as soon as one practice is addressed by new federal regulations, the states and their private contractors simply employ new methods. The "catch me if you can" approach includes a long list of federal regulatory attempts to curb the practices, including a CMS regulation requiring improved transparency and accountability requirements for DSH payments (which have often been the target in the revenue schemes). Also, President Barack Obama's Patient Protection and Affordable Care Act includes cuts to federal DSH payments, under the theory that more of the previously uninsured will now have access to health insurance, and the DSH payments designed for hospitals serving the uninsured will be less necessary. However, neither the tighter CMS requirements nor the cuts to DSH payments address what are categorized as "non-DSH supplemental payments." As states see the DSH payments as a shrinking means of incorporating their schemes, the targeting of the non-DSH supplemental payments is quickly increasing. From 2006 to 2010, federal Medicaid matching non-DSH supplemental Medicaid payments grew by more than $8 billion, with $2.3 billion of that increase caused by only one state—Texas.[94]

Further, despite the regulatory efforts, states have continued the revenue maximization schemes and corresponding diversion of the federal aid. The following examples illustrate evidence of the ongoing state strategies using disproportionate share hospitals:

- The budget estimates for Indiana shows $58 million from the state's disproportionate share hospital program going into the general fund each year for FY2012 and FY2013.[95]
- North Carolina's general fund budget documents for FY2012 and FY2013 include $115 million in funds generated from the disproportionate share program each year.[96]
- Texas dwarfs the other two states' efforts, explaining how it puts federal aid intended for the poor in the general fund "available for general purpose spending." The Texas budget estimate explains: "With respect to federal payments, General Revenue-related revenues from the Disproportionate Share Program, which helps pay for indigent care at state and local hospi-

tals and the closely related Upper Payment Limit Program . . . are expected to total $669 million in 2012–13."[97]

Also, California will apparently claim even more than those three states combined, using just a bed tax on hospitals. Governor Jerry Brown signed a 2013 bill extending the fee on hospitals for three years. Plans for the resulting federal Medicaid funds resulting from the bed tax include routing the money to state general funds (some related to healthcare expenditures unrelated to the hospitals) and using the federal Medicaid money to claim yet more federal Medicaid funds (and continue the cycle):

> In 2013, the fee raised $3 billion. The state received $620 million, some $40 million went to hospitals as grants and the remainder was used as leverage to attract an additional $1.9 billion in federal funds . . .
>
> It is estimated that extending that fee for three more years beginning next year will generate $3 billion for the state's General Fund.[98]

Moreover, Florida has been blatant in its use of intergovernmental transfers (IGT's) to save state general revenue, the illusory practice described above:

> Over the years the amount of dollars that have been used for these activities has grown substantially. A significant portion of the funding in the Medicaid budget for hospitals for inpatient and outpatient services is funded by IGT's in lieu of state general revenue funds. For FY 2009–2010, there was $880,351,951 in IGTs in the Florida Medicaid budget.[99]

With states always seeming to stay one step ahead of the regulatory efforts to halt the diversion of federal aid funds by employing poverty industry revenue maximization consultants, the federal government has grown increasingly frustrated. But despite the frustration, the poverty industry just continues to grow.

5

Cost Recovery

Poverty Industry Taking Child Support from Children and Families

As the preceding chapters illustrate, the poverty industry's scope and effect are immense. Abused and neglected children, the sick, and the elderly are used in revenue strategies almost as if they are resources on industry conveyor belts to tap into as much federal aid as can be extracted. And the reach and impact of the poverty industry does not end with the diversion of federal aid. This chapter explains how even child support has not escaped. Rather than supporting children, much of what we call child support is often converted into a government revenue strategy that is harming children and families.

Children in low-income single-parent households desperately need child support payments. However, reports from the Federal Office of Child Support Enforcement indicate that $28.5 billion—over a quarter of the national child support debt—is owed to the government. The targets of strategies to convert child support into government funding are poor families and children involved in the welfare and foster care systems.[1]

As with the practices described in previous chapters, private companies are again intricately involved with child support revenue strategies. In addition to helping states obtain children's Social Security benefits and maximizing federal Medicaid funds, MAXIMUS also runs entire child support offices. The military contractor Lockheed Martin has also contracted to run state child support offices and even has a contract with the Federal Office of Child Support Enforcement. The national Federal Parent Locator Service Child Support Services Portal, and its access and use of confidential government information regarding millions of people across the country, is housed at the following: "System Location: Lockheed Martin, Building 101, 9500 Godwin Drive, Room F12, Manassas, Virginia 20110-4157."[2]

The first way that states convert child support into a government revenue stream is through our nation's welfare assistance program, called Temporary Aid to Needy Families (TANF). When low-income custodial parents need welfare assistance, states force those parents to transfer their children's rights to child support to the government. States' rationale for taking child support from poor children is to pay themselves back for the costs of welfare assistance, in a forced tradeoff and resulting government debt: mothers and children owing their child support rights and the impoverished fathers owing the paymehts.[3] For most poor families, the ability to pay back the cost of welfare is not a reality and the resulting debt and harm never cease.

The poverty industry's conversion of child support to replenish government revenue is largely unknown to the public. Most people view child support as purely beneficial and only intended for children and custodial parents. But for the millions of children whose child support rights have been taken by the government, the child support enforcement efforts are anything but beneficial. Although initially it may seem to be a fair policy that absent parents should be pursued for government-owed child support to repay welfare costs, the reality of the practice results solely in harm—harm to mothers, fathers, children, and society.

States require poor mothers to identify absent fathers and then to sue them, over and over again. When mothers are poor, the fathers are almost always poor too. Thus, most of the resulting government-owed child support cannot be paid, and huge back payments (arrearages) quickly accumulate. Poor fathers who try to catch up almost always fail, as the poverty industry lines up against them and the relentless enforcement mechanisms never slow: a poor father finally obtains a new job but then is fired after he is jailed for unpaid child support; a truck driver trying to catch up on child support arrearages has his license suspended due to the back payments of child support, so he can't work; a construction worker has 65 percent of his wages garnished for child support and as a result he can't afford his rent or insurance on his old work truck.

As a result of the forced welfare cost recovery mechanisms, the poverty industry is further harming the already fragile relationships between poor mothers and fathers, and poor children often lose contact with their fathers as the insurmountable child support mechanisms drive the fathers away. Moreover, society is also harmed by the welfare cost recovery focus. Poor fathers who are unable to pay child support retreat from their families and are driven into the underground economy, reducing legitimate work and resulting tax payments—and increasing crime.

Worse still, states do not even benefit financially from the fiscal strategy of taking child support from children to recoup welfare costs. With the large administrative costs of the enforcement efforts against poor fathers—including paying private contractors—states may be spending more money seeking to collect child support to repay welfare costs than they are actually collecting. And when government-owed child support is actually collected, taking the money from low-income families increases the economic struggles of the families and increases their likelihood of needing additional welfare assistance, thus increasing state costs.

Mothers, fathers, children, the social fabric, and even the state finances all lose. The only winners, perhaps, are the private contractors of the poverty industry who are profiting from state contracts.

The story of Derek Harvey and his children, discussed in more detail later in this chapter, illustrates the harm. Mr. Harvey took custody of his four children after the mother of his oldest daughter died and the mother of his other children abandoned the children due to substance abuse. He also took custody of a fifth child who was not his own, the half sister to one of Mr. Harvey's daughters. He tried his best to raise all five children as a single father, making only $10.96 per hour working for the city of Baltimore as a landscaper.[4]

Already struggling financially, Mr. Harvey's efforts to raise his children were undermined when the Baltimore City Office of Child Support Enforcement—operated by MAXIMUS—started pursuing him for government-owed child support. According to the company, Mr. Harvey owed about $10,000 in back payments that accrued prior to the change in custody, all of which were owed to the state because both mothers had received welfare assistance (and at which time Mr. Harvey was struggling with unemployment).[5]

A poor father stepped up and took custody of his four children and even another child not his own. He found a low-wage job to try to support them, but then the Maryland Child Support Agency operated by MAXIMUS harmed his efforts to support his children—in the name of child support.

In the second method of converting child support into government revenue, the poverty industry is taking child support from abused and neglected children—and again, the only winners in the practice are private contractors. Similar to welfare cost recovery, states pursue the child support payments when children are in foster care to recoup the state costs of care. So, in addition to the practice of foster care agencies taking children's Social Security benefits discussed in chapter 3, states also take the foster children's rights to child support.

The poverty industry pursues child support in foster care cases against parents who have the least ability to pay. The collection effort is only required when children are removed from poor families: when foster children are removed from prosperous families, the requirement to pursue child support to pay back the cost of care does not exist.[6]

As with welfare cost recovery, it may initially seem appropriate for states to pursue the impoverished parents of foster children for government-owed child support payments to pay back the costs of care. But again, the states' cost recovery effort has only caused harm.

When children enter foster care, the parents struggle to overcome poverty and other barriers with the hope of reuniting with their children. However, the additional debt obligation from government-owed child support can often derail the parents' struggle for economic stability and family reunification. Many states include the child support payments as a requirement in plans before reunification can be considered. States convert foster children into collateral, with the parents only able to seek reunification if they can pay off the government debt first.

When the parents are unable to make the support payments, some states use the government debt as the sole reason to terminate parental rights. For example, as discussed in more detail later in this chapter, an incarcerated father in North Carolina was scheduled for early release due to good behavior and he had an approved reunification plan to regain custody of his daughter. But the state foster care agency terminated his parental rights for not paying child support to reimburse foster care costs. The father only made forty cents a day working in the prison kitchen, thus making only $72.80 during the relevant statutory period, and was not even under a court order or otherwise made aware that he needed to pay support. However, the court found he nonetheless should have been paying over his money toward the cost of foster care and terminated his parental rights for that reason alone. The father lost his daughter for $72.80 owed to the government.[7]

Unfortunately, the case is not unique. As foster care agencies face dwindling state funding, they have increasingly turned to other revenue strategies even when the strategies harm the children in their care—and taking child support is no exception.

Both the welfare and foster care cost recovery strategies using child support enforcement result in the diversion of agency and program purposes. The core purposes of the foster care, welfare, and child support agencies are to serve the best interests of children and families. However, as the agencies focus more on revenue and cost recovery, often aided by private contractors, the self-interested government financial interests undermine the agencies' primary goals.

This chapter explores the practices and concerns regarding revenue strategies of the poverty industry using child support. The policy issues are set out, illegalities exposed, the impact on vulnerable children and families explained—and how we all are harmed by the diversion of purpose when agencies created to serve others instead seek to serve themselves.

Welfare Cost Recovery: Modern-Day Bastardy Acts

The poverty industry's pursuit of child support as a government cost recovery strategy harkens back to the time when children born out of wedlock were considered bastards and their mothers treated as criminals. Over 400 years ago, the old "Poor Laws" of England authorized local parishes to protect society from the risk and burden of supporting children born outside of marriage. Single mothers were forced before public tribunals to name the fathers of their "illegitimate" children and pay bonds to protect the towns from the possible financial burden of their children. State laws in early America mimicked the Elizabethan Poor Laws, including the American "bastardy acts." For example, in 1781, Maryland's "Bastardy and Fornication" law put unwed mothers in jail until they paid security to indemnify the county against the potential cost of their children or until they named the absent father:

[A]ny justice of the peace . . . informed of any female person having an illegitimate child . . . shall call on her for security to indemnify the county from any charge that may accrue by means of such child, and, upon neglect or refusal, to commit her . . . to be . . . safely kept until she shall give such security; but in case she shall on oath discover the father, then the said justice is hereby required to discharge her . . . and directed to call such father . . . before him, and shall cause him to give security . . . to indemnify the county from all charges that may arise for the maintenance of such child.[8]

Still today, although children born to unmarried parents luckily are no longer referred to as bastards in current laws, modern paternity and child support policies are not far removed from the old bastardy acts. States still force unwed mothers applying for public assistance to provide the names of possible fathers of their children in order to indemnify society for the cost of their children. States require the mothers to make their children and themselves available for DNA testing to determine paternity, and then force the mothers to sue the fathers for child support—requiring the mothers to divulge intimate details in courtrooms that are often crowded, dingy, chaotic, and open to the public. Then, the government generally takes any resulting child support payments. States impose these paternity and child support requirements on low-income mothers applying for welfare cash assistance, Medicaid, food stamps, or even childcare assistance necessary for the mothers to work.

States take choices that are available to middle-class and wealthy women away from poor mothers, and strip dignity from the fathers. The long outdated notions of bastardy acts still exist, but there is a key difference today: Governments also collaborate with companies of the poverty industry, seeking to profit by helping to enforce the outdated and harmful welfare cost recovery requirements.

History of Conflicting Purpose

From its beginnings, child support has not been just about supporting children. The origins of child support include English common law, state poor laws, divorce codes, bastardy laws, and criminal nonsupport laws. The purposes of the support obligation were also varied, and a tension emerged between society's interest in providing support to children and the countervailing interest in protecting society from the burden of supporting children. The conflict began more than 200 years ago, and continues today.

EARLY HISTORY: SUPPORTING CHILDREN OR PROTECTING SOCIETY

In England during the 1800s, the duty of parents to support their children was considered a principle of natural law, but there was no legal remedy to enforce the obligation.[9] However, a different and enforceable support obligation also existed at the time, but for the benefit of local governments. The Elizabethan Poor Laws sought to indemnify towns from the potential burden of supporting poor children, giving local parishes the power to pursue fathers for support obligations to protect against the cost of providing public aid to single mothers. Thus, two competing purposes for child support existed from the obligation's English beginnings.

As the child support obligation emerged in America, courts initially recognized support obligations through divorce proceedings and most states began formalizing such support obligations through divorce laws in the 1930s. However, while a child support obligation owed for the benefit of children developed through the divorce laws, other conflicting support obligations were already entrenched in early American law— again for the benefit of local governments rather than for the children. Many states enacted laws modeled on the old Elizabethan Poor Laws so that towns could sue absent fathers to reimburse public aid provided to the mothers and children. States also enacted "bastardy" statutes aimed at protecting society from the burden of "illegitimate" children.

As the child support obligation continued to develop in America, the conflicting interests between state and child became even more entrenched. Courts increasingly described the best interests of children as the overriding concern in child support proceedings. But simultaneously, states and local governments—armed with new federal laws— continued to ramp up their efforts to seek child support as a means of reimbursing welfare costs rather than providing support to children.

FEDERAL CHILD SUPPORT LAWS CONTRIBUTING TO THE CONFLICT

When the U.S. Congress first enacted legislation regarding child support, it initially focused on the government's fiscal interests. Early federal legislation provided requirements to help states pursue support obligations to pay back the costs of public assistance, rather than to benefit children. Then, Congress enacted Title IV-D of the Social Security Act in 1975 as a partnership between the federal and state governments to collect child support. Title IV-D formalized the structure of welfare cost recovery that still exists today: poor mothers applying for public aid must establish paternity, sue the fathers for child support, and simultaneously assign the rights to receive the child support over to the government to repay the costs of the public assistance. Thus, like the Elizabethan Poor Laws of England and the American bastardy acts, the primary goal of the Title IV-D child support program at its creation was not to help poor children but to take child support from poor families to repay public aid.

Almost as an afterthought, Congress also added authority to provide child support enforcement services for parents not receiving welfare and thus not required to sign over their child support to the government. The child support program in America was born in conflict, pitting the government fiscal interests against the interests of the children.

THE BASTARDY ACTS CONTINUE

After creation of the IV-D child support system, the outdated policies from the old bastardy acts were brought forward—and strengthened. With sweeping changes to the welfare assistance program in 1996, called Temporary Aid to Needy Families (TANF), Congress continued the forced child support program with increased sanctions. Under the prior AFDC welfare program, a mother's failure to sufficiently cooperate with child support enforcement resulted in a reduction but not a complete loss of welfare assistance for the family. Under TANF, a mother and her family can lose all benefits.

State laws only allow narrow exceptions to the child support cooperation requirements, and they are rarely provided—although a low-income mother may have several concerns with helping in the child support process. For example, she may fear retaliation from the father, either in the form of abuse toward her and the children or through threats of custody litigation, where the absent parent seeks custody not for the benefit of the children but to avoid child support. The mother may prefer not to name the father, following rape, incest, or other circumstances whereby leaving the father out of the child's life is preferred. She may also hope to either preserve or build a positive relationship with the father, whereas being forced to sue the father for child support owed to the government will often harm the fragile relationship.

Legal Confusion from Conflicting Agency Purposes: Agency Fiscal Interests versus Best Interests of Children

When child support agencies value their own fiscal self-interests above the interests of supporting children, legal confusion results. The conflict goes to the core of child support agency purpose, but has largely been ignored. The analysis provided here illustrates the nonsensicalness that results from child support's conflicting goals, and how something called child support can actually cause harm to children and families.

In all matters regarding child support, the controlling legal standard is the best interests of the children. However, in welfare cost recovery cases, states force custodial parents to assign the child support to the government with the goal of serving the fiscal interests of the state child support agency. Thus, a clear legal question emerges: When the agency's fiscal interests conflict with the best interests of the children, whose interests prevail?

Few courts or state legislatures have addressed or even acknowledged the conflict, despite the fact that such a significant percentage of child support arrearages are owed to the government rather than to children. The following are examples of three states that at least acknowledged the competing goals, but failed to resolve the conflict. The failure is no surprise, because—as the examples illustrate—it's impossible to resolve the conflicting goals when child support agencies are working to take funds from children.

IRRESOLVABLE CONFLICT: VERMONT AND ALASKA

Vermont is one of the few states, if not the only one, to recognize the conflict between the agency self-interests and the best interests of children in state legislation. A Vermont statute seemingly addresses the conflict: explaining that even when child support has been assigned to the state to pay back the costs of welfare, the best interests of the child standard still controls and no support actions should occur that are not in the child's best interests:

> When an assignment is in effect, the state shall be guided by the best interests of the child for whose benefit the action is taken.
>
> * * * *
>
> (2) If, after reasonable inquiry into the circumstances of the family, it is determined by the office of child support that an action would not be in the best interests of the affected child, a support action should not be undertaken.[10]

The statutory language is clear. However, the irresolvable conflict remains. Any dollar of child support the agency takes as assigned support rather than providing the payment to the child is contrary to the child's best interests. Thus, under the language of the statute, *no* support action taken "when an assignment is in effect" could ever be in the child's best interests.

A decision by the Vermont Supreme Court also leaves doubt as to whether the statute will ever be truly applied. In *Powers v. Office of Child Support*, the court addressed whether the child support agency could be sued for not doing its job well.[11] In ruling that the child support agency did not waive sovereign immunity, the court recognized the legislative requirement to protect the best interests of children but nonetheless concluded that "Vermont's statutory scheme was not intended to benefit individual children and custodial parents, but was intended to benefit Vermont society as a whole." The court noted the statutory requirement that the child support agency must always be guided by the best interests of the child, and that the agency purpose does not change when child support has been assigned to the state. However, the court concluded that the state agency's fiscal interests were at least equal to the interests of children: "In neither case does the service provided by [the child support agency] flow to an individual, but instead it flows to the welfare of the state, its children, and its fisc."[12] Thus, when the state's fiscal interests come head-to-head with the interests of children in Vermont, it is doubtful after *Powers* whether the courts will honor or enforce the statutory priority of the best interests of children.

In Alaska, a hopeful decision by the state's Supreme Court acknowledged the conflict between agency fiscal interests and the best interests of children in *Department of Revenue, Child Support Enforcement Division v. Pealatree.* The court even suggested there are some circumstances when the agency's fiscal interests should give way to the best interests of children.[13]

In the *Pealatree* case, the parents divorced and the father received custody of their minor son. As part of the divorce agreement, the parents agreed the mother would not owe child support in exchange for her relinquishment of possible claims to the father's tools that he needed in his job as a laborer. The tools were worth about $5,000. The trial court judge in the divorce ruled that the agreement was a proper offset against child support the mother would otherwise owe of $50 per month, because the agreement allowed the custodial father to keep his tools and better support his son.

Three years later, the father needed welfare assistance and the state child support office began pursuing the mother for child support that was assigned to the state. The agency thus challenged the $5,000 offset against the child support obligation. On appeal, the Alaska Supreme Court ruled that the mother's $5,000 offset against her child support obligation was still valid. The court explained that "situations may exist in which [the child support agency's] direct and derivative rights to recoupment of public assistance payments should yield to equitable considerations," and that "one such circumstance would be a child support offset agreement that a court approved as serving a child's best interest."

However, while recognizing that the best interests of children might be considered in some instances, the *Pealatree* ruling did not fully resolve the conflict between the agency and children. As with the Vermont legislation described above, the core question still remains: If the best interests of children are the guiding standard for child support decisions, when could it ever be in the best interests of children for the child support agency to pursue and take the child support from the children?

Then in Maryland, opportunity was presented to resolve the conflict—but again without success. Child support enforcement actions were contrary to the children's interests, and were driven in large part by a poverty industry contractor, MAXIMUS, Inc. The next section describes the case.

HARVEY V. MARSHALL: THE BEST INTERESTS OF CHILDREN VERSUS THE STATE AND MAXIMUS, INC.

Mr. Harvey is the father of four children born to two different mothers. Both mothers applied for welfare assistance when they initially had custody of the children, which resulted in Mr. Harvey owing child support payments that were assigned to the state.[14] Mr. Harvey was unemployed for much of the time, and the government-owed child support continued to mount.

Then, after finding employment as a landscaper for the city of Baltimore, Mr. Harvey was able to step up for his children. He took full custody of his children when one of the mothers died and the other mother abandoned the children. He also began taking care of a fifth child (not his own), the half sister to one of Mr. Harvey's daughters. He struggled to raise all five children making only $10.96 per hour working for the city.[15]

Mr. Harvey received very little communications from the child support agency, but the arrearages quietly and quickly increased. Then, after all the children came to live with him, the child support agency began its effort to collect the back payments. A private contractor, MAXIMUS, was hired to operate the Baltimore City Office of Child Support Enforcement and asserted that Mr. Harvey owed $32,000 in child support to the government—including for alleged child support obligations that accrued even while he had custody of all the children.[16]

Mr. Harvey obtained a clarified custody order that affirmed he had custody of the children, and the child support obligations that MAXIMUS claimed accrued while the children lived with Mr. Harvey were accordingly dismissed. However, MAXIMUS continued to pursue about $10,000 in back payments that the company said accrued prior to the change in custody, all of which were owed to the state. MAXIMUS pursued child support orders, in the name of Mr. Harvey's children, in order to take money from the household where the children lived.[17]

Mr. Harvey pleaded that the child support was reducing his ability to support the children, harming his credit rating and hopes to finance and purchase a family home, and undermining his effort to save money for the children to attend college. When MAXIMUS refused to stop its collection efforts,[18] Mr. Harvey asked the state child support agency (which oversees the local child support offices) to use its statutory discretion to waive the state-owed arrearages.

The Maryland state agency initially agreed, recognizing the harm to the children. The head of the state child support agency issued a written request to MAXIMUS, indicating that it was in the children's best interests to halt all enforcement efforts against Mr. Harvey other than collecting $1.00 per year as a nominal amount. But MAXIMUS—although under contract with the child support agency—refused the agency's request. MAXIMUS expressed concern that stopping the collection effort would harm its collection rates and thus harm the company's financial interests. At trial, an employee testified that MAXIMUS did not like the proposal because it "would potentially harm the numbers that show the local enforcement office's collection rate."[19]

Despite harm to the children, the state agency acquiesced to the company's refusal. The state gave priority to the fiscal interests of MAXIMUS over the best interests of the children, and the trial court unfortunately agreed.[20]

Mr. Harvey appealed the decision, arguing that the child support agency illegally failed to adhere to the best interests of the child standard but rather submitted to the private interests of MAXIMUS. But the Maryland Court of Special Appeals ruled in favor of the financial interests of MAXIMUS and the state agency. Even though MAXIMUS had contracted to run the Baltimore child support office whose primary purpose is to help children, the court concluded that the purpose of the MAXIMUS contract was not to help children but rather was "expected to increase revenues for the State."[21] The court even concluded that it was appropriate to put the purely private financial interests of MAXIMUS over the interests of children:

> In enacting the pilot program to privatize the Administration's "child support enforcement functions," the legislature evidently sought to take advantage of efficiencies achievable in private enterprise as compared to government operations. In delegating such responsibility, it was obviously necessary to give the private company financial incentives to per-

form the work. The record in this case suggests that one of BCOCSE's financial incentives was measured by its "collection rate" with respect to child support arrears.[22]

The court reasoned that the financial incentives to MAXIMUS were more important than the children served by the child support office that MAXIMUS was hired to run:

> We are persuaded that this motivation is a legitimate one in this context, because financial incentives for performance and achievement are an integral part of private enterprise. The legislature, in enacting [the privatization pilot project], undoubtedly understood that when a private company undertakes to collect monies owed to the State, its success in doing so may benefit both the company and the State. Although this financial incentive may work to the detriment of a debtor like Harvey, as well as his children, it also may work to the benefit of the State's citizens as a whole.[23]

Maryland's top appellate court, the Court of Appeals, agreed and ruled in favor of the state's fiscal interests, and found it appropriate to favor the private interests of MAXIMUS over the interests of the children.

As Mr. Harvey's case moved up through the courts, the conflict between the fiscal interests of the state and its contractor with the best interests of the children was brought to a head. The child support agency looked to the past, even citing the old Maryland Bastardy Act, and argued that the main purpose of Maryland's child support and paternity statutes is to protect the public from the burden of supporting illegitimate children and to increase state revenues through welfare cost recovery. Mr. Harvey argued for the children, pointing out that the Maryland Bastardy Act was repealed long ago and that the primary purpose of child support is now to promote the best interests of children.[24]

The arguments become circular. The pursuit of government-owed child support is established by statute, so the practice seems to be an appropriate statutory goal. However, the best interests of the child standard has not been un-linked from assigned child support, and courts and statutes refer to the primacy of the best interests of children as the standard in all matters regarding child support. The arguments highlight the irresolvable conflict when an agency created to serve children turns against the children. There is never a time when the state's fiscal interests in taking child support payments are not in direct conflict with the best interests of children. And adding the private interests of a company's profit goals into the mix, the conflict deepens—as evident in the Harvey case.

The Harvey case illustrates that as long as child support agencies are turning their efforts against the best interests of children, conflict will result. As discussed below, the conflicts and resulting legal confusion have an enormous impact on children, families, and society.

Impact from the Conflict: Harm Caused by Child Support Agencies and Private Contractors Turning against the Best Interests of Children

When custodial parents can choose whether to initiate child support proceedings, and any payments are provided to the children and their families, the benefit can be great. Although the government IV-D child support program was initially created to collect child support assigned to the government, the services are also available to families not receiving welfare assistance. The side of child support that provides payments to children and families has been effective. Child support collections in the non-welfare cases have grown much faster than collections of the government-owed child support, in significant part because when custodial parents are poor and in need of welfare assistance, the noncustodial parents are also often poor. Total non-welfare child support collections now account for more than 90 percent of all child support collections.

Thus, while not the initial goal of the child support program, the increase in child support collections for non-welfare families provides a significant benefit to families and to society. But the other side of child support, that which forces the child support process on poor families and takes the payments from children, is a different story.

In addition to the poverty industry goal of turning child support into revenue, some proponents contend the welfare cost recovery policies help society by increasing paternal responsibility and improving family relationships. According to the reasoning, if a state forces a poor father to pay government-owed support, he will view himself with greater value and self-respect and will increase contact with his children. However, the theory is not supported by research and the argument fails within the reality of how the child support system impacts poor fathers, mothers, and children.

First, when states take child support from the families, the fathers are less likely to pay or feel any pride and increased family attachment when they are able to pay. Second, when the mothers are poor the fathers are often poor too. The child support orders are often set at unrealistic levels for poor fathers, and large arrearages result. Almost two-thirds of the parents responsible for unpaid child support arrearages had incomes of less than $10,000.[25] Even child support agency officials recognize that because of the economic situation of fathers in the families receiving welfare, the child support arrearages are often uncollectible.

Despite the recognition of poor fathers' inability to keep up with support payments, the fathers are hauled into packed courtrooms and berated by frustrated family court judges, often with the mothers and children present. Many feelings are present during such child support dockets, but self-respect and pride are usually not among them.

Moreover, the poverty industry treats poor custodial mothers the same as the noncustodial fathers, if not worse. Child support can be a tool to enforce the financial rights of women and children. However, in the side of child support where the payments are taken to repay welfare costs, paternalistic and harmful treatment of poor mothers reigns. Rather than enforcing the mother's rights, state welfare cost recovery policies diminish the ability of a mother to choose the best course for her family— whether or not to pursue the absent father for child support—and take any resulting support payments from the mother. The outdated ideas of the bastardy acts, when single mothers were treated as criminals and forced into court to protect society from the burden of their illegitimate children, are still very much alive in the world of welfare cost recovery. The states' treatment of poor fathers and mothers has not resulted in societal benefits, and as the next sections explain, only harm has resulted.

CULTURE OF CONFLICT: STATE VS. STATE VS. MOM VS. DAD VS. CHILD

The child support requirements pit the states' competing interests against themselves and lead to greater turmoil between family members.

For a young low-income single mother in need of public assistance, the forced trip to the child support office has become almost a rite of passage—and not a good one.

The conflict begins within the state child support agency. The agency's competing interests are aligned squarely against each other: serving the best interests of children, while taking money from the children—and further weakening the bonds in the children's already fragile families through the forced child support system.

The child support agency's competing interests fall into two categories, looking forward and outward, and looking back and inward. The outward- and forward-looking interest hopes to support the future best interests of children and to help the families' struggle for economic stability, so that future public assistance is not needed. Looking inward and back, child support agencies have short-term fiscal self-interests of forcing the child support system on families receiving public assistance and taking the resulting payments. The agencies have a shortsighted goal of using child support as government revenue, at the expense of the long-term hopes for the children and families.

When a family is receiving public assistance, allowing the custodial parent to decide whether to pursue child support and giving any payments to the family will serve the state interests in encouraging family economic stability and reducing the family's need for public assistance in the future. However, if the agency provides child support to the families, the money is then not available for the agency's goal of bolstering government revenue. In fact, the competing state interests often collide within a single case. When a custodial parent has left public assistance, back-owed child support is owed to the state to repay welfare costs while current support is owed to the parent. The child support agency will thus strive to take child support from the family while simultaneously trying to get child support to the family. Consider the following example:

Maryland Child Support Agency Argues Against Supporting Children
In child support cases where support payments are owed both to the government and to the families (because the custodial parents stopped receiving welfare assistance), the traditional rule is that families should be paid first before the government. However, an exception to the "families first"

rule has been applied to child support payments received by intercepting tax refunds—which is often the most successful method of collecting support in cases where the parents are poor. Thus, legislation was introduced in Maryland in 2014 to clarify that when child support is collected through tax refund intercepts, the families should be paid first before the government.

The head of the Maryland child support agency argued against prioritizing payments to families and children. The bill did not eliminate any money owed the government, but simply indicated the families should be paid first. However, the agency director incorrectly testified that the bill "requires that taxpayers are not reimbursed for these [welfare] costs even when child support is collected."[26]

Further, similar to the agency's argument regarding foster children's Social Security benefits discussed in chapter 3, the child support agency argued that by taking child support payments from low-income children, the agency could help more children: that these "reimbursements allow the Department to provide services for many more vulnerable children."[27]

In addition to the states' internal competing interests, the forced child support system pits the interests of poor families against each other. Studies of fragile families show that young, poor families have potential for healthy relationships between the parents, and the possibility to become two-parent families. Most mothers want the fathers to be significantly involved in their children's lives, and most of the fathers want to be involved. However, rather than supporting the families with services targeted to encourage healthy relationships, states force the mothers to sue the fathers—with any payments routed away from the families. The result is not positive for the relationships.

Further, the child support cooperation and assignment requirements also add conflict between the children and the parents. The poverty industry alienates low-income fathers from their children as the fathers are not able to keep up with support payments owed to the government, and the fathers may reduce contact with the children because of embarrassment or the desire to avoid enforcement efforts. Most children want their fathers involved in their lives, and the children likely cannot understand the forced child support system. As the children see their mothers suing the fathers, the children may blame both parents as the fathers retreat from family involvement.

Thus, the diversion of child support into state revenue and private profit comes at a high cost of conflict. The competing agency interests collide and the poverty industry's revenue goals cause a weakening of the already fragile relationships in struggling families. Our welfare program has a stated legislative goal of encouraging and supporting two-parent families. Why then is a policy continued whose conflicting interests tear fragile families apart?

SOCIETAL COSTS

In addition to the conflict described above, society is harmed by the poverty industry's diverted use of child support. When child support is provided to families, the payments have a significant impact on reducing the number of children living in poverty. When states and their contractors use support payments as revenue, fewer children can escape poverty. The impact is felt by all of us. A study found that the costs to the U.S. economy resulting from child poverty amount to about $500 billion annually, or almost 4 percent of the GDP.[28]

Also, societal harm results as the child support requirements cause low-income noncustodial parents to retreat from the workforce. The impact is felt disproportionately by young African American men. As the poverty industry initiates pursuit, the fathers face unrealistically high support orders, license suspensions, and having their wages garnished as much as 65 percent. As a result, many poor fathers will retreat from the "above-ground" economy. A recent economic study found that stricter child support enforcement causes an increase in criminal activities among low-income fathers, as the fathers seek to avoid the regular labor force.[29]

The ripple effect of low-income noncustodial fathers leaving the formal economy is immediate. The obligors are more likely to engage in criminal activities, less likely to seek medical care without employer-sponsored health insurance, less likely to pay taxes, less likely to pay child support, and less likely to have a positive relationship with the custodial parents or their children.

IMPACT ON FAMILY ECONOMICS
They don't want to cooperate, because it will only hurt their
family. They don't want to have the State collect their children's support, because it will hurt their children.
—Child support caseworker[30]

States require single parents applying for welfare assistance to establish and pursue child support and simultaneously trade away their
children's rights to the child support payments. Proponents have con-
tended the tradeoff is a good bargain. In exchange, the families receive
regular welfare assistance payments (although with time limits and
work requirements). However, considering the economic realities of
families receiving welfare, the harm of the forced tradeoff becomes
apparent.

Children and families are forced to give their child support rights to
the government when the families have the greatest need for additional
financial support. Families on welfare are the most economically fragile
at the time when they try to leave welfare for work. If the families were
also able to receive child support payments, the payments could enhance
their ability to build up greater economic stability in preparation for
leaving welfare.

A policy experiment in Wisconsin uncovered what should be
obvious—that allowing child support to benefit children is better for the
children and their families, and better for the state as a result. The state
received a waiver from the welfare cost recovery rules in 1997 so it could
pass any child support payments directly to families receiving welfare.
Studies examining the waiver program indicated significant success, including "increased paternity establishment, increased child support collections, and little additional government cost."[31] In fact, allowing child
support to benefit children can reduce the cost of welfare:

> Child support may also reduce the costs of public assistance. If child
> support provides sufficient income to help a single parent become self-
> sufficient—perhaps by packaging child support with own earnings and
> other work-related supports—child support may (indirectly) reduce reli-
> ance on, and the costs of, welfare.[32]

Further, the child support cooperation and assignment requirements cause additional negative family economic impact by reducing informal and "in-kind" support from noncustodial parents. When states require poor mothers to sue poor fathers for payments that are then taken from the children, the fathers are less likely to provide informal financial help, buy food and clothing, or help with transportation needs and so on. The Department of Health and Human Services Office of Inspector General (OIG) investigated problems with the child support requirements and warned of the harm: that "child support enforcement may actually make some TANF families worse off. "[33] The OIG explained that noncustodial parents may stop providing informal or in-kind support to custodial parents who cooperate in establishing and enforcing child support obligations owed to the government. To counter the possible harm, the OIG recommended that states should take advantage of flexibility available within federal child support rules and reconsider their current child support policies to ensure they are not "counter-productive to long-term goals of helping clients attain independence and self-sufficiency."[34]

IMPACT ON PUBLIC ECONOMICS

Finally, even the fiscal motive of the poverty industry in converting child support to revenue is not successful. At first glance, the cost-effectiveness of the child support program seems excellent and improving every year. For the side of child support providing payments to children, that conclusion is true. But for the other side of child support, the program is a fiscal failure.

In 2011, the total administrative costs for child support collections reached $5.7 billion, resulting in $25.1 billion in support payments provided to the families and children. The social value of such payments to families is enormous. As a comparison, the total amount of child support provided to families was more than $8 billion greater than the approximately $17 billion in total federal spending on the nation's welfare program. The additional financial support greatly increases the families' economic stability, and the support payments also create an additional "cost avoidance" benefit: When child support payments are provided to families, the families are less likely to need public assistance and savings to public finances result. For example, a study found that the increased family economic stability from child support paid to families in 1999 resulted in $2.6 billion in avoided public assistance costs.

However, whereas the $5.7 billion in total administrative costs resulted in $25.1 billion in child support collections that were owed to families, the administrative costs resulted in only $1.6 billion in welfare cost recovery payments.

Even dividing out the administrative costs to only consider the welfare cost recovery caseload, the cost effectiveness is minimal and likely even negative. The total administrative costs are not broken down by type of case, but the costs of enforcement in child support cases where the parents received welfare are often significantly higher—because the obligors are poor and collections more difficult. To put it simply, we may likely be spending more on child support enforcement in cost recovery cases than the resulting collections. Further, this fact does not even take into account the lost cost avoidance benefits when support payments are not provided to families, as described above.

Thus, the poverty industry's practice of converting child support into government revenue and private profit causes conflict and harm—and creates no benefit to children, families, the government, or society. Perhaps the only beneficiaries of the revenue strategy using poor children and families are the private contractors who profit from helping states pursue the payments. Further, the harm does not stop with families receiving welfare. The next section explains how child support is also converted into government revenue in the foster care system.

Using Foster Children as Collateral for Poverty Industry Revenue

Similar to welfare cost recovery, child support is also used in a revenue strategy involving foster children. The poverty industry targets abused and neglected children removed from poor families, pursues child support against the parents, and takes any resulting support payments away from the children. This policy does not apply to children removed into foster care from well-off families—only poor children. The practice again harms the children, families, and society. And again, the only winners are the private contractors.

Some of the same private contractors that help foster care agencies obtain foster children's Social Security benefits also help states with this foster care revenue strategy using child support. For example, foster children may encounter MAXIMUS when the company contracts with the state to help obtain children's disability payments, and then also when the company contracts to help enforce child support obligations.

This revenue strategy targets parents who have the least ability to make support payments. When their children are removed, often due to neglect caused by the circumstances of poverty, the parents struggle to improve their economic stability in order to reunify with their children. However, the government-owed child support obligation can undermine the reunification efforts by saddling the low-income parents with debt obligations they cannot afford to pay—and that do not help their children.

States use the foster children as collateral, mortgaged to secure the debt for their own care. Rather than only using federally required case plans to help parents overcome barriers in order to reunify with their children, states often illegally convert the case plans into debt collection tools. The parents can only get their children back if they can pay off the poverty industry. Almost like repossession of a car, the poverty industry may permanently terminate parental rights if the parents are not able to pay the government-owed debt.

Losing a Daughter for $72.80
A North Carolina foster care agency terminated a father's rights while he was incarcerated for the sole reason of not paying child support to the government.[35] The child had done well in her father's care prior to his temporary incarceration. Because his parents were deceased and he had no siblings or other family able to care for his daughter, she was taken into foster care.

He called the social worker as often as he could to check on his daughter. He sent letters. He arranged to have a Christmas gift sent to his daughter through the Angel Tree organization. And he had opportunity for good work after release: "During his service in the U.S. Army from 1978–1983, from which he received two honorable discharges, T.D.P.'s father earned his GED . . . Prior to his incarceration, he worked as a restaurant cook and the restaurant manager told him she would rehire him upon his release . . ."

While the girl "was in her father's care, DSS concluded the minor child was happy, healthy, clothed and well-fed . . . ," and "[d]ue to his good be-

havior, his release date had been changed to an earlier date . . ." The social worker thus approved a plan for reunification with the father after his
pending early release date from prison. But the agency simultaneously initiated proceedings to terminate parental rights.

Although the father made only pennies a day working in the prison
kitchen, and he did not even know he owed support because there was
no child support order in place, the court found he should have paid to
reimburse the costs of foster care. The court found he could have paid "an
amount greater than zero." At 40 cents a day, the father earned $2.80 per
week. Thus, considering his total earnings and the maximum amount of
support he could have paid during the statutory period, the father's parental rights were terminated for a government debt of $72.80.[36]

The case illustrates the result when the poverty industry subordinates
the child welfare system's primary goals to a focus on cost recovery,
and unfortunately the case is not alone in its Dickensian approach. As
underfunded state agencies desperately seek revenue, combined with
federal laws and funding rewarding fast termination of parental rights,
such examples will likely continue.

The revenue tactic of taking child support from foster children results in diverted agency missions. The core purposes of child welfare
agencies are to protect the welfare of children and to strengthen and
preserve families. The purpose of the child support program is to serve
the best interests of children. However, through the forced intersection
of the two programs in order to obtain foster children's child support,
the poverty industry causes a shift that subverts the agencies' intended
missions to a fiscal pursuit.

Caseworkers often oppose the revenue strategy, expressing concern
that parents of foster children "are 'too poor to pay,'" that "enforcing
child support will be detrimental to the parent/child relationship."
Further, "[t]hey do not believe that child support serves to stabilize
the family unit and help insure its future integrity."[37] States imposing
government-owed child support on already poor families creates a barrier to parents' efforts to obtain economic stability and reunify with their
children. Foster children face longer stays in foster care and weakened
parent-child relationships. Also, like with welfare cost recovery, there is
little if any revenue gain to the government. The impoverished parents

of foster children cannot meet the child support obligations, and the government administrative costs in pursing the support likely outweigh the resulting collections.

Illegality also results. States take plans required to help parents re-unify with their children and often turn them into debt collection tools, requiring the parents to pay the government debts before reunification is allowed. The practice conflicts with statutorily required reunification efforts as impoverished parents are even further impoverished. And if the parents cannot make the payments, an unconstitutional practice can occur as in the case described above—terminating parental rights for a government-owed debt.

The stated goal of turning foster children's child support into revenue is simple: paying back the government costs of foster care. Our initial emotional response to the cost recovery effort may be equally simple: parents who abuse and neglect their children should be held legally responsible to pay child support to the government for the resulting foster care costs. However, the simple goal and emotional desire to punish the parents and hold them accountable come to a halt when confronted by reality.

Targeting Impoverished and Broken Families

Foster children don't come from rich families. When states remove children into foster care, their parents have often endured years of hardship: homeless and unemployed parents unable to find work; parents who grew up in the foster care system repeating the cycle; disabled parents unable to obtain adequate services; mothers who have been subjected to domestic violence; parents trying to overcome addictions; and single mothers who received welfare struggling to make it on their own.

A national study found that children in poor families were twenty-two times more likely to experience some form of maltreatment than children in better-off families.[38] This poverty correlation doubles when considering only child neglect (children in poor families are 44 times more likely to experience neglect), and neglect is the most common type of maltreatment. Foster care agencies often treat such circumstances of poverty as grounds for child removal.

The poverty correlation in foster care is heightened by the lack of services to help poor families stay intact. Federal law requires state foster care agencies to make "reasonable efforts" to prevent the need for child removal. The requirement could trigger needed assistance to poor families prior to child removal, but unfortunately state agencies often overlook the "reasonable efforts" requirement, and services are therefore not adequate. A survey of foster care caseworkers found that parents of foster children were in need of services at the time of removal. Needed services included child care so the parents could work; domestic violence services; treatment for addictions; assistance with housing; services for mental health problems; and access to medical care, but the needs were often unmet.[39]

Further, the disproportionate impact on the poor is exacerbated by the funding structure of the child welfare system. Although some federal funds are available under Title IV-B to help struggling families stay together, the funds are capped. But the funds available under Title IV-E to pay foster care costs after children are removed are not capped and are only limited by the number of eligible children. About ten times the amount of funding has been made available for foster care services after child removal, as opposed to funds available to help poor families stay together.

In addition to the funding discrepancy, the federal funds for foster care services are targeted so that foster care agencies are incentivized to remove children from poor families. States agencies can only receive the IV-E funds on behalf of children removed from poor families that would have been eligible for welfare assistance. States often hire poverty industry contractors to develop strategies to increase the "penetration rate," the percentage of foster children who come from poor families and are eligible for the IV-E funds. Children growing up in poor families face greatly increased risk of being assessed for abuse and neglect, and then states further target the children because they come with federal funds attached.

The Law Behind the Revenue Strategy: Discretion to Serve the Best Interests of Foster Children Ignored

States pursue child support obligations against the parents of foster children and divert the resulting payments to replenish government revenue, under the laws governing the Title IV-E foster care program. The requirements only apply when a child is removed from a poor family, and then the child welfare and child support agencies work together to pursue child support payments from the parents. States take any resulting payments in order to repay the costs of foster care.

The revenue strategy formally began in 1984, when Congress inserted language into Title IV-E that formed the basis of foster care cost recovery through child support enforcement that continues today. The following requirement was imposed upon state child welfare agencies:

> [W]here appropriate, all steps will be taken, including cooperative efforts with the State agencies administering the program funded under part A of this subchapter and plan approved under part D of this subchapter, to secure an assignment to the State of any rights to support on behalf of each child receiving foster care maintenance payments under this part.[40]

Even with the cost recovery law in place, foster care agencies still have wide discretion to serve the best interests of foster children and only initiate child support cases when no harm is done. But the discretion is usually ignored.

The "where appropriate" clause in the statutory language gives states flexibility to consider the children's interests and family circumstances before referring a foster care case for child support enforcement. Federal guidance explains that states have discretion to determine "which cases are appropriate for referral." And "[t]o determine if a case is 'appropriate' to refer to the title IV-D agency," the guidance continues, "the State should evaluate it on an individual basis, considering the best interests of the child and the circumstances of the family."[41] Suggested factors include whether reunification is a goal and whether the state-owed child support obligation would be a barrier to reunification.

A few states, like Ohio, California, and Rhode Island, implemented policies to take advantage of the discretion by considering the children's best interests and reunification concerns. However, many states only provide exceptions to the child support requirement in instances of domestic violence. Other states, like Maryland, Nebraska, and Texas, provide no exceptions at all regardless of any harm that may result.[42]

As explained in earlier sections of the book, taking foster children's child support is just one of many poverty industry revenue strategies—

and the strategies often overlap. For example, just considering the various forms of cost recovery strategies, a foster child's mother may likely have received cash welfare assistance prior to her child's placement in foster care. Because of the welfare receipt, the state would force her to sue the noncustodial father for child support to repay the costs of the welfare assistance, as described in the first part of this chapter. If the mother then encounters difficulties and the state places her child in foster care, the state may initiate simultaneous child support collection efforts against both parents to repay the costs of foster care services. Further, if the child suffers from a learning disorder or other disability, the child may be eligible to receive Social Security benefits—which the child welfare agency will also take to reimburse foster care costs. The result is a bureaucratic cost recovery focus that diverts the agency missions, harms the children and families, and creates significant social costs.

Child Welfare Agencies' Missions Diverted by the Poverty Industry

Child welfare agencies exist to serve dual goals—protecting the interests of children and strengthening and preserving families. The agencies are supposed to help families with services to prevent the need for child removal. And if a child is removed, the agencies will provide care and services for the child while also assisting the parents with reunification efforts.

Thus, protecting the best interests of the children is at the forefront of the agencies' goals, with a simultaneous mission of preserving the families. But the poverty industry is undermining the missions. The industry ignores the best interests of children and harms family preservation and reunification, diverting the agency goals of protecting children to revenue maximization.

SERVING CHILDREN AND FAMILIES VERSUS RACE FOR THE MONEY

A child removed from her family into foster care will encounter a swirling world that will determine the fate of the parent-child relationship. The child and her parents will be surrounded by a blur of meetings with caseworkers, reports, court hearings, discussions with lawyers, counseling and therapy, classes to improve parenting skills, and visits to doctors and mental health professionals. Ideally the interests of the child and parents are not lost in the confusing mix. However, states will also initiate the cost recovery focus, as well a powerful force: legal requirements and financial incentives that will encourage a race toward terminating parental rights.

The child welfare system's policies were significantly altered through the Adoption and Safe Families Act (ASFA) in 1997. The goal of assisting family reunification in foster care cases was not eliminated, but ASFA also shifted focus toward promoting adoptions due to concern about children languishing in foster care. Parental rights must be terminated before an adoption can occur, so ASFA set short time limits for states to begin the termination process. Along those lines, "concurrent planning" is encouraged, where child welfare agencies actively pursue adoption while simultaneously providing required reunification services.

ASFA provides some discretion to allow more time for reunification when doing so is in the best interests of the children, but money trumps all. States often ignore the discretion because the financial incentives are all geared toward quickly terminating parental rights. For example, agencies are worried they may not maximize federal funds if they do not terminate parental rights quickly. Also, financial awards are provided to foster care agencies for each finalized adoption but no similar financial incentive is provided to work toward family reunification.

Even with states' race to terminate parental rights encouraged by financial incentives, child welfare agencies have a core mission of providing reunification services to strengthen and preserve families. The agencies are supposed to "prevent or eliminate the need for removing the child from the child's home . . . ," and if child removal occurs the agencies must provide reunification services "to make it possible for a child to safely return to the child's home."[43] Thus, despite ASFA encouraging states to terminate parental rights as quickly as possible, family reunification continues as a key component of required case planning goals. However, the reunification requirements are often weakened as a result of the government's cost recovery focus. Again, private contractors are often present. In addition to contracting with states to pursue government-owed child support, the poverty industry companies also help states maximize revenue through strategic compliance with the ASFA and other Title IV-E requirements.

POVERTY INDUSTRY REVENUE VERSUS
FAMILY REUNIFICATION

Although the child welfare system is structured against the poor, hope remains for some parents. A good caseworker may work through the bureaucratic barriers, develop a relationship of trust with the parents, and develop a case plan with reunification assistance. For example, if a child is taken into foster care because the parents are facing homelessness, unemployment, and substance abuse, the caseworker might help locate housing assistance, a drug treatment program, and help with job training.

Overcoming poverty is not easy, but the parents can make good progress with effective caseworker assistance. However, when the parents face the greatest vulnerability and need for services, the foster care agency shifts its role as social services provider to the goal of revenue maximization. And while the agencies and their private contractors initiate government-owed child support, the financial pursuit will increase the parents' economic difficulty and harm their struggles to reunify with their children.

A report by the OIG found that most foster care caseworkers don't approve of the child support cost recovery requirements. The caseworkers often "expressed opinions that families of IV-E Foster Care children are 'too poor to pay,'" that the child support requirements could hamper family reunification, and "that enforcing child support will be detrimental to the parent/child relationship." The caseworkers explained they "do not believe that child support serves to stabilize the family unit and help insure its future integrity."[44] The report recognized that foster care caseworkers were reluctant to refer cases to child support enforcement because they cared about helping their clients:

> Foster care staff are oriented to talk in terms of an individual child. They form interpersonal relationships with the families they serve. On the other hand, most IV-D Child Support Staff view themselves as adversaries of "absent parents." The child support staff tend to be "bottom line oriented."[45]

Despite the concerns and harm, the OIG expressed a belief that foster children might benefit from the child support cost recovery requirements. Although any child support payments are taken from the children, the OIG asserted foster children might benefit indirectly through paternity establishment that could trigger possible inheritance and insurance rights and also information regarding genetically linked medical problems. Further, the report explained that the paternity establishment could help a child potentially form social relationships with the father that otherwise might not occur.

However, the U.S. Department of Health and Human Service's Assistant Secretary for Planning and Evaluation (ASPE) disagreed with the OIG's positive view that child support cost recovery can be helpful in some foster care cases—expressing concern about the conflicting missions:

> I believe your draft does not address several important issues, and therefore oversimplifies the extent to which Child Support collections for foster care children can or should be pursued. . . . The report does not adequately address the real and perceived conflicts between the activities and goals of the IV-D [child support] program (maximizing collections) and those of the IV-E [foster care] program (maximizing family reunification).[46]

Unfortunately the focus on government revenue apparently won out in the OIG report, which called for improved collaboration with child support staff in order to increase child support enforcement in foster care cases. The OIG acknowledged but quickly disregarded the concerns of HHS leadership: "We agree that child support should only be pursued in 'appropriate' cases. However, we continue to believe that the majority of children in foster care can benefit from IV-D Child Support services, such as paternity establishment and locating absent parents."[47]

The OIG's conclusion that child support cost recovery in foster care cases can actually help the children does not withstand scrutiny. Most children enter foster care due to family poverty. Pursing government-owed child support against impoverished parents does not help the children, undermines parents' reunification efforts, and harms the parents' relationships with their caseworkers. Further, while the child welfare program has expressed desire to increase the involvement of noncustodial fathers in their children's lives, increased cost recovery efforts have the reverse effect. The government-owed child support obligations can further alienate parents from each other, and cause the noncustodial fathers to further retreat from the agency in pursuit. If the primary agency interaction with fathers takes the form of child support obligations the fathers cannot afford to pay, threatening the fathers with incarceration due to contempt, suspending their driver's licenses, and garnishing 65 percent of their paychecks for support payments that are taken from the children, the fathers will seek to avoid rather than embrace agency involvement.

Moreover, the OIG's claim that foster children can receive benefit from child support enforcement because of the parent identification and location services is based on a misunderstanding of the law. Foster care agencies can request parental location assistance from child support offices, and paternity can be established, without referring a child's case for child support enforcement.

With all harm and no benefit to families or children, the only potential beneficiary of child support cost recovery in foster care cases is the poverty industry: the state agencies looking to replenish government revenue and the private contractors seeking to maximize profit. And in fact, states also do not win because government agencies receive little or no financial benefit—and likely incur a loss. As explained regarding child support cost recovery used in welfare cases, payments from child support enforcement in foster care cases are overshadowed by the cost of enforcement. The parents of foster children are almost always poor, and collecting support payments from impoverished parents is not a successful undertaking. The administrative costs of collections are likely close to if not greater than the resulting collections Also, states taking child support payments from families and children results in the loss of "cost-avoidance" benefits, the cost savings when parents and children are less likely to need public assistance in the future when child support is paid to families rather than routed to government coffers.

Children are harmed. Families are harmed. Social costs are increased. Any revenue gain to the government is questionable at best. Only the poverty industry contractors stand to benefit. The conclusion is simple. When child support benefits children, the collection effort can be worth the cost. When states divert child support toward cost recovery, the questionable fiscal benefit to the government is simply not worth the harm that results.

Illegality of Using Foster Children as Collateral

The poverty industry's effort to use foster children's child support as revenue is a fiscal failure and includes negative policy implications. Further, illegality can result.

ILLEGAL DIVERSION OF AGENCY MISSION

Agencies enforcing government-owed child support obligations against the parents of foster children conflicts with the required goal of family reunification. The diverted agency mission conflicts with federal law.

Foster care agencies must make reasonable efforts "to preserve and reunify families." A case plan is required, and the plan must include services to help the parents overcome difficulties so that a safe reunification may be possible.

Agencies are supposed to provide services and plans to help make reunification more likely, not more difficult, and not add burdens irrelevant to the children's interests or that do not address the causes for child removal. However, the agency enforcement of government-owed child support in foster care cases has nothing to do with the causes for child removal, is harmful to the children, and the additional obligation will make reunification less likely.

Many state foster care agencies even insert the government-owed child support as an element in the required reunification plans. The agencies use foster care children as collateral: If the parents do not meet the case-planning requirement of paying child support to the government, the children are not returned.

When states pursue government-owed child support obligations that harm family reunification goals, or when the government debt is inserted into required reunification plans, the federal statutes that require a focus on family reunification are violated. The conflict has a significant negative effect on case planning goals, and as the next section explains, the conflict can lead to the termination of parental rights.

UNCONSTITUTIONAL PRACTICE: TERMINATING PARENTAL RIGHTS FOR A GOVERNMENT-OWED DEBT

We have not rid ourselves of debtors' prisons only to substitute for that Dickensian horror, the termination of the debtor's parental rights.[48]

Several states include the failure to pay government-owed child support as a statutory factor for terminating parental rights. Some states even allow the unpaid debt alone to serve as grounds for termination. Such statutory grounds for terminating parental rights are unconstitutional, subordinating the constitutionally protected parent-child relationship to the fiscal interests of the poverty industry.

The government interest in termination of parental rights proceedings is supposed to be protecting the welfare of children, not pursing government-owed debts. For example, if a parent owes money to repay government loans for a child's education, should the parent lose her child if she falls behind on the loan payments? A child placed in foster care is obviously different, because the child is removed due to abuse or neglect. However, the reasons for ultimately terminating the parent-child relationship must always be based on the best interests and welfare of children, and support payments owed to the government are not related to those interests.

Agencies terminating parental rights due to government-owed child support divert the child welfare mission toward agency cost recovery, with the children used as collateral. The parents can try to reunite with their children if they can keep up with payments owed to the government, but they can lose the child-collateral if they fall behind.

In fact, several state court decisions have upheld the termination of parental rights due to the government-owed debts. For example, in the case discussed earlier, the appeals court in North Carolina allowed a termination of an incarcerated father's parental rights for the sole reason that the father failed to make government-owed support payments. Although the agency caseworker developed a plan for the father to reunite with his daughter after prison release, the agency also initiated the process to terminate his parental rights—and the only reason provided was the government debt. The agency relied on the following North Carolina statute:

(a) The court may terminate the parental rights upon a finding of one or more of the following:

. . . (3) The juvenile has been placed in the custody of a county department of social services. . . . and the parent, for a continuous period of six months next preceding the filing of the petition or motion, has willfully failed for such period to pay a reasonable portion of the cost of care for the juvenile although physically and financially able to do so.[49]

The father was actually not even under a court order to pay child support, and he only made 40 cents a day working as a cook in the prison.

However, the court found he should have paid some "amount greater than zero" and used his failure to do so as the grounds to permanently remove his daughter.

Similar examples exist in other states. In Georgia, a teenage girl gave birth to a daughter while she was in foster care. The seventeen-year-old mother was separated from her daughter because the foster care agency did not find a placement that would let them stay together. Once separated, the agency required the young mother (who was still in foster care herself) to make support payments to repay the costs of her daughter's foster care. The agency made the government debt part of her reunification plan.[50] The mother then had to leave foster care when she turned eighteen, but the agency kept her daughter and filed a petition to terminate parental rights six months after the mother aged out of care. The juvenile court explained: "[T]here is no doubt that this mother loves this child. However, her own circumstances have placed her in the position of not being able to provide the basic necessities for the child since the child's birth one and one-half years ago."[51]

The Georgia appellate court noted several difficulties the young mother faced as reasons for terminating her parental rights. The mother could not maintain stable housing, she had not finished high school, she struggled with mental health difficulties including post-traumatic stress disorder, and she did not have health insurance. Further, in addition to such difficulties faced by many foster children trying to transition to independence, the court emphasized another factor as reason to take away her daughter: The struggling mother was $220 behind on the government-owed child support payments.[52]

Unfortunately, such examples are not uncommon. In South Carolina, courts have ruled that unpaid child support owed to the government can be the sole reason for terminating incarcerated parents' parental rights.[53] Other Georgia cases have allowed termination of parental rights of an incarcerated mother and disabled father, explaining that the state's "law requires a parent to financially support his or her child while the child is in foster care, even in the absence of a court order"[54] and "even if personally disabled"[55] or "unable to earn income."[56] And in other North Carolina cases, a parent's rights were terminated because the parent was only able to pay $136 of $300 owed toward the cost of foster care,[57] and a court found it appropriate to terminate parental rights for unpaid support where a young struggling mother was not even told she was supposed to pay support to the government.[58]

The parent-child relationship is constitutionally protected, and the grounds for termination of parental rights can only occur when in the best interests of the children. Thus, the agency focus on debt collection as a reason to terminate parental rights is an unconstitutional infringement on the parent-child relationship, in violation of substantive due process.

Supreme Court Justice Ruth Bader Ginsburg explained that the U.S. Supreme Court has been "unanimously of the view that 'the interest of parents in their relationship with their children is sufficiently fundamental to come within the finite class of liberty interests protected by the Fourteenth Amendment'" and "that '[f]ew consequences of judicial action are so grave as the severance of natural family ties.'"[59] The Court recognized a fundamental liberty interest in the parent-child relationship that requires meaningful inquiry into the substantive content of state statutes providing for terminating the relationship.

Substantive due process is about more than process. The Supreme Court explained in *Troxel v. Granville* how the doctrine requires a focus on fair content—not just fair procedures:

> We have long recognized that the Amendment's Due Process Clause, like its Fifth Amendment counterpart, "guarantees more than fair process." . . . The Clause also includes a substantive component that "provides heightened protection against government interference with certain fundamental rights and liberty interests."[60]

As Supreme Court Justice Antonin Scalia explains, the heightened scrutiny is a "a substantive component, which forbids the government to infringe certain 'fundamental' liberty interests *at all*, no matter what process is provided, unless the infringement is narrowly tailored to serve a compelling state interest."[61]

That test is not met when a state statute allows the termination of the parent-child relationship due to a government-owed debt. When a state seeks to terminate parental rights, a clear and compelling state interest exists to protect the welfare of children. But a state agency ending the parent-child relationship because of money owed to the government is not related to that state interest.

Refocusing Child Support Toward Helping Children

The conclusions to be drawn from this chapter are simple. When multiple agencies that exist to serve vulnerable children and fragile families are engaged in collaboration, the result should help the children and families—not cause harm.

Child support enforcement actions should not work against the interests of children and their families. The agency pursuit of government-owed child support when families receive public assistance or when children are in foster care causes harm and results in no benefit: The agency cost recovery effort harms the best interests of children; further divides fragile families as the parents are pitted against each other; weakens the economic stability of impoverished families; undermines the efforts of families to reunite with children in foster care; alienates poor fathers from their families and from the above-ground economy; and there is little if any positive revenue effect for the state agencies, and more likely a fiscal loss.

As long as states continue their cost recovery efforts using child support, the interests of children and families will conflict with the states' fiscal pursuits and the only winners will be the private contractors. The harm can be remedied by ensuring child support is only pursued and used to help children. More detailed recommendations to realign the agencies' missions are included in the conclusion to this text.

PART III

Looking Forward, and Reclaiming the Safety Net

6

The Expanding Web of the Poverty Industry

This chapter sheds light on how the poverty industry and its practices are continuing to expand with a growing web of interconnections and revenue schemes between private contractors, human service providers, and states. Examples illustrate the increasing and varied efforts to use the most vulnerable among us as revenue tools.

For example, companies that run nursing homes have sought to maximize profits by drugging the elderly residents with psychotropic drugs for unapproved reasons. With the residents sedated to a state of submission, the companies cut costs by hiring fewer nursing home staff while Medicare and Medicaid funds become company profit. Similar fiscal motives have led to alarming growth in the use of psychotropic drugs for children in foster care and juvenile detention facilities. Simultaneously, pharmacies have profited by illegally promoting the use of their psychotropic drugs to these nursing home residents and institutionalized children for off-label uses, including illegal incentives to doctors.

Another alarming practice involving nursing homes has emerged in Indiana. A municipal agency in Indianapolis has been buying up for-profit nursing homes all across the state, using the nursing homes as a means to claim higher amounts of federal Medicaid funds, and then diverting the resulting federal aid for other purposes rather than increased services and quality of care for the nursing homes' residents.

And the poverty industry keeps growing, with seemingly endless examples of the industry using vulnerable populations to bolster revenue. States are outsourcing probation services and collections of court fines and fees, with the effect of bringing back debtors' prisons. Private companies are contracting with state and county courts that serve the poor, almost to the point of running entire court systems. Increasingly, private contractors run state juvenile detention centers, foster care group homes, and even entire foster care systems. Companies that provide hospice care, services intended to aid the dying, are targeting patients who may not actually be dying in order to maximize profits from government aid.

The creative energy of the public/private partnerships could be used by human service agencies to explore new and better ways to serve the intended beneficiaries of the agencies' services. However, rather than adhering to a mission of best serving the impoverished, the poverty industry is perfecting and growing its abilities to use the vulnerable in order to serve itself.

Drugging the Vulnerable for Profit

Another poverty industry revenue strategy that uses the vulnerable involves drugs—lots of drugs. Nursing homes have often drugged the elderly to the point of sedation, reducing the need for nursing home staff and thus maximizing nursing home profits. Foster care homes and juvenile detention centers have used similar tactics, with doctors accepting gifts and speaking fees from pharmaceutical companies while prescribing their drugs for off-label uses to children. Facilities and agencies find doctors to prescribe psychotropic and anti-psychotic drugs to foster children at high rates, often related to categories of disabilities linked to revenue strategies using the children's Social Security benefits and Medicaid funds from special education services. Further, some hospitals have used a national discount drug program intended to help the poor to generate revenue: receiving the discounted drugs, selling them for a higher price, and then pocketing the difference. And lawsuit after lawsuit brought against pharmaceutical companies have uncovered illegal marketing and kickback schemes to increase profits through increased use of psychotropic drugs to foster children and nursing home residents.

Nursing Homes Drugging the Elderly to Reduce Costs

Nursing homes have often become more about revenue and profit, and less about providing high-quality care for our nation's elderly. The facilities have looked to decrease operational costs as a primary way of improving the bottom line, often leading to a reduction in staffing. And to allow for reduced staffing, nursing homes often drug elderly patients so that less staffing is needed to care for them. The nursing homes prescribe medications to their elderly residents for off-label purposes, such as multiple strong anti-psychotic drugs when no psychosis is present. The nursing homes reduce costs and increase revenue, provide the elderly with poor care, and Medicaid and Medicare foots most of the bill.

Both privately run and government-run nursing homes have used the revenue strategy, but the private for-profit nursing homes employ the drugging strategy more frequently. Studies and investigations have found that nursing home residents are frequently prescribed psychotropic medications when not needed and for unintended purposes. For example, at one nursing home in Connecticut, "two-thirds of long-stay residents are receiving antipsychotic drugs, even though they do not have a psychosis or related condition that regulators say warrants their use."[1] As of 2013, nursing homes have been giving more than one out of five residents antipsychotic drugs despite mounting concerns and a federal initiative aimed at reducing the practice.[2] An article in the *Wall Street Journal* explains the economic incentive nursing homes receive:

> Nursing homes often find it difficult to balance the demands of caring for certain patients against the pressure to keep staff costs down. The economics of elderly care can work in favor of drugs, because federal insurance programs reimburse more readily for pills than people.[3]

Harm often results from the extent to which nursing homes use such drugs. An investigation by the *Chicago Tribune* explained: "Frail and vulnerable residents of nursing homes throughout Illinois are being dosed with powerful psychotropic drugs, leading to tremors, dangerous lethargy and a higher risk of harmful falls or even death."[4] For example, a seventy-four-year-old man "was in a nursing home near Peoria for less than a day before staff members held him down and injected him with a large amount of an antipsychotic drug," and "[a] few hours later he fell, suffering a fatal head injury."[5] The drugged nursing home residents often become so lethargic they are living out their last years in almost lifeless fashion. Again from the *Tribune* investigation:

> Some residents on antipsychotic drugs become so lethargic they must be hospitalized. They cannot feed themselves, attend physical therapy or talk

with loved ones. Residents once capable of caring for themselves become immobile and incontinent. It is common for nursing staff to struggle to wake up residents at mealtimes.[6]

At one of the Illinois nursing homes, the inspectors encountered an elderly female resident affected by the drugging:

[I]nspectors described a 78-year-old woman walking around with a blank look on her face. Her eyes were wide open, and she rarely blinked. When health inspectors checked her medical records, they discovered that the nursing home had been giving her large doses of antipsychotic drugs, even though she was not psychotic. The woman could barely speak to inspectors. But with the same blank expression on her face, she did manage to tell them this: "I want to go home."[7]

Rather than nursing homes providing treatment that is really needed, antipsychotics have seemingly become the sedative cure-all. For example, an elderly woman was often upset and repeatedly asking to use the bathroom, and the response was as follows:

Nurses responded by giving her injections of two antipsychotics, inspection reports state. When that didn't work, the woman was sent to a hospital for a psychiatric evaluation. The psychiatrist reported back that the woman had a urinary tract infection.[8]

Juvenile Facilities Drugging Children as Fiscal Strategy

The poverty industry has applied the same drugging revenue strategy to children. Foster care homes, detention centers, and residential treatment centers often prescribe children psychotropic medications to reduce costs and increase revenue. In Florida, for example, the agency entrusted with the care of troubled youth opted to drug the children to reduce costs and because of ties between the state psychiatrists and pharmaceutical companies:

A relatively small percentage of young inmates pumped full of pills actually suffer from the serious psychiatric disorders that the FDA allows to be treated by these powerful drugs. But adult doses of anti-psychotic drugs have a tranquilizing effect on teenage prisoners. *Prescribing anti-psychotics for so many rowdy kids may be a reckless medical practice, but in an era of budget cuts and staffing shortages, it makes for smart economics.*[9]

The numbers are staggering: "[T]he Florida Department of Juvenile Justice has been buying twice as many doses of the powerful anti-psychotic Seroquel as it does ibuprofen. As if the state anticipated more outbreaks of schizophrenia than headaches or minor muscle pain."[10]

A 2007 investigation by the *Palm Beach Post* found that "in 24 months, the department bought 326,081 tablets of Seroquel, Abilify, Risperdal and other antipsychotic drugs for use in state-operated jails and homes for children."[11] The investigation concluded: [t]hat's enough to hand out 446 pills a day, seven days a week, for two years in a row, to kids in jails and programs that can hold no more than 2,300 boys and girls on a given day.[12]

In addition to children cared for by the Department of Juvenile Justice, an investigation found that children in foster care in Florida have also been prescribed psychotropic medications at much higher rates than other children. The suicide of a seven-year-old boy in foster care prompted the investigation. Gabriel Myers was taken into foster care when found with his mother, who was passed out on drugs. The boy, who had been sexually abused, ended up hanging himself with an extendable shower chord in his foster care home. Although the agency had no records for the drugs, the autopsy determined he was on multiple psychotropic medications including at least one that had been flagged for associations with suicide.[13]

The overuse of psychotropic medications among children in foster care or detention centers is not limited to Florida. Reports by the GAO in 2011 and 2012 found agencies and facilities were prescribing psychotropic medications to foster children at very high rates. Thousands of foster children were prescribed five or more of such drugs at the same time. Even infants in foster care are being given the drugs.[14] The report found that the child welfare system in Massachusetts prescribed psychotropic medications to almost 40 percent of all foster children. A 2004 study found that the Texas foster care system gave the drugs to 42 percent of the state's foster children. And of foster children in group homes or residential treatment centers, the centers prescribed psycho-tropic medications to almost half the children in their care.[15] A longtime Texas court-appointed special advocate (CASA) for children described her concerns:

> [The CASA volunteer] recalled seeing a 3-year-old foster child who was "drooling on the couch," because he had been prescribed behavior-altering and anxiety drugs soon after he went into foster care.
>
> "Foster homes are using psychotropic drugs to control these children. They can have more children in their home that way," she said. "I have cried with kids who have been so messed up on this medication. . . . If they're on the medication, their need is shown to be higher, and the pro-viders get a higher reimbursement rate."[16]

In Georgia, a 2010 investigation by the *Atlanta Journal-Constitution* similarly found that private foster care agencies were drugging children to reduce costs. Morningstar Treatment Series, a private foster care agency that runs the "Youth Estate" group home, was cited multiple times by the state for inappropriately using antipsychotic drugs on the children. The drug usage was described as improper chemical restraints used "as a means of convenience" for the group home's staff:

> One resident, for instance, was drugged for "non-compliance," accord-ing to an incident report prepared by Morningstar. The resident had argued over serving an in-school suspension, so a nurse gave the child Ativan, an anti-psychotic, and Benadryl, an over-the-counter antihis-tamine also used as a sedative. After "lying on the bench for a little while," the incident report said, the child completed the suspension "without fighting it."[17]

Subsequent to the citations for improper use of drugs, the state ordered the private foster care agency to revise its drug policies. But the agency did not stop. For example, a child "received Valium for 'agitation and aggression'; when the child still didn't calm down, a nurse gave him the powerful anti-psychotic drug Thorazine."[18] No prescriptions were pres-ent: "In those instances, as in others, inspectors noted, "there was no valid prescription for the medications given."[19] The state warned the private agency after the multiple violations that adverse action would be imposed, and then imposed its penalty—only a $450 fine. And another private agency received a similar slap on the wrist:

> Inspectors documented numerous deficiencies in oversight by Bethany Christian Services of Atlanta, for instance . . . Two other foster parents with Bethany forced a child to swallow a Benadryl tablet. The foster parents, the child said, called it a "sleep vitamin." From 20 investigations and four other inspections since May 2008, the state has cited Bethany Christian eight times for a total of 27 rules violations. Just once, however, did the state impose a penalty: a $500 fine this January.[20]

Drug Industry Encouraging the Drugging Revenue Strategies

In addition to the incentive of nursing homes and foster care facilities to reduce staffing costs by prescribing more psychotropic medications, pharmaceutical companies have also encouraged increased drugging of foster children and elderly nursing home residents. Illegal marketing, gifts, and kickbacks are not uncommon. Lawsuits have resulted in multiple billion-dollar settlements, but have not seemed to slow the practice.

The investigation by the *Chicago Tribune* and ProPublica into the use of psychotropic medication in nursing homes, noted above, uncovered the impact of one psychiatrist—Dr. Michael Reinstein. Many of the nursing home patients to whom he was prescribing the drugs "suffered from side effects so severe that they trembled, hallucinated or lost control of their bladders."[21] In 2007, this one psychiatrist wrote more prescriptions for the antipsychotic drug clozapine than all of the doctors in Texas combined.[22] According to the investigation, "[d]ocuments filled out by Reinstein suggest that if each of his patient visits lasts 10 minutes, he would have to work 21 hours a day, seven days a week."[23] Three of his patients died of clozapine intoxication, and one of the nursing home residents who died had five times the toxic level of the drug in his blood.[24]

The extent of Reinstein's prescriptions apparently did not go unnoticed by the large pharmaceutical company AstraZeneca. The *Tribune* reported that head of the company's U.S. sales wrote that the doctor might be worth half a billion dollars to AstraZeneca, that "'we need to put him in a different category,'" and "should answer 'his every query and satisfy any of his quirky behaviors.'"[25] The company paid him $490,000 over a decade to promote the antipsychotic drug Seroquel. And "Reinstein provided the company a vast customer base: thousands of mentally ill residents in Chicago-area nursing homes."[26]

In a 2014 investigation by the Denver Post, similar practices were exposed regarding psychotropic medications targeted toward foster children. The story notes how "[p]harmaceutical companies wooed academic leaders, ghostwrote articles, suppressed damaging health data and lavished doctors with gifts to make prescribing powerful psychotropic drugs to children a blockbuster profit center," with particularly strong impact on foster children where the drugs are often used for "off-label" uses.[27] The investigation found that the Colorado child welfare system prescribed antipsychotic drugs to foster children at twelve times the rate of other children on Medicaid.

> In Colorado, nine of the top 10 most prescribed drugs for foster children in the Medicaid program are psychotropics, according to the most recently available data. In contrast, for non-foster children, only one psychotropic is among the top 10 most prescribed drugs in Medicaid.[28]

The investigation addresses a lawsuit against GlaxoSmithKline regarding marketing and other practices to encourage use of psychotropic drugs on poor children. An insider salesperson at the company noted how "he became disgusted with Glaxo's all-expense-paid trips to Jamaica and Hawaii for physicians and their guests to train them how to give speeches touting the drugs," and the investigation exposed how speakers received over half a million dollars annually to promote the use of antidepressants on children despite lack of FDA approval.[29] To promote the antipsychotic drug Risperdal for children, Glaxo reportedly created a "Back to School Bash" and a marketing plan to increase use of the drug on children—even providing "starter kits" to child psychiatrists that included free samples and coupons for the drug, along with lollipops and toys.[30]

The *Palm Beach Post* investigation of Florida juvenile detention and residential treatment centers, discussed above, similarly found that psychiatrists hired to care for the troubled youth were taking "huge speaker fees from drug makers—companies that profit handsomely when doctors put kids on antipsychotic pills."[31] According to the *Post*, one out of every three child psychiatrists hired by the state juvenile justice system within the five years prior to the investigation had taken speaker fees or gifts from companies making antipsychotic medications.[32]

An investigation in California by the *San Jose Mercury News* also uncovered similar concerns. For example, the investigation found that California doctors who prescribed psychotropic medications to foster children received more than double the money from drug companies as typical California doctors.[33]

Lawsuits have been plentiful, brought by government and insiders against the pharmaceutical companies for inappropriately pushing their psychotropic drugs for use in nursing homes and for children in foster care, group homes, or detention centers. Below are some example settlement agreements:

- 2014—The U.S. Department of Justice announced that Omnicare—the largest supplier of drugs and pharmacy services to nursing homes—will pay $124 million to settle allegations that the company paid kickbacks to obtain contracts to supply drugs to nursing homes with Medicare and Medicaid patients. Omnicare had previously agreed to a $98 million settlement in 2009, including for allegations that Omnicare "solicited and received kickbacks from a pharmaceutical manufacturer, Johnson & Johnson (J&J), in exchange for agreeing to recommend that physicians prescribe Risperdal, a J&J antipsychotic drug, to nursing home patients.[34]
- 2013—Johnson & Johnson agreed to pay $2.2 billion to settle civil and criminal charges that the company illegally promoted its antipsychotic drugs for unapproved use on elderly nursing home residents, the mentally ill, and vulnerable children.[35]
- 2012—Abbott Laboratories agreed to pay $1.6 billion to settle claims of illegal marketing of the anti-seizure drug Depakote. The Justice Department explained that Abbott admitted to marketing the drug to nursing homes for off-label uses, including controlling the behavior of elderly dementia patients.[36] "The company trained its sales representatives to promote Depakote to nursing homes as a way to sedate patients without running afoul of a federal law intended to prevent overuse of certain medications."[37]

- 2012—GlaxoSmithKline (GSK) agreed to plead guilty and pay $3 billion to settle criminal and civil claims, including illegal promotion of Paxil for off-label uses to children. "GSK unlawfully promoted Paxil for treating depression in patients under age 18, even though the FDA has never approved it for pediatric use."[38]

- 2010—AstraZeneca agreed to pay $520 million to settle claims and to resolve allegations that the company illegally promoted its anti-psychotic drug Seroquel for unapproved uses on the elderly and children. "According to the settlement agreement, AstraZeneca targeted its illegal marketing of the anti-psychotic Seroquel towards doctors who do not typically treat schizophrenia or bipolar disorder, such as physicians who treat the elderly, primary care physicians, pediatric and adolescent physicians, and in long-term care facilities and prisons."[39]

- 2009—Ely Lily agreed to plead guilty and pay $1.415 billion to settle criminal and civil claims that the company illegally promoted its antipsychotic drug Zyprexa for unapproved uses, including for vulnerable children and elderly nursing home residents.[40] "In one marketing effort, the company urged geriatricians to use Zyprexa to sedate unruly nursing home patients so as to reduce 'nursing time and effort,' according to court documents."[41]

- 2009 Pfizer and its subsidiary Pharmacia & Upjohn Company agreed to pay $2.3 billion to settle criminal and civil claims regarding illegally marketing and providing kickbacks to promote multiple drugs, including promoting the use of the antipsychotic drug Geodon for unapproved use on children.[42]

- 2007—Bristol Myers Squibb agreed to pay $515 million to settle claims, including promoting its antipsychotic drug Abilify for unapproved use on children and the elderly in nursing homes. The claims also alleged that the company "paid illegal remuneration to physicians and other health care providers to induce them to purchase BMS drugs," including consulting fees and "travel to luxurious resorts."[43]

However, even the growing list of multi-billion-dollar settlements seem to be just minor bumps in the road for the pharmaceutical industry practices.

Buying the Elderly to Maximize Revenue

According to studies, the use of psychotropic drugs on residents has often been more prevalent in for-profit nursing homes than in non-profit or government-owned nursing homes—and the for-profit facilities have also used lower staffing levels and have experienced greater numbers of deficiencies.[44] The profit potential of privately run nursing homes has not gone unnoticed as lucrative investment firms have begun to buy up the companies. For example, the Carlyle group—often known for buying defense contractors, among other types of companies—acquired HCR Manor Care in 2007 for $6.3 billion.[45] HCR Manor Care is one of the largest private operators of nursing homes in the United States.

The potential to make money from for-profit nursing homes also became the foundation for a creative revenue scheme in Indiana, where a municipal hospital agency has bought up private nursing homes all across the state. Rather than bringing the nursing homes under government control to improve services, the aim has been to use the elderly to increase revenue for other purposes.

Health and Hospital Corporation (HHC) is an Indiana municipal corporation and government agency that operates the Marion County Health Department and hospital system (which includes Indianapolis). Back in the early 2000s, HHC was losing money—operating at a $30 million annual deficit. Urged by state legislators who were looking broadly toward ways to maximize federal funds, HHC collaborated with the state human service agency to come up with ideas to increase federal aid as a revenue source.[46]

HHC's target became the elderly residing in for-profit nursing homes across the state. In essence, HHC has been buying up the elderly in their last remaining years and using them to leverage more federal aid to use for other purposes—rather than using the aid to improve nursing home care as intended.

HHC and state officials recognized an opportunity related to federal Medicaid funding policies for nursing homes.[47] The federal government sets maximum payment limits for federal Medicaid matching payments, and states have discretion to decide what service providers receive the maximum payments. So in 2001, the Indiana legislature passed legislation to allow the state's government-owned nursing homes to re-

ceive higher Medicaid payments.[48] The fiscal impact statement of the
legislation explains that the bill allows "the Office of Medicaid Policy
and Planning (OMPP) to increase Medicaid reimbursement rates for
government-owned and operated nursing facilities to the extent allowed
by federal statutes and regulations." The analysis further describes how
the increased rates are designed to maximize federal Medicaid funds:

> In addition, the bill requires that each governmental transfer or other
> nursing home payment mechanism that OMPP implements must maxi-
> mize the amount of federal financial participation that the state can ob-
> tain. This provision can be interpreted as requiring the state to investigate
> and implement alternative means of leveraging federal dollars through
> the Medicaid program potentially increasing federal reimbursement with
> little or no additional state funding.[49]

Then, after using the nursing homes to increase Medicaid funds, HHC
routed the funds to uses other than improving care in the nursing
homes.

Actually, during the same legislative session, the Indiana House and
Senate passed separate legislation to add language requiring that any
increased federal Medicaid payments must be provided to the nursing
homes. The bill required that "[a]ll money used to generate additional
federal financial participation under this chapter through an intergovernmental transfer or other payment mechanism and any additional
payments that are received by the state through an intergovernmental transfer or other payment mechanism under this chapter shall be
distributed to Medicaid nursing facilities."[50] However, then Governor
Frank O'Bannon vetoed the separate bill and thus stripped the language
that would have required all additional federal aid claimed in the name
of nursing homes to be distributed to the nursing homes.[51] Governors
Joe Kernan, Mitch Daniels, and Mike Pence continued where O'Bannon
left off and allowed the strategy to grow.

With legislation in place allowing higher Medicaid claims for
government-owned nursing homes, HHC started buying up poorly
performing for-profit nursing homes—buying its first twelve in 2003.[52]
The municipal agency started "buying" the nursing homes but did not
actually buy the physical properties and did not take over management

of the nursing homes. HHC purchased nursing home licenses and leased the properties from the private companies that owned the rights. Rather than manage the nursing homes itself, HHC hired a private company, American Senior Communities, to operate the nursing homes, which is the same company that was running the nursing homes prior to the initial HHC "purchases" in 2003.[53]

Thus, the shift in ownership of the nursing homes to the government in order to increase Medicaid claims has been illusory. Although it doesn't manage the nursing homes, HHC claims ownership to reap the higher maximum federal Medicaid funding rates.

HHC has a mission of serving the public health and the interests of its individual beneficiaries (those receiving care). Thus, the municipal agency could and should use any additional federal Medicaid funds intended for nursing home care to improve the care for the elderly in such nursing facilities—especially in a state with some of the worst statistics regarding nursing home care in the country. However, when HHC buys nursing homes across the state, its motive has not been to improve care for the nursing home residents.

After buying a nursing home, HHC received at least an extra $55 per day per elderly person in federal Medicaid funds and then routed the bulk of the extra money away from the nursing homes.[54] HHC has used most of the money for other purposes, including building a new $750 million hospital complex. The revenue strategy developed by the Indiana legislature and HHC has allowed the agency to buy poorly performing nursing homes, leave the elderly residents in poor care, and redirect their Medicaid funds to build a new hospital system that otherwise would have required an increase in property taxes or state and local spending. A professor of bioethics explained the immorality of the HHC practice, that "[a]s a general moral principal when dealing with vulnerable persons, your first duty is to make sure they have adequate protection and services to meet their needs."[55]

As of 2010, HHC (located solely in Indianapolis) had purchased 39 nursing home licenses in 22 counties.[56] By 2013, the number increased to 59 nursing homes.[57] Further, following HHC's lead, other county hospital systems have followed suit and it's been a race to buy up as many for-profit nursing homes as possible. As of 2013, county hospitals had purchased 205 nursing homes across the state.[58]

After HHC purchased the nursing homes, an investigation showed that the quality of nursing home care had not improved but rather often worsened. The result is not surprising, because HHC's contract with the private companies managing the nursing homes does not require any minimum staffing levels, provides no standards for acceptable care, and provides no incentives to improve care.[59] According to the *Indianapolis Star*, as of 2010:

- Ten out of the 17 nursing homes HHC purchased in 2003 had worse state report card scores seven years later.
- In nationwide federal five-star rankings, 16 out of 27 nursing homes purchased from 2003 to 2008 received the lowest rating possible. And the amount of time nurses spent with patients declined at 25 out of those 27 nursing homes.
- Eight nursing homes owned by HHC, including four homes that HHC owned since 2003, appeared on the federal government's 2009 list of "most poorly performing homes."
- The amount of time residents in HHC nursing homes received from nursing aides was lower than the statewide average.[60]

The president and executive director of HHC actually argued that using the funds to increase nursing staff at the nursing homes would not necessarily improve care. But his assertion flies in the face of long held expert views that nursing staff ratios is a key indicator of quality care in nursing facilities.[61]

The funds HHC obtained from the revenue strategy were used primarily to build the $750 million hospital complex, renamed Eskenazi Health after a $40 million gift from a real estate developer.[62] However, much more of the cost was funded on the backs of elderly nursing home residents. The revenue scheme of buying up nursing homes and taking Medicaid funds from the elderly netted HHC $218 million by 2010, including $49 million in just one year in 2009. By 2012, the cash flow from the scheme increased to $104 million annually.[63] Taking so much federal aid from the elderly resulted in a nice hospital system, to say the least:

> Indiana has never seen a hospital quite like this. From the spiraling wooden sculpture suspended from the ceiling in the main concourse to

the vegetable garden on the roof, the brand-new Eskenazi Hospital keeps you wondering what you will see around the next corner . . . The massive complex, spread out on 37 acres, will replace Wishard Hospital, a deteriorating hodgepodge of buildings, some a century old . . .

Inside and out, the hospital has distinctive touches. The front of the building features tall decorative fins that shimmer colorful light . . .

Up on the rooftop, a 5,000-square-foot "Sky Farm" features a produce and flower garden laid out in neat rows. A nearby shed is filled with gardening tools. Patients and employees will be able to plant and pick fruits, vegetables and flowers, or just sit on a bench and gaze at the horizon.[64]

The $40 million gift from Mr. Eskenazi and his wife resulted in a sculpture of the couple placed in the hospital's main concourse.[65] The president and chief executive of HHC explained: "'We wanted to make this beautiful and unique,' [the HHC executive] said. 'But we didn't want to forget our history. We want to look forward while honoring where we came from.'"[66]

However, the long-term care policy director for United Senior Action has a clear explanation of where the hospital came from: "[T]hey are funding this hospital literally on the backs of these [nursing home] residents."[67] Rather than "honoring" the elderly nursing home residents, HHC has taken hundreds of millions in federal Medicaid funds intended to aid the residents and instead used it to build a new hospital system. The state and local government saves revenue, HHC gets a new hospital complex, the companies profit, and the elderly poor have been trapped in poor care.[68]

Indiana governors and the state legislature have likely allowed this practice to continue because most of the public do not understand the scheme. Also, the strategy results in a benefit to many taxpayers by reducing the need for higher property taxes or other means to pay for the hospital system. And the elderly poor are quiet, stowed away in nursing facilities as HHC designates their federal aid to other purposes.

Crime Doesn't Pay . . . Except in the Poverty Industry

Many states and counties are now working with private companies to turn courts serving the poor into revenue and profit generators. Much like the old debtors' prisons where the poor were jailed for owing debts, courts are partnering with private companies to maximize revenue in the form of fees and fines from defendants—most of whom are impoverished. Those who can't afford to pay are jailed.

In such strategies, a county court system might be working with one company to collect court fines and fees, another company to run the probation system, another company to operate an electronic monitoring system for probationers, and possibly another company to help manage the entire court system through computerized systems.

Debtor Prisons Used to Maximize Revenue as the Poor Become Poorer

As the counties and states seek revenue from the debtor prison revenue strategies, and as the companies profit, the poor become poorer. For example, if a low-income individual gets caught up in the criminal courts, he may serve a short sentence or be put on probation. He then owes fines and restitution and court fees. Private collection and probation companies jump into action. Collection and probation fees are tacked on. He can't keep up. The fines, interest, and penalty charges increase. He is jailed for not making payments. And the cycle starts over.

Similar to concerns with other revenue tactics, these poverty industry strategies using the courts can cause the diversion of intended government purpose. In this case, rather than focusing solely on justice, public safety and rehabilitation, agencies and courts are focused on revenue production. Judges and probation officers are forced to act as collection agents rather than agents of justice.

Jurisdictions vary in how the resulting money is spent. States or counties may use the funding for the court systems in order to save government revenue, such as a criminal court in New Orleans where fees and fines amounted to two-thirds of the court-operating budget.[69] Or in other jurisdictions, the states and counties route much of the money away from the courts to state and county general funds. Out of the $163 million collected in such court fees and fines in one year in Iowa, the state took $106 million for general fund revenue and most of the remainder went to government entities other than the courts. Similarly, in Philadelphia, the city routed the full amount of the $2 million in collections from the revenue strategy to the city's general coffers.[70]

But regardless of how governments use the revenue, the private companies are always taking a large percentage as profit—and adding more to the amount owed by the poor. A Pennsylvania state law first explains how the courts "may refer the collection of costs, fines and restitution of a defendant to a private collection agency whether or not the defendant's maximum sentence or probationary term has expired with or without holding a hearing."[71] A collection fee owed to the collection agency, of an additional amount equal to up to 25 percent of the total costs and fees already owed, "shall be added to the bill of costs to be paid by the defendant."[72] And to encourage the debtor/defendant to pay, the judge wields the jail cell: "Nothing in this subchapter limits the ability of a judge to imprison a person for nonpayment."[73]

The following summarizes how the debtor prison revenue strategy works in an Oregon court system:

Clakamas County Circuit Court: Fees upon Fees upon Fees
In Clakamas County, Oregon, the circuit court explains: "All fines, restitution and fees assessed are due and payable the day of sentencing," and as soon as the account is delinquent it will be referred to a collection agency.[74] The collection agency is Alliance One Credit Company, which "has served the court and government industry in comprehensive collection service since the early 1980's," whose "current client base includes over 500 courts and government entities," and has "grown into an industry leader with offices throughout the United States, South America, Latin America, Canada, India, Philippines and the Caribbean."[75]

The court website then explains a few of the additional fees that will be tagged onto the fines and fees already owed. "The law allows the following fees to be automatically added and collected, without further notice or action by the court to recover administrative and collection costs."

- "Payment Assessment/Fee"—A fee of up to $200 "will automatically be added to any judgment that includes a monetary obligation that must be collected by the court."

- "Collection Referral Assessment Fee"—"A separate fee (28% of the case balance) will be added to recover costs for any judgment referred for collection to the Department of Revenue (DOR) or private collection firm."
- "License Sanction Assessment Fee"—If the debtor fails to comply with payment order, a "$15.00 License Sanction Assessment Fee and a docketed judgment will be added each time and for each case in which the court is required to notify the Oregon Department of Motor Vehicles for Failure to Appear or Failure to Comply."
- "Fee Waiver/Deferral" Fee—There is even a fee charged to seek a deferral of the court fees and costs. Unless the court clerk immediately grants the fee waiver or deferral, the "request will go before a judge to make your request for a fee waiver or fee deferral." If the fees are deferred, a $25 fee will be charged to defer the fees.
- And if you don't pay? "If you discover that a warrant has been issued for your arrest you may check with any law enforcement office or check with the Warrants office."[76]

The incentive for states and counties to employ private companies to increase collections of court fines and fees is strong. The court systems are underfunded, local governments and states are unwilling to provide sufficient funding, and the cost of targeting the poor for increased fees and costs initially appears to be free. The private collections agencies don't charge the government entities, but rather tack their large fees onto the amounts already owed by the debtors. If the companies don't collect, they don't get paid.

In 2012, the City of Bridgeton became the first New Jersey local government to take advantage of a new state law allowing municipalities to hire collection agencies to pursue municipal court fees and fines. According to the *Daily Journal*, Mayor Albert Kelly explained the reasoning for hiring Duncan Solutions and allowing the company to tack on an additional 22 percent to the total amount owed. The mayor explained that, "[g]iven the economic landscape the last few years, we, like so many others, have had to do more with less," and "[t]hat means using new tools provided by the state to enable us to collect potentially lost revenue."[77] In 2014, when Brick Township took advantage of the same New Jersey law, the mayor explained why he wanted to hire Pioneer Credit to pursue $650,000 in unpaid municipal court fines:

"This was a no-brainer since there is so much money sitting there and absolutely no cost to the town."[78] According to the *Asbury Park Press*, the Council president Susan Lydeker echoed the reasoning: "A fee will be added to the fine by the contractor," Lydecker said. "We don't pay anything."[79]

But they do pay. There are significant costs resulting from the debtor prison revenue strategy: harm to the vulnerable populations, and harm to the governments that pursue their money. Individuals who are already struggling with poverty become caught in a mire of continuously growing debts as they are required to pay endless court fees and fines: charged for initial court appearances; charged for trials; charged to file an appeal; charged for other administrative court costs; charged for "court technology" fees; charged for public defenders, even though they are supposed to be free; charged for prosecution reimbursement; charged for their own warrants; charged for fines and restitution; charged for any time served in jail; charged when their driver's licenses are suspended; charged for their probation; charged for drug testing; charged for electronic monitoring; charged interest on the growing amount owed; charged for entering into payment plans; charged a penalty if unable to make timely payments; charged for the collection agencies that pursue the charges; charged when they become jailed again for not paying the charges; and more.

As the poor become poorer, governments are harmed too. Pursued by the collection agencies for the unmanageable court debts, the individuals are less likely to obtain economic stability and more likely to be a cost to society. Many of the impoverished individuals will avoid "above ground" employment to avoid harsh wage garnishments, or if they are working they will lose their jobs when their driver's licenses are suspended or after being locked up for not paying the debts. States and counties will report the increasing court fines and fees on credit histories, which in turn make it more difficult for the individuals to find housing or jobs, as landlords and employers frequently require credit reports. When unable to make ends meet, the individuals will more likely need public assistance. The chances of successfully reentering society after even a short prison sentence are hampered. The chances of going back into prison again are greatly increased. Even the right to vote can be lost if unable to pay the court debts.

Also, the unmanageable debtor prison debts don't exist in a vacuum but become entangled with other conflicting debt obligations. A low-income father struggling to get on his feet in Florida may briefly encounter the criminal justice system for a minor crime. An initial $500 criminal misdemeanor fine can balloon to several thousand dollars in court fees and costs. An additional fee charged by a private collection agency of up to 40 percent of the total fines and costs is then added. The father may already be facing thousands of dollars in back-owed child support, so he must decide between supporting his children and paying the court debts—both of which may be using private debt collectors. If he chooses the court debt over paying to support his children, the mother and children will be financially harmed and more likely to need government assistance. If he chooses to pay child support, he might avoid a driver's license suspension that would occur if child support is not paid, but then his unpaid court debts will trigger the license suspension anyway. And if he is locked up for not paying the court debt, he will lose any employment—and everyone is harmed.

Further, states and counties fail to consider the fiscal costs of the debtor prison revenue strategy (in addition to the social costs noted above). Jurisdictions attempting to use the strategy have encountered a difficulty that should have been obvious: It's hard to collect money from the poor. A study of court collection efforts in Florida by the National Association of State Courts examined barriers to collecting court fees and fines. One of the reported "barriers to success" was that "over 30 percent of the county criminal cases involve homeless individuals." The governments may spend more money in the collection effort in pursuing the poor than in the resulting collections. According to an investigation by the Brennan Center for Justice, the collection effort backfired in Mecklenburg County, North Carolina. As a part of the collection strategy, the county arrested 564 people for failing to pay the court fines and fees, and jailed 246 of the individuals—at a cost of $40,000 for $33,746 collected.[80]

Although the U.S. Supreme Court concluded in *Bearden v. Georgia* that a person should not be jailed for falling behind on such court fines and fees if unable to pay, the ruling is often ignored. According to an investigation by NPR, during a four-month period in Benton County,

Washington, about 25 percent of the people in jail for misdemeanor offenses were there because they were not able to pay their court fines and fees.[81]

The poverty industry does not even spare children from the debtor prison revenue strategies. According to an ACLU 2010 investigation and report, some jurisdictions will also impose court fines and fees on juveniles—and will jail the youth or the parents if they are not able to make the payments. For example, the ACLU report notes an example where a homeless and unemployed mother was jailed when she could not pay $104 per month in fees to a juvenile detention facility holding her son.[82]

Probation as Revenue

In addition to working with private collection agencies, states and counties have also hired private probation companies for the debtor prison revenue strategies. Many misdemeanor and traffic courts have begun hiring probation companies to help increase revenue, with the money to be used either by the courts or by the counties and municipalities.

MAXIMUS apparently did not want to miss out on this revenue strategy when it bought National Misdemeanant Private Probations Operations for an undisclosed amount in 2003. In its third quarter revenue report for that year, MAXIMUS described its increase in Human Services revenue as "due primarily to the acquisition of National Misdemeanant Private Probation Operations (NMPPO), the largest U.S. provider of community corrections services."[83]

Again, the courts have become revenue production centers, and the poor are the revenue source. A report by Human Rights Watch explains that "an increasing number of counties and municipalities depend on local courts as sources of revenue by trying to fund through misdemeanor fines what they cannot or will not fund through taxation."[84] Once charged with a misdemeanor and placed on probation, the for-profit companies charge service fees on top of fines, as well as costs for mandated classes and behavioral programs—sometimes provided by the same companies. As with private collection agencies, the local governments and courts pay nothing because the probation services are completely "offender-funded."

Electronically Monitoring the Poor for Profit

Further, states and local governments are also contracting with companies that provide electronic monitoring services to increase government revenue. For example, Mountlake Terrace, Washington explains that its contract with "the Electronic Home Monitoring company costs the City $5.75 per client, per day." The city then charges each "client" who is court ordered to wear the monitoring device $20.00 per day, "resulting in a revenue for the City of $14.25 per client, per day." Thus, "[a]t an average of 10 to 14 clients per day, the City receives approximately $50,000 to $60,000 in revenue per year."[85]

Seemingly Endless Ways of Profiting from the Poor

The ways in which the poverty industry uses vulnerable populations to maximize profit and revenue are seemingly endless. If one revenue strategy is slowed after investigations uncover questionable practices, new strategies quickly emerge. Children and impoverished adults are sorted, juggled, and sorted again—as the poverty industry uses its creative energies to serve itself rather than serving those in need.

For example, after the 340B Drug Discount Program was created to reduce costs of prescription medications for the poor, the goal of expanding needed access to medication has sometimes been shifted toward revenue production. The program requires pharmaceutical companies to sell drugs at a discounted rate to hospitals and clinics that serve the poor and uninsured. However, some healthcare providers have turned the discounts into revenue. An investigation by Senator Charles Grassley of Iowa found that Duke University Hospital was able to purchase drugs in 2012 at a discount for $65.8 million, but then sold the drugs for $135.5 million—resulting in $69.7 million in revenue.[86]

Several companies have cropped up that specialize in helping to use the discount drug program to maximize revenue. A "340B Coalition" now organizes two conferences a year, and according to the *New York Times* a past conference in San Francisco attracted about fifty companies as exhibitors.[87] The pharmaceutical industry does not like this revenue strategy because it forces the companies to charge less to participating healthcare organizations. In fact, Billy Tauzin, who left Congress in 2004 to lead the lobbying effort for pharmaceutical companies, has changed sides. He left his lucrative position with the drug industry for another opportunity—to help lead a new lobbying group for healthcare providers seeking to benefit from the 340B program.[88]

As another example, some for-profit hospice companies have been criticized for cherry-picking their clients to maximize profit. According to investigations, these companies who are intended to provide care and comfort to the dying are sometimes targeting patients who may not actually be dying in order to maximize payments from Medicare. The $17 billion industry received $15 billion of its revenue from Medicare.[89]

To be eligible for hospice care, a patient generally must have only six months or less to live. However, companies are incentivized to find patients who need fewer services and will have longer stays in hospice care. An investigation by the *Washington Post* found that at one branch of AseraCare in Alabama, one of the largest for-profit hospice chains, almost 80 percent of the patients were discharged alive.[90] Lawsuits have charged that such hospice companies use aggressive marketing techniques to increase the number of patients regardless of whether they are dying, including tying employee pay and bonuses to enrollment, and paying kickbacks to referral sources such as nursing homes—and even to patients directly.[91]

And the list of poverty industry strategies continues to grow, from isolated fraudulent practices using the vulnerable in moneymaking schemes to entire government agencies being taken over by private companies. For-profit companies are now virtually running county courthouse computer systems. States and private contractors are partnering to turn juvenile detention centers, foster care group homes, and entire foster care systems into profit centers. And in the infamous "kids for cash" scandal, federal prosecutors alleged two Pennsylvania judges were receiving kickbacks for several years from a private detention center in return for sentencing children to the private facility. Kids were often denied lawyers, and were locked away for long sentences at the private facility for very minor offenses. The judges received $2.6 million. Although found guilty, one of the judges later argued the payments he received were not kickbacks but rather a "finder's fee."[92]

The poverty industry's expanding revenue strategies are diverting the missions of human service agencies, undermining programs for the poor, harming the vulnerable, and harming all of us as billions in aid funds are misused. The next and concluding chapter provides a path forward to begin reeling in the poverty industry practices, and to restore fiscal integrity to the safety net.

7

Reeling In the Poverty Industry

Restoring Agency Purpose, and Restoring Fiscal Integrity to the Safety Net

This book does not support arguments to cut government aid programs. The fact that the poverty industry is misusing aid funds does not mean that the funding should be cut. It means we need to stop the poverty industry from misusing the funds. The analysis provided in this book, and the practices that are exposed, are intended to call out for broader policy debate and reforms in order to improve the programs and targeted funding so that needed assistance truly reaches those in need.

We can all disagree about the best way to help vulnerable populations. And we will. But we all should be able to agree that when aid funds are generated with specific intent to help those in need, those funds should be used as intended.

This book also does not condemn contracts with private companies to help with government services. However, the book does condemn private contracts that use the vulnerable as a revenue source and that help to redirect aid funds to government coffers and private profit.

States have underfunded their human service agencies, and states themselves are also cash-strapped. Having faced years of poor fiscal climates and a political environment opposed to raising revenue through general taxation, states are desperate for other ways to raise revenue. However, the fact that states and human service agencies need more money does not rationalize using the vulnerable in revenue schemes.

Rather than focusing on how to use the vulnerable in revenue strategies, the poverty industry should use its collective energy and resources to determine the best way to help those in need. In the process of considering improved ways of providing assistance, several simple principles should be followed. Medicaid funds intended to help care for the elderly in nursing homes should be used to care for the elderly. Funds intended to help hospitals serve the poor should be used to help hospitals serve the poor. Impoverished schoolchildren with special needs should not be used as a tool to route their aid funds to general revenue. Child support should only be pursued and used to help children. Survivor and disability benefits belonging to abused and neglected children should only be used to benefit those children. Veterans' benefits received by a child whose parent died in the military should only be used to help that child. Elderly nursing home residents and vulnerable children should not be drugged to the point of sedation to save money and increase revenue. Courts and probation officers should focus on justice, public safety, and rehabilitation, not be transformed into debtor-prison revenue centers.

Obvious. But the shift will not be easy. Revenue maximization schemes that use the vulnerable as revenue tools have become entrenched in the mind-set of state and human service agency leadership, and the practices are bipartisan. Democrats and Republicans alike have increasingly used children and the poor as revenue tools, and have been able to do so because the rest of us have been unaware. Hopefully, increased awareness will help shed light on the poverty industry practices and to encourage needed change.

Much discussion and debate are needed to begin reeling in the poverty industry and realigning the mission of human service agencies with best serving the needs of their beneficiaries. Some suggestions are provided here, with the goal of providing a beginning to the discussion.

Purpose: Restoring the Mission of Human Service Agencies

The conflict between the purpose and fiscal self-interests of human service agencies, introduced in chapter 1, laid the groundwork for the poverty industry practices discussed in this book. To reduce the resulting harm, the conflict must be resolved.

In feudal England, the *parens patriae* doctrine provided power to protect the vulnerable, but the power was often misused for fiscal gain. The king used the protective power to assert guardianship over the children of wealthy landowners in order to increase riches for the Crown. The king considered it his right to take assets from the children of landed gentry after their parents died, in return for providing wardship services. And the king also often sold off wardship and marriage rights to the children. Thus, the purpose of parens patriae to protect children in the king's realm in turn rationalized the power to assert dominion over the children and the children's property and funds. Children were used rather than helped.

Eventually, enlightenment and awareness led to societal revulsion that forced the end of such practices. But similar practices have begun again.

The parens patriae doctrine still exists today, and provides the purpose and power of human service agencies to serve vulnerable children and adults. As today's agency inheritors of the parens patriae power face their own search for increased revenue, they have looked back and taken hold of the doctrine's unfortunate beginnings. Although wealthy children are no longer targeted, the rich targets have been replaced with the poor. Revenue maximization strategies concocted with private consultants again target children and adults with revenue-producing potential—but today's targets are the vulnerable rather than the entitled: abused and neglected children, the poor, the disabled, and the elderly.

In fact, today's agency practices are in many ways worse than those of feudal times. Whereas children born into the privileged class structure of the feudal tenurial system might maintain their social status and privilege after reaching the age of adulthood and no longer needing wardship care, children today enter foster care poor and leave care poor—if not worse.

Similarly, impoverished adults, the disabled, and the elderly are often not faring well under the care of their agency protectors. Agencies created to help these populations are instead using them to bolster revenue, while the vulnerable languish in Dickensian conditions. Further, rather than supporting low-income families, the agencies pursue a revenue strategy of forcing poor mothers to sue poor fathers and then taking any resulting child support as government revenue—weakening the already fragile families.

So, as human service agencies have sought to turn the clock back hundreds of years to rationalize their treatment of their beneficiaries as a source of funds, enlightenment is necessary again. Despite the agencies' loathing of judicial review, litigation must continue to bring the practices to the attention of the courts. Despite the agencies' seeking confidentiality in their practices, the public must be made aware. And despite the agencies' preference for unfettered discretion, Congress and state legislatures must force the agencies to only act in the best interests of their beneficiaries—if the agencies will not do so of their own accord.

In the end, it's not complicated. Agencies created with the purpose of serving the vulnerable should only use their power to serve that goal. The following sections provide some initial discussion regarding how this principle can be upheld to begin remedying the harm of the revenue strategies discussed in this book.

Using Foster Children's Survivor and Disability Benefits to Help the Children

When a child enters foster care, the child welfare agency requires flexibility and discretion to determine the best way to meet the child's evolving needs. The best mix of services and assistance is not always clear, and may continuously change. However, within such necessary discretion, one thing is certain: the agency charged with protecting an abused and neglected child should not use that child in a revenue scheme to take the child's resources. If a child is potentially eligible for Social Security benefits due to disabilities or a deceased parent, the agency should use any such benefits belonging to the child in order to help that child. If a child is eligible for VA benefits because a parent died in the military, the agency should only use the funds for the child's benefit.

Again, this is obvious. But unfortunately, as discussed in chapter 3, foster care agencies are partnering with private contractors to maximize federal funds that belong to foster children and then taking the funds as government revenue. Under revenue maximization contracts, private contractors receive confidential information about foster children and then work with the agency to maximize the number of children determined disabled—and to find all those children with parents who are deceased. This is done not to help the children, but to take the children's money. Stated simply, the practice needs to stop.

The ideal way to end the misuse of foster children's federal benefits—social security benefits or VA benefits—is through federal law. Through either federal statute or regulation, clarification could prohibit foster care agencies from using the children's funds for the fiscal self-interests of the agency or state. In fact, former congressman Pete Stark's office developed legislation to accomplish this needed realignment of foster care agency purpose and practices.[1] Stark introduced the Foster Children Self Support Act in 2007 and again in 2010, which would have helped ensure that foster children's own resources are used to benefit the children. The bill would have also established a planning process, so that the children's funds are used and conserved as part of a plan to help with the children's future transition to independence.

Unfortunately, the Foster Children Self Support Act has not yet gained sufficient congressional attention to receive a committee hearing or vote. The hope is that members of Congress will recognize the importance of this issue and give foster children the attention they deserve. While we wait, states should take action now.

Foster care agencies and their parent states should follow a simple strategy: Stop taking children's assets. When agencies use the children for revenue, the agency's short-term focus on financial gain ignores the long-term harm to children and to society.

Instead of contracting with private companies to maximize survivor and disability benefits in order to take the money from foster children, the foster care agencies could still contract with the revenue maximization contractors—but to actually help the children.

Companies like MAXIMUS could help states decide when to apply for disability benefits for a child—not based on the most revenue potential for the state, but when it is best for the child. Instead of "dissecting" the foster care population for the order of applying for Social Security benefits based on what children will bring in the most money for the state, companies like the Public Consulting Group could help prioritize applications based on the children's needs and best interests. The companies could help foster care agencies manage the children's funds and use or conserve the money in plans to help the children in their future transition to independence.

If foster care agencies refuse to do what's right for children, legislation and litigation can seek to correct the practices. For example, Maryland legislation was introduced in 2014 and 2015 for "Protecting the Resources of Children in State Custody."[2] The bill had strong support, but after active lobbying against the legislation by the secretaries of the Maryland Department of Human Resources (under both Governor O'Malley and Governor Hogan) the bill has not yet been enacted. The hope is that the legislation will be introduced again and lawmakers will vote for the children.

In addition to legislative reform, attorneys for children should pursue state litigation to try to stop this practice. Such a lawsuit was filed on behalf of Alex, the foster child described earlier in the book.[3] Unfortunately, Alex's case was dismissed because the Maryland foster care agency convinced the court that the time limit for Alex bringing a claim began when the agency first began taking his money—although Alex was a child in foster care at the time and was given no notice of the agency's actions.

Attorneys also pursued litigation on behalf of Ryan, another foster child described earlier in the book.[4] Ryan's case reached Maryland's top appellate court, and his case became the first in the country to find that the foster care agency violated a child's constitutional rights in the process of taking his money. As explained in more detail in chapter 3, the Maryland Court of Appeals ruled that the agency failed to give any notice whatsoever to Ryan regarding the agencies' actions, in violation of his due process rights. If other state courts similarly provide foster children protection for their due process rights to notice of agency actions, advocates for the children can seek to prevent the agencies from taking the children's funds and can suggest more preferred representative payees for the children—such as family members, pro bono attorneys or accountants, other volunteers, or nonprofit organizations. Also, we hope litigation in other states can go further and directly prohibit foster care agencies from taking children's resources.

Involvement of juvenile courts can also help realign the purpose of foster care agencies toward always helping children rather than maximizing government revenue. The Social Security Administration has experienced difficulty in administering or monitoring the representative payee system for foster children's disability and survivor benefits. The juvenile court system is overwhelmed too, but the two systems could help each other through communications and coordinated actions.

For example, if juvenile courts received notice when a foster care agency applies to become a child's representative payee, the notice could help the courts and parties in the foster care proceedings to provide additional information to the SSA in its investigation for the most preferred payee. Further, the juvenile courts could then engage in investigation regarding the foster child's resources and plans for the child's transition to independence—to help ensure the child's funds are used in the best way for the child. Federal and state laws already require foster care agencies to submit progress reports to juvenile courts at least every six months regarding foster children. If federal or state law also required the agencies to include information about the use of children's Social Security benefits or other resources, the judge and the parties in the juvenile court case could take a more active role in monitoring the agencies' actions to ensure the children's best interests are followed. Agencies could also file such progress reports with the SSA to provide additional information not gathered through the Administration's accounting system.

Child Support Should Support Children

Child support enforcement actions should not harm children or their families. This is a simple point to understand. But as long as the poverty industry seeks to use child support as revenue rather than to support children, harm will result.

As explained in chapter 5, state agencies are often partnering with private companies to force child support obligations on impoverished families involved in the welfare or foster care programs, and then taking any resulting child support from the children and their families as government revenue. The practices conflict with the purposes of the foster care, social services, and child support agencies.

When these multiple human service agencies work together, the result should help the children and families—not cause harm. But the poverty industry strategy of taking child support as revenue directly hurts the best interests of children. The practice further divides already fragile families as the parents are pitted against each other. Already poor families become poorer. Families' attempts to reunite with children in foster care are undermined. Poor fathers are alienated from their families and from the workforce. Even the states suffer a fiscal loss: any government-owed child support collections are likely outweighed by the administrative costs of collecting the payments and by the additional costs when the struggling families are more likely to need additional government assistance as a result of the practice. As long as this revenue strategy is continued, the only winners will be the private contractors of the poverty industry.

Again, the principle necessary to stop the harm is not complicated. Human service agencies should only pursue child support for the benefit of the children, not for themselves.

To achieve this needed correction of agency purpose, reform to federal law is the most direct method. Two of the primary goals of the welfare cash assistance program (TANF) are supporting the "formation and maintenance" of two-parent families and helping families to achieve economic self-sufficiency, but the child support revenue strategies undermine both goals. Requirements that poor custodial parents applying for welfare must sue the poor noncustodial parents and assign any child support to the government should be replaced with policies that support families and children. Caseworkers could help custodial parents decide if pursuing child support is in the best interests of the children, and the decision for whether to pursue child support should belong to the custodial parent or other relative caretaker, not the government.

For example, a mother applying for public assistance might consider her relationship with the father and whether opening a child support case would harm the fragile relationship that often exists. Some parents may decide that forgoing child support services will allow the relationship to grow, encouraging more informal support and cooperative assistance in raising the child, and even possibly leading to cohabitation or marriage. Parents will also be able to assess whether the potential benefits of pursuing child support are outweighed by the risk of domestic violence from an abusive, absent parent.

For cases where children are in foster care, Congress could amend federal law to require states to exercise discretion and only refer foster care cases for child support enforcement if not contrary to the children's best interests or in conflict with case-planning goals. For example, when the case plan is reunification with the mother, then an agency's pursuit of child support against the mother would conflict with that goal. Further, federal law should also rectify current illegal practices by prohibiting states from using foster children as collateral—where children are only returned if government-owed support is paid. And an agency should only seek to terminate parental rights if doing so is in the child's best interests, not because of a government debt.

If a decision is made to pursue child support, the child support assignment requirements should be eliminated so that any collected child support is used to care for the children. As confirmed by a study in Wisconsin, such a policy would lead to increased child support payments, increased family economic stability, and lower child poverty rates. If an agency pursues child support when a child is in foster care, the child support could be used to improve the child's care by directing the payments to increase the inadequate financial assistance provided to the child's foster home. Or, the payments could be conserved in trust to assist the child with the difficult transition to independence after aging out of foster care.

Until federal law reform occurs, states and their human service agencies already possess the ability to do what's right for children and families. States have broad discretion to define good cause exceptions to current child support cooperation requirements, to protect the best interests of the children and support the relationships in fragile families. Similarly, states already have discretion to only refer foster care cases for child support enforcement when not harmful to the best interests of children or case planning goals.

Further, even if government-owed child support is pursued, federal policy encourages states to "pass through" some of the assigned child support back to the families and allow payments go to families first. Unfortunately, despite the federal encouragement for "pass through" and "families first" policies, most states have not used such discretion to help children and families. For example, Maryland is ranked as one of the richest states in the country, but thus far Maryland has declined to implement the families first policy and does not pass through a single penny of child support to families on public assistance. In comparison, West Virginia is 48th in the rankings of the richest states but passed through more than $2.6 million in child support to families on public assistance in 2013.[5] And Tennessee, which ranks as 44th in per capita wealth, passed through almost $22 million in child support to families receiving public assistance.[6]

Ultimately the solution to stopping the harm from poverty industry strategies using child support lies in the words of the child support obligation. Child support should only provide support to the children. Hopefully, more states will begin to embrace this simple but crucial principle.

Medicaid Funds Should Be Used to Provide Medicaid Services

Continuing obvious but needed change to realign the purpose of human service agencies, when an agency or state receives federal Medicaid funds, the funds should only be used for the intended Medicaid purposes. Again, the poverty industry collaboration of government with private contractors should benefit, not use, the vulnerable populations.

The structure and process for states claiming federal Medicaid funds is complex, and improvements from the federal government are needed. However, although the structure is complex, the principle that Medicaid funds should be used for intended Medicaid purposes is simple. States and human service agencies know when they are doing wrong.

For example, when New Jersey requires school districts to use poor children to maximize school-based Medicaid claims and then diverts more than 80 percent of the funds to general state coffers, the state knows the aid funds are not being used as intended. When Texas uses illusory Medicaid maximization strategies to divert $1.7 billion in Medicaid funds to general revenue over a five-year period, the state knows the aid funds are not being used as intended. And when Maryland uses a bed tax scheme to divert up to 35 percent of Medicaid funds from poor-performing nursing homes to general funds, the state knows that the aid funds are not being used as intended.

But perhaps the most alarming aspect about the poverty industry's revenue maximization schemes and diversion of government aid is what we don't know. Although significant data and examples are provided in this book, no national data exist to determine exactly how much Medicaid funding is being diverted by the poverty industry to other purposes. We know it's a lot, in the billions, but we don't know exactly how much. Some schemes are at the state level, some at the county level, and some at the agency level, and many are hidden from public view through Enronesque budget and accounting gimmicks.

Thus, states must be more accountable in how they use aid funds. When the federal Center for Medicare and Medicaid Services provides Medicaid funds to states, the federal agency should be able to better monitor how the states use the money. When states request and receive the federal Medicaid funds, they should be able to accurately explain how they use the funds. To fully fix the problem, the scope of the problem needs to be fully exposed. As a beginning, further investigation and audits by the General Accounting Office and the U.S. Department of Health and Human Services Inspector General's Office can better account for the full extent of how Medicaid funds are actually used.

In addition to the need for increased monitoring and accountability, the following section describes additional structural reforms to consider—in order to begin restoring integrity to our safety net programs.

Structure: Restoring Fiscal Integrity to the Safety Net

Chapter 2 described fiscal federalism, the economic structure in which the federal and state governments collaborate to administer America's largest aid programs. The chapter also explained how the poverty industry has undermined the intended benefits of the federal-state partnership and resulted in the misuse of billions in aid dollars intended to help the vulnerable. Several possible reforms should be considered to begin putting a stop to the harm of the poverty industry and restoring fiscal and legal integrity to safety net programs.

Clarify and Enforce Statutory Purpose of Aid Programs

First, the core statutory purpose of federal matching grant programs like Medicaid and the Title IV-E Foster Care program must be preserved. Congress created these programs to match federal dollars with state dollars to increase needed services to maltreated children and the poor. For example, if a state receives $50 in federal matching funds for $50 in state spending on Medicaid, the result should be $100 used for the intended Medicaid services. But in the illusory revenue strategies discussed in chapter 4, the $50 in federal dollars is claimed without any actual state spending, and sometimes even part or all of the federal aid is directed to other uses.

This widespread gaming needs to stop. Congress should further clarify statutory language regarding the purpose of matching grant program funds so that funds intended to increase services to the vulnerable must not be used for other purposes. For example, strict requirements can be added that federal matching funds must supplement, not supplant, the state funds. Illusory revenue maximization schemes that result in state agency claims for federal matching funds without any actual additional state spending should be prohibited. At the beginning of the Medicaid program, Congress included a "maintenance of state effort" provision to help ensure the federal aid was used to increase needed healthcare services rather than be diverted by states for other purposes. The language required that the funds "shall be used directly in the public assistance program and may not be withdrawn from the program by the States."[7] Although such requirement is already inherent in the statutory purpose of the Medicaid program, the directive may be necessary again.

When the poverty industry misuses aid funds intended for the vulnerable, the government actors and private companies involved in the schemes should be held accountable for the misuse. For example, the Center for Medicare and Medicaid Services (CMS) has broad authority to protect the integrity of the Medicaid program. CMS should improve its use of that authority to clamp down on state practices that are not consistent with the statutory purpose of the Medicaid program. If more authority is ultimately needed, Congress should provide it. But in the meantime, CMS already has discretion to deny a state's proposed Medicaid plan if inconsistent with the statutory purposes and framework. CMS could also construe its authority as a means to prohibit the poverty industry's illusory claiming practices or inappropriate use of federal aid payments.

Further, a state engaged in such inappropriate practices should be subject to fines and additional audits, and should be required to redirect the funds to provide Medicaid services as intended. If a private company causes such illusory or fraudulent practices, the company should be pursued under the False Claims Act. If found to be responsible for illusory claims or the misuse of aid funds, the company should be barred from further contractual participation with the federal aid programs.

Reining in Revenue Maximization Contractors

Both sides of the poverty industry collaboration have spurred the poverty industry practices. Cash-strapped states and human service agencies, unwilling to raise sufficient revenue through general taxation, are seeking funding anywhere else they can find it. Private revenue maximization contractors have discovered a lucrative way to cash in on the cash-strapped states, helping to guide them in the process of seeking revenue from the children and the poor.

Rather than helping states and agencies to best serve the vulnerable, too often the contractors are helping states and agencies to use the vulnerable. The contractors frequently entice states and agencies through contingency-fee contracts, in which the companies help increase claims for aid funds and the states and agencies pay nothing as the companies take a percentage of the increased funds.

In chapter 2, the inappropriateness and likely illegality of using contingency-fee contracts to maximize claims for federal aid is explained. Thus, as part of the process of reining in revenue maximization contractors, the federal government should prohibit the use of such contingency-fee contracts. Even without a prohibition, states should recognize that contingency-fee contracts greatly increase the occurrence of incorrect and sometimes fraudulent claims for aid funds— increasing the likelihood of federal audits. Further, the contingency-fee arrangement causes the focus to be all about the money, rather than about the best interests of the vulnerable. For example, strategies of private contractors in chapter 3 discussed how the companies looked for potentially disabled foster children and "dissected" the population and ranked the children based on the ease and speed with which they would produce revenue—rather than evaluating the extent of the children's needs.

Because of the complexity of the claiming process for federal aid, revenue maximization contractors can serve a helpful role if the contracts are structured and monitored appropriately to improve integrity. The contracts could include flat-fee payment arrangements rather than contingency fees, or performance incentives could be used that focus on accuracy or the best interests of vulnerable populations rather than maximizing money to the state.

Consider Structural Improvements to Aid Programs

As we consider ways to improve the integrity of how states and their contractors claim and use federal aid funds, the federal government should also consider structural improvements to the aid programs and claiming process. The rules governing claims for funds should be simplified and include improved targeting toward programmatic purposes, and federal guidance and enforcement of the rules must be consistent.

The federal government should continually improve its auditing and monitoring of how states claim and use federal aid but also recognize that the use of private contractors for such audits can cause further harm to fiscal federalism's goals. While states have been hiring contingency-fee contractors to increase claims for federal aid, the federal government has also been using private contingency-fee contractors to audit and recover improper claims. Just as states should stop using contingency-fee contracts, the federal government should stop as well. Although lucrative for the poverty industry contractors—because they can make money coming and going—the conflicting roles increase harm to fiscal federalism's hope for a harmonious collaboration between the federal government and states in the provision of needed aid.

Debate and analysis should continue regarding other possible structural reforms, including how to balance the administration and financing of aid programs between the federal and state governments. However, significant caution and concern should guide any consideration of the theme in GOP proposals to restructure poverty programs by just giving all the federal money to states and letting them do what they want. Senator Marco Rubio termed the proposal "flex funds," through which he basically proposes to consolidate most or all federal aid funds and give it all to states as flexible money to do what they wish.[8] Similarly, Congressman Paul Ryan proposed an "opportunity grant" that would take our largest safety net programs—including food stamps (SNAP), housing vouchers, and childcare assistance—and terminate those programs and instead give all the money to states in a block grant for flexible use.[9]

The theory behind these flexible block grant proposals is simple: Because states should be better able to understand regional needs of the vulnerable, all the money should be given to states—without controls—in order to let states flexibly meet those regional needs. However, the flaw with the theory is glaring. As shown throughout this book, even with stringent program rules and multiple audits such as in the Medicaid program, states and their revenue contractors seek out loopholes and illusory schemes to maximize and divert the aid to other uses. As explained in the *Boston Globe* regarding Mitt Romney's Medicaid maximization schemes: "It's not hard to imagine how a governor—one that employs complex shell games to find loopholes in federal rules in order to maximize and divert federal aid—would use the federal funds if handed to the state without any federal oversight."[10] A proper response to state misuse of federal aid is not to give those states even more discretion to do whatever they wish—but to simplify the claiming process, reduce loopholes allowing the revenue schemes, and improve oversight to ensure Medicaid funds are used as intended.

Conclusion

Mission matters. When the poverty industry places the mission of maximizing revenue and profit over serving those in need, the vulnerable are harmed. And when the vulnerable are harmed, we are all harmed.

As explained earlier in the book, vulnerability does not imply weakness. We are all vulnerable. And, like it or not, we are all interdependent— with each other and with our government institutions. Some of us are just more vulnerable at times than others. In fact, writers and researchers such as Brené Brown have recognized that vulnerability and connectivity are traits that should be embraced by leaders in both the public and private sectors.[11]

The poverty industry includes the vast combined powers of government and private enterprise. This collaboration has the capacity to do immense good, if the right goals are pursued.

States and their human service agencies must lead the way, because they ultimately control the purpose of their partnership with private contractors. And in order for the partnership to realize its true potential to best serve our country's vulnerable populations, the agencies must first have the strength to embrace their own vulnerabilities—because truth and strength lie in vulnerability.

The temptation for underfunded agencies to prioritize their own fiscal interests through the revenue strategies discussed in this book is strong, and can temporarily help the agencies to feel more secure in their existence. However, if agency existence takes priority over purpose, then the meaning of that existence is lost.

NOTES

INTRODUCTION

1 Maryland Department of Human Resources, *MAXIMUS Benefits & Eligibility Advocacy Services*, SSI/SSDI Assessment Report, February 2013 (on file with author).

2 Campbell Robertson, "For Offenders Who Can't Pay, It's a Pint of Blood or Jail Time," *New York Times*, October 19, 2015.

3 Juan Thompson, "Lawsuit Challenges a Mississippi Debtors Prison," *The Intercept*, October 22, 2015.

4 Martha Albertson Fineman, Vulnerability and the Human Condition Initiative, http://web.gs.emory.edu/vulnerability/index.html (accessed December 18, 2014).

CHAPTER 1

1 *In re* Ryan, No. 802023006, at 3 (Balt. City Cir. Ct. June 16, 2011) (on file with author).

2 I was lead counsel for Alex in his litigation challenging the practice of the Maryland foster care agency taking his survivor benefits. I served as co-counsel for amici supporting Ryan in his appeal challenging the same practice.

3 *Ryan*, 3; emphasis added.

4 Ibid.

5 The United States Conference of Mayors, *2009 Status Report on Hunger and Homelessness Survey, A Status Report on Hunger and Homelessness in America's Cities* (December 2009), http://usmayors.org/pressreleases/uploads/USCMHungercompleteWEB2009.pdf (accessed October 16, 2014).

6 The United States Conference of Mayors, *2012 Status Report on Hunger and Homelessness Survey, A Status Report on Hunger and Homelessness in America's Cities* (December 2012), http://usmayors.org/pressreleases/uploads/2012/1219-report-HH.pdf (accessed October 16, 2014).

7 The United States Conference of Mayors, *2013 Status Report on Hunger and Homelessness Survey, A Status Report on Hunger and Homelessness in America's Cities* (December 2013), http://usmayors.org/pressreleases/uploads/2013/1210-report-HH.pdf (accessed October 16, 2014).

8 Gordon M. Fisher, Dept. of Health and Human Services, "The Development and History of the U.S. Poverty Thresholds—A Brief Overview," in *Newsletter of the Government Statistics Section and the Social Statistics Section of the American Statistical Association* (1997), 6–7, http://aspe.hhs.gov/poverty/papers/hptgssiv.htm (accessed October 16, 2014).

9 Mark E. Courtney, et al., *Midwest Eval. of the Adult Functioning of Former Foster Youth: Outcomes at Age 23 and 24* (Chapin Hall at the University of Chicago, 2010), http://www.chapinhall.org/sites/default/files/Midwest_Study_Age_23_24.pdf (accessed December 18, 2014).

10 Jennifer L. Hook and Mark E. Courtney, *Employment of Former Foster Youth as Young Adults: Evidence from the Midwest Study* (Chapin Hall at the University of Chicago, 2010), 9, www.chapinhall.org/sites/default/files/publications/Midwest_IB3_Employment.pdf (accessed October 16, 2014).

11 Bureau of Justice Statistics, "Study Finds More than Half of all Prison and Jail Inmates have Mental Health Problems," http://www.bjs.gov/content/pub/press/mhppjipr.cfm (accessed November 17, 2014).

12 National Alliance on Mental Illness, "State Mental Health Cuts: The Continuing Crisis," http://www.nami.org/Template.cfm?Section=state_budget_cuts_report (accessed November 17, 2014).

13 Kathleen Short, "Current Population Reports," in *The Research Supplemental Poverty Measure: 2011* (2012), 60–244, http://www.census.gov/prod/2012pubs/p60-244.pdf (accessed October 16, 2014).

14 National Women's Law Center, "Steep Rise Seen in Deep Poverty Among Elderly, http://www.nwlc.org/media/steep-rise-seen-deep-poverty-among-elderly (accessed November 17, 2014).

15 Catherine Saint Louis, "In Nursing Homes, an Epidemic of Poor Dental Hygiene," *New York Times*, August 4, 2013, http://well.blogs.nytimes.com/2013/08/04/in-nursing-homes-an-epidemic-of-poor-dental-hygiene/?_php=true&_type=blogs&_r=0 (accessed October 16, 2014).

16 Ibid.

17 Daniel R. Levinson, "Skilled Nursing Facilities Often Fail to Meet Care Planning and Discharge Planning Requirements," in *Department of Health and Human Services OEI-02-09-00201* (2013), http://oig.hhs.gov/oei/reports/oei-02-09-00201.pdf (accessed October 16, 2014).

18 Daniel R. Levinson, "Adverse Events in Skilled Nursing Facilities: National Incidence Among Medicare Beneficiaries," in *Department of Health and Human Services OEI-06-11-00370* (2014), http://oig.hhs.gov/oei/reports/oei-06-11-00370.pdf (accessed October 16, 2014).

19 Daniel L. Hatcher, *Purpose vs. Power: Parens Patriae and Agency Self-Interest*, 42 N. MEX. L. REV. 159 (2012). (Article provided foundational research and material for this chapter in the book.)

20 Neil Howard Cogan, *Juvenile Law, Before and After the Entrance of "Parens patriae,"* 22 S.C. L. REV. 147, 161 (1970).

21 Lawrence B. Custer, *The Origins of the Doctrine of Parens Patriae*, 27 EMORY L.J. 195, 199 (1978).

22 Maryland Department of Human Resources, "About DHR," http://www.dhr.state.md.us/blog/?page_id=921 (accessed December 19, 2014).

23 *In re Gault*, 387 U.S. at 16–19.

24 Bernardine Dohrn, "Seize the Little Moment: Justice for the Child 20 Years at the Children and Family Justice Center," *NW J. L. & Soc. Pol'y* 6, no. 334 (2011) (describing the state of a Chicago juvenile court).

25 In the Interest of: A.V.B. A Minor Child, 1996 WL 33482529, 24 (Ga.) (Brief for Appellant Georgia Department of Human Resources).

26 Ibid., 25–26.

27 Barbara Bennett Woodhouse, "Children's Rights," in *Youth and Justice*, ed. Susan O. White (New York: Plenum Press, 2001), http://papers.ssrn.com/sol3/papers. cfm?abstract_id=234180 (accessed October 16, 2014).

28 Reply Brief of Appellants, *L.J. v. Donald*, 2010 WL 2639447 at 9 (July 1, 2010).

29 *Indiana Protection and Advocacy Services v. Indiana Family and Social Services Admin.*, 603 F.3d 365 (7th Cir. 2010).

30 *In re Gault*, 1966 WL 100788, Brief for Ohio Association of Juvenile Court Judges as Amici Curiae (U.S. Oct. 11, 1966).

CHAPTER 2

1 Nicholas Riccardi, "Political Struggle Centers on Welfare-to-Work Contractor," *Los Angeles Times*, June 20, 2000.

2 MAXIMUS, "MAXIMUS Reports Fourth Quarter and Full Year Financial Results for Fiscal 2014," news release, November 13, 2014, http://investor.maximus.com/ press-release/earnings-and-dividends/maximus-reports-fourth-quarter-and-full-year-financial-result-0 (last accessed December 7, 2014).

3 Daniel L. Hatcher, "Poverty Revenue: The Subversion of Fiscal Federalism," 52 ARIZONA L. REV. 675, 682 (2010). (Article provided foundational research and material for this chapter of the book.)

4 The investigation was spurred by a qui tam complaint filed by a former MAXI-MUS division manager. U.S. Department of Justice, "Virginia Company Enters into Deferred Prosecution Agreement and Agrees to Pay $30.5 Million," news release, July 23, 2007, http://www.justice.gov/opa/pr/2007/July/07_civ_535.html (accessed October 16, 2014); Complaint at 1, 4, *United States* ex rel. *Turner v. Maximus Inc.*, No. 1:05-cv-01215 (D.D.C. June 22, 2005).

5 Deferred Prosecution Agreement at 3, *United States* ex rel. *Turner v. Maximus Inc.*, No. 1:05-cv-01215, (D.D.C. July 23, 2007); see also, U.S. SEC, *Form 8-k: Maximus, Inc.* (Virginia, 2007), http://edgar.brand.edgar-online.com/EFX_dll/EDGARpro. dll?FetchFilingHTML1?ID=5318470&SessionID=c_QaWFq_OCzCG47 (accessed December 18, 2014) (providing language from the deferred prosecution agreement as part of the SEC filing).

6 U.S. Dept. of Justice, news release.

7 United States' Notice of Intervention and Settlement at 7, *United States* ex rel. *Turner v. Maximus Inc.*, No. 1:05-cv-01215 (D.D.C. July 20, 2007) ("In consideration of the obligations of Maximus in this agreement . . . the OIG-HHS agrees to release and refrain from instituting, directing, or maintaining any administrative action seeking exclusion from Medicare, Medicaid or other Federal health

care programs . . . against Maximus under 42 U.S.C. § 1320a-7a . . . or 42 U.S.C. § 1320a-7a(b)(7).").

8 "New York Awards Medicaid Fraud Contract to MAXIMUS," Business Wire, news release, September 13, 2007, http://www.businesswire.com/news/home/20070913005083/en/York-Awards-Medicaid-Fraud-Contract-MAXIMUS#.VJMinEsipuY (accessed December 18, 2014).

9 Bill Myers, "D.C. Hands Money to Company Tied to Fraud Scandal," *The Examiner*, October 30, 2007, http://www.washingtonexaminer.com/d.c.-hands-money-to-company-tied-to-fraud-scandal/article/82673 (accessed December 14, 2014).

10 "MAXIMUS Awarded $15 Million Medicaid Contract by Indiana," Business Wire, news release, November 19, 2007, http://www.businesswire.com/news/home/20071119005095/en/MAXIMUS-Awarded-15-Million-Medicaid-Contract-Indiana#.VJMjxksipuY (accessed December 18, 2014); "MAXIMUS Wins Rebid for California Medicaid Program," Business Wire, news release, April 9, 2008, http://www.businesswire.com/news/home/20080409005119/en/MAXIMUS-Wins-Rebid-California-Medicaid-Program#.VJMkFUsipuY (accessed December 18, 2014) ($208.4 million contract); "MAXIMUS Awarded Renewal on Medicare Appeals Contract," Business Wire, news release, May 14, 2008, http://www.businesswire.com/news/home/20080514006442/en/MAXIMUS-Awarded-Renewal-Medicare-Appeals-Contract#.VJMkdosipuY (accessed December 14, 2014); "MAXIMUS Awarded $7.2 Million Medicare Task Order," Business Wire, news release, May 21, 2008, http://www.businesswire.com/news/home/20080521005005/en/MAXIMUS-Awarded-7.2-Million-Medicare-Task-Order#.VJMkoUsipuY (accessed December 14, 2014); "MAXIMUS Awarded Medicare Part A West Appeals Contract, Expands Company's Role as a Leading Medicare Claims Processor," Bloomberg, news release, November 20, 2008, http://www.bloomberg.com/apps/news?pid=newsarchive&sid=araB1CRafkqE (accessed December 18, 2014).

11 "MAXIMUS Awarded Professional Services Contract to Support U.S. Department of Justice," Business Wire, news release, July 21, 2008, http://www.businesswire.com/news/home/20080721005148/en/MAXIMUS-Awarded-Professional-Services-Contract-Support-U.S.#.VJMepEsipuY (accessed December 18, 2014).

12 Emily Berry, "WellCare Settles SEC Probe; Announces Layoffs," *American Medical News*, June 12, 2009, http://www.amednews.com/article/20090612/business/306129999/8/ (accessed December 19, 2014).

13 Jacob Goldstein, "Feds: WellCare 'Misled and Confused Medicare Beneficiaries,'" *Wall Street Journal*, Health Blog, February 20, 2009, http://blogs.wsj.com/health/2009/02/20/feds-wellcare-misled-and-confused-medicare-beneficiaries/ (accessed December 19, 2014).

14 Gary Fineout, "Illegal Cash Went to Many Officials," *Health News Florida*, August 20, 2009, http://health.wusf.usf.edu/post/illegal-cash-went-many-officials (accessed December 19, 2014).

15 Robert Green, "WellCare Enters Into Deferred Prosecution Agreement," Bloomberg, May 5, 2009, http://www.bloomberg.com/apps/news?pid=newsarchive&sid=aVHxoFQYy8To (accessed December 19, 2014).

16 "WellCare Whistleblower Suit Claims Financial Improprieties," *Tampa Tribune*, June 29, 2010, http://tbo.com/news/business/wellcare-whistleblower-suit-claims-financial-improprieties-32016 (accessed November 29, 2014).

17 Ibid.

18 Brittany Alana Davis, "Saying It's Changed, WellCare Wants In On State Medicaid Contracts," *Tampa Bay Times*, June 10, 2010, http://www.tampabay.com/news/health/saying-its-changed-wellcare-wants-in-on-state-medicaid-contracts/1234720 (December 19, 2014).

19 Department of Justice, "Office of Public Affairs, Florida-Based WellCare Health Plans Agrees to Pay $137.5 Million to Resolve False Claims Act Allegations," news release, April 3, 2012, http://www.justice.gov/opa/pr/2012/April/12-civ-425.html (accessed October 16, 2014).

20 WellCare, "WellCare Announces Successful Medicare Part D Bid," news release, September 28, 2007, http://www.wellcare.com/WCAssets/corporate/assets/PressReleasePDP092407.pdf (accessed October 16, 2014).

21 WellCare, "WellCare Earns Senior Choice Gold Award for Medicare Advantage Benefits Plan," news release, November 16, 2007, http://wellcare.com/WCAssets/corporate/assets/SeniorChoiceGoldAward111607.pdf (accessed October 16, 2014); Lewis Krauskopf, "Agents Search WellCare Headquarters in Tampa," *Reuters*, October 24, 2007, http://www.reuters.com/article/2007/10/24/us-wellcare-warrant-idUSN2460433220071024 (accessed October 16, 2014); Jacob Goldstein, "WellCare Probe Triggered by Alleged Medicaid Fraud," *Wall Street Journal*, November 2, 2007, http://blogs.wsj.com/health/2007/11/02/wellcare-probe-triggered-by-alleged-medicaid-fraud/ (accessed October 16, 2014).

22 Jacob Goldstein, "WellCare Employee Pleads Guilty to Fraud; Shares Rise," *Wall Street Journal*, October 8, 2008, http://blogs.wsj.com/health/2008/10/08/wellcare-employee-pleads-guilty-to-fraud-shares-rise/ (accessed October 16, 2014).

23 Terry Boyd, "WellCare, Centene, Passport Winners in Kentucky's Medicaid Managed-Care Bonanza," *Insider Louisville*, July 7, 2011.

24 Brittany Alana Davis, "Company with Fraud Record Lines Up for New Medicaid Contract," *Miami Herald*, June 10, 2012.

25 Daniel L. Hatcher, "Poverty Revenue: The Subversion of Fiscal Federalism," 52 ARIZONA L. REV. 675, 682 (2010).

26 Wallace E. Oates, "Toward A Second-Generation Theory of Fiscal Federalism," 12 *Int'l Tax & Pub. Fin.* 350 (2005).

27 Deloitte Development, LLC, "Centers for Medicare & Medicaid Services (CMS), Medicaid and Children's Health Insurance Program (CHIP) Policy Implications and Evaluations 'MACPIE,'" Deloitte, http://www.deloitte.com/view/en_US/us/Industries/US-federal-government/government-contract-vehicles/cms-macpie/index.htm (accessed September 15, 2014).

28 Northrop Grumman, "Northrop Grumman Selected to Set Up, Sustain Tennessee's Medicaid and Children's Health Insurance Eligibility System," news release, July 9, 2013, https://www.globenewswire.com/newsarchive/noc/press/pages/news_releases.html?d=10039519 (accessed December 10, 2014).

29 Northrop Grumman, "Health IT, Child Support Enforcement Consulting," http://www.northropgrumman.com/Capabilities/BenefitSystems/Documents/Child_Support_Enforce_card.pdf (accessed December 10, 2014).

30 Social Security Administration, Office of the Inspector General, *Audit, Report: Contract with Lockheed Martin Government Services, Inc. for Digital Imaging Services 2*, A-04-08-18066 (November 2008), http://www.ssa.gov/oig/ADOBEPDF/A-04-08-18066.pdf (site now discontinued).

31 Public Consulting Group, "About Public Consulting Group (PCG)," http://www.publicconsultinggroup.com/About/index.html (accessed December 19, 2014).

32 HMS, "State of Alaska Awards Post-payment Recovery and Cost Avoidance Contract to HMS," news release, July 11, 2012, http://files.shareholder.com/downloads/ABEA-4GAAQJ/1965182160x0x582322/4c278ba1-0e1f-4f00-8936-49dacbcfbc65/HMSY_News_2012_7_11_General_Releases.pdf (accessed December 19, 2014).

33 "MAXIMUS Increases Quarterly Cash Dividend to $0.12 per Share," news release, December 17, 2008, Reuters, http://www.reuters.com/article/2008/12/17/idUS224081+17-Dec-2008+BW20081217 (accessed December 19, 2014).

34 Seeking Alpha, "MAXIMUS F4Q08 (Qtr. End 9/30/08) Earnings Call Transcript," statement of Richard Montoni, President and Chief Executive Officer, November 13, 2008, http://seekingalpha.com/article/105919-maximus-f4q08-qtr-end-9-30-08-earnings-call-transcript?page=-1&find=maximus (accessed October 18, 2014).

35 Seeking Alpha, "HMS Holdings Corp., Q3 2008 Earnings Call Transcript," statement of Walter Hosp, Senior Vice President and Chief Financial Officer, November 13, 2008, http://seekingalpha.com/article/103287-hms-holdings-corp-q3-2008-earnings-call-transcript (accessed October 18, 2014).

36 Seeking Alpha, ibid., statements of Bill Lucia, President and Chief Operating Officer, and Bob Holster, President, Director, and Chief Executive Officer.

37 Ibid.

38 OpenSecrets.org Center for Responsive Politics, "Influence & Lobbying: Ranked Sectors," Center for Responsive Politics, http://www.opensecrets.org/lobby/top.php?indexType=c&showYear=2011 (law updated July 28, 2014) (accessed October 18, 2014).

39 Ibid.; Influence Explorer, "Pharmaceuticals/Health Products," Sunlight Foundation, http://influenceexplorer.com/industry/pharmaceuticalshealth-products/08c1fa7788994f148eddfb78c10032cf?cycle=2012 (accessed September 15, 2014); Influence Explorer, "Hospitals/Nursing Homes," Sunlight Foundation, http://influenceexplorer.com/industry/hospitalsnursing-homes/0b4aba987b6e4cb5931b8060b40a0c7f?cycle=2012 (accessed September 15, 2014).

40 OpenSecrets.org, "Influence & Lobbying, Defense: Summary," Center for Responsive Politics, http://www.opensecrets.org/industries/indus.php?ind=D (accessed August 19, 2014).

41 OpenSecrets.org, "Influence & Lobbying, Health: Summary," Center for Responsive Politics, http://www.opensecrets.org/industries/indus.php?ind=H (August 19, 2014).

42 OpenSecrets.org, "Influence & Lobbying, Hospitals & Nursing Homes: Summary," Center for Responsive Politics, http://www.opensecrets.org/industries/indus.php?ind=H02 (accessed August 19, 2014) (23 million compared to 24 million for defense industry).

43 See, e.g., Dave McKinney, "Governor's Donor Gets Chance at Contract," *Chicago Sun Times*, 8, March 7, 2005; Dave McKinney, "Lawmakers Say Firm Awarded State Pact Had 'Inside track,'" *Chicago Sun Times*, 26, July 18, 2005.

44 McKinney, *Governor's Donor*.

45 Ibid.

46 Garrett Therolf, "Firm Courts Supervisors, Wins Reprieve," *Los Angeles Times*, November 19, 2008, http://articles.latimes.com/2008/nov/19/local/me-maximus19 (accessed October 22, 2014) (noting that MAXIMUS spent $200,000 on lobbying fees, compared to $25,000 spent by Policy Studies, Inc.).

47 Garrett Therolf, "Low-Rated Firm Fights to Keep Rich County Work," *Los Angeles Times*, October 30, 2008, http://articles.latimes.com/2008/oct/30/local/me-maximus30 (accessed October 22, 2014).

48 Ibid.

49 Ibid.

50 Jim Doyle, "Centene Wins Missouri Medicaid Contract," *St. Louis Post-Dispatch*, February 23, 2012, http://www.stltoday.com/news/local/metro/centene-wins-missouri-medicaid-contract/article_b25fa40d-fdbe-5df7-a776-bf56a640c687.html (accessed October 22, 2014).

51 Jim Doyle, "Clayton-based Centene Wins Missouri Medicaid Contract," *St. Louis Post-Dispatch,* February 22, 2012, http://www.stltoday.com/business/local/clayton-based-centene-wins-missouri-medicaid-contract/article_72e45b08-5d64-11e1-8a9a-001a4bcf6878.html (accessed October 22, 2014).

52 "Board of Directors," Centene Corporation, http://www.centene.com/investors/corporate-governance/board-of-directors/ (accessed August 1, 2010); "Solutions," Centene Corporation, http://www.centene.com/about-us/solutions/ (accessed August 1, 2010); see also Christopher Lee, "Thompson's Medicaid Reforms Could Benefit His Employers," *Washington Post*, August 8, 2006, http://www.washingtonpost.com/wp-dyn/content/article/2006/08/07/AR2006080701088.html (accessed October 22, 2014).

53 Barbara Martinez, "In Medicaid, Private HMOs Take a Big Role," *Wall Street Journal*, November 15, 2006, http://www.wsj.com/articles/SB116354350983023095.

54 Jan Murphy, "Consultant Reaps State Windfall," *Patriot-News*, A1, February 24, 2008.

55 Ibid.

56 Brad Bumsted, "Rendell Denies Use of 'Pay-to-Play' Deals," *Pittsburgh Tribune-Review*, March 10, 2009, http://www.pittsburghlive.com/x/pittsburghtrib/news/s_615249.html (accessed October 22, 2014).

57 Jan Murphy, "Deloitte's $250 Million State Department of Public Welfare Contract Object of Court Fight," *Patriot-News*, April 24, 2011, http://www.pennlive.com/midstate/index.ssf/2011/04/tech_firm_fights_deloittes_250.html (accessed October 22, 2014).

58 Ibid.

59 *Pittsburgh Business Times*, "Ridge to Consult for Deloitte and Touche," November. 2, 2006.

60 Brad Bumsted, "GOP: No-Bid Smacks of Favors," TribLive, March 4, 2008, http://triblive.com/x/pittsburghtrib/news/regional/s_555380.html#axzz3LGgaPKGf (last accessed December 7, 2014).

61 Ibid.

62 *Patriot-News*, "Pennsylvania's Payouts to Deloitte Consulting Near Half-Billion Dollars," February 25, 2008, http://cloud-computing.tmcnet.com/news/2008/02/25/3289847.htm (last accessed December 7, 2014).

63 Ibid.

64 See, e.g., Paul Kengor, *Competitive Contracting and Privatization Options in Wisconsin State Government*, Wisconsin Policy Research Institute Report, April 2001, 1 (accessed October 22, 2014). ("The seeds are there for more privatization in Wisconsin. The receptivity is shown by the encouragement of the State Legislature and Governor Thompson, who together created the bipartisan Wisconsin Commission on Privatization, which in 1998 called for a comprehensive privatization plan.")

65 E.g., Susan Page, "Medicare Scrap Could Shove Aside Prescription-Drug Benefit," *USA Today*, January 29, 2003, http://www.usatoday.com/news/health/2003-01-29-bush-healthcare_x.htm (describing Thompson's support for legislation that conditioned access to a prescription-drug benefit on enrolling in a private managed-care program).

66 *Washington Business Journal*, "Tommy Thompson Joins Akin Gump," March 9, 2005, http://www.bizjournals.com/washington/stories/2005/03/07/daily16.html (accessed December 19, 2014).

67 Ibid.

68 "Board of Directors," Centene Corporation, http://www.centene.com/investors/corporate-governance/board-of-directors/ (accessed December 7, 2014); "Tommy G. Thompson Elected to Medco Board of Directors," news release, October 16, 2006, PR Newswire, http://www.prnewswire.com/news-releases/tommy-g-thompson-elected-to-medco-board-of-directors-56490612.html (accessed December 19, 2014); WRAL.com, "Former HHS Director Tommy Thompson Joins Voyager Board," *Capitol Broadcasting Company*, March 2, 2006, http://www.wral.com/news/local/story/155109 (accessed October 22, 2014); Bard, "Tommy

Thompson Elected to Bard's Board of Directors," news release, August 16, 2005, http://www.crbard.com/prlanding.aspx?releaseID=743558 (accessed December 19, 2014).

69 Public Consulting Group, Management Team, William S. Mosakowski, http://www.publicconsultinggroup.com/about/management_team/index.html (accessed December 8, 2014).

70 Ibid., Rich Albertoni.

71 Ibid., Tom Entrikin.

72 Ibid., Brian Howells.

73 Ibid., Jill Reynolds.

74 Ibid., Jim Waldinger.

75 Public Consulting Group, Medicare-Medicaid, Janice Paterson, Esq., PMP, http://www.publicconsultinggroup.com/health/medicaidmedicare/index.html (last accessed on December 8, 2014).

76 Public Consulting Group, Cathy Anderson, Subject Matter Expert, http://www.publicconsultinggroup.com/humanservices/sme/CathyAnderson.html (accessed December 8, 2014).

77 Public Consulting Group, Jamie Kilpatrick, Early Intervention Services Subject Matter Expert, http://www.publicconsultinggroup.com/humanservices/sme/JamieKilpatrick.html (accessed December 8, 2014).

78 Public Consulting Group, Sam Fish, Human Services Law Subject Matter Expert, http://www.publicconsultinggroup.com/humanservices/sme/samfish.html (accessed December 8, 2014).

79 Public Consulting Group, Judge James Payne, Subject Matter Expert, http://www.publicconsultinggroup.com/humanservices/sme/JamesPayne.html (accessed December 8, 2014).

80 MAXIMUS, President, Human Services North America, http://www.maximus.com/kathleen-kerr (accessed December 7, 2014).

81 MAXIMUS, Human Services President & General Manager, http://www.maximus.com/akbar-piloti (accessed December 7, 2014).

82 MAXIMUS, Board of Directors, http://investor.maximus.com/corporate-governance/board-of-directors (accessed December 8, 2014).

83 Aaron Blake, "Jindal: GOP Scandal Response Should Focus on Big Government," *Washington Post*, May 24, 2013, http://www.washingtonpost.com/blogs/post-politics/wp/2013/05/24/jindal-gop-scandal-response-should-focus-on-big-government/ (accessed October 22, 2014).

84 Associated Press, "Louisiana to Rebid Medicaid Eligibility Contract," April 22, 2013, http://neworleanscitybusiness.com/blog/2013/04/22/louisiana-to-rebid-medicaid-eligibility-contract/ (last accessed December 8, 2014).

85 Elizabeth Montalbano, "Microsoft Adds Health Care to Global E-Government Platform," *ComputerWorld*, April 23, 2009, http://www.computerworld.com/s/article/9132042/Microsoft_adds_health_care_to_global_e_government_platform (accessed October 22, 2014).

86 Laura Maggi, "Investigators Looking into Possible Perjury by Former Louisiana Health Chief," *Times-Picayune*, May 4, 2013, http://blog.nola.com/politics/print. html?entry=/2013/05/investigators_looking_into_pos.html (accessed October 22, 2014).

87 Melinda Deslatte, "Greenstein Resigns Post," *Advocate*, April 3, 2013, http://theadvocate.com/home/5571651-125/jindal-health-secretary-resigns (site now discontinued).

88 Melinda Deslatte, "Governor's Office: Greensteign, CNSI had Improper Communications," *Fox 8 WVUE-TV,* May 3, 2013, http://www.fox8live.com/ story/22092450/jindal-administration-outlines-contract-problems (accessed October 22, 2014).

89 Jeff Adelson, "Louisiana Cancels Medicaid Claims Contract in Wake of Federal Investigation," *Times-Picayune*, March 21, 2013, http://www.nola.com/politics/index.ssf/2013/03/louisiana_cancels_medicaid_cla.html (accessed October 22, 2014).

90 See FAR 9.5 (incorporating FAR 2.101's definition of a conflict of interest that arises where, "because of other activities or relationships with other persons, a person is unable or potentially unable to render impartial assistance or advice to the government, or the person's objectivity in performing the contract work is or might be otherwise impaired, or a person has an unfair competitive advantage").

91 U.S. Department of Health and Human Services, Office of Inspector General, *Conflicts and Financial Relationships Among Potential Zone Program*, no. OEI-03-10-00300 (July 2012), http://oig.hhs.gov/oei/reports/oei-03-10-00300.pdf (accessed October 22, 2014).

92 Ibid.

93 North Carolina Department of Health and Human Services, DHHS/DMA Program Integrity Contract with Public Consulting Group, http://www.ncdhhs.gov/ dma/bulletin/0411bulletin.htm#pcg (accessed November 29, 2014).

94 "Revenue Management," Public Consulting Group, http://www.publicconsulting-group.com/health/publichospital/revenuemanagement.html (accessed September 15, 2014).

95 U.S. Government Accountability Office, GAO-05-748, Medicaid Financing: States' Use of Contingency-Fee Consultants to Maximize Federal Reimbursements Highlights Need for Improved Federal Oversight 15–43 (2005).

96 University of Massachusetts Medical School, Center for Health Care Financing, Medicaid Claiming, http://chcf.umassmed.edu/services/school-based-medicaid-claiming/medicaid-claiming (accessed November 29, 2014).

97 GAO, Medicaid Financing, 35–36, 88–89.

98 Ibid.

99 Office of Management and Budget, Executive Office of the President, "OMB Circular no. A-76," Attachment A (2003), http:// www.whitehouse.gov/omb/circulars/a076/a76_incl_tech_correction.pdf (site now discontinued); see also Martha Minow, *Outsourcing Power: How Privatizing Military Efforts Challenges Accountability, Professionalism, and Democracy*, 46 B.C. L. REV. 989, 1014–15 (2005).

100 Administrative Costs for Children in Title IV-E Foster Care, 70 Fed. Reg. 4803, 4805 (proposed January 31, 2005) (to be codified at 45 C.F.R. pt. 1356).

101 See Joint Legislative Committee on Performance Evaluation and Expenditure Review (PEER), *Report to the Mississippi Legislature on the Department of Human Services' Use of Revenue Maximization Contracts* (2000), no. 413, 19, http://www.peer.state.ms.us/reports/rpt413.pdf.

102 U.S. Department of Health and Human Services, Office of Inspector General, *Review of Washington State's Administrative Costs Claimed for Medicaid School-Based Health Services in State Fiscal Year 2000,* no. A-10-01-00011 (2002), 8, http://oig.hhs.gov/oas/reports/region10/h0100011.pdf (accessed October 23, 2014).

103 Ibid., 8–9.

104 Department of Health and Human Services, Substance Abuse and Mental Health Services Administration, *Cost Analysis and Audit Support for the Substance Abuse and Mental Health Services Administration,* no. 283-09-0275 (2009), https://www.fbo.gov/index?s=opportunity&mode=form&id=5dee21914813105b1270b1c153dee391&tab=core&_cview=0&cck=1&au=&ck= (accessed October 22, 2014).

105 GAO, Medicaid Financing, 4.

106 Ibid.

107 Senator Chuck Grassley, "Grassley Seeks Answers on States' Use of Consultants to Increase Medicaid Funds," news release, February 13, 2004, http://www.grassley.senate.gov/releases/2004/p04r02-13.htm (site now discontinued).

108 GAO, Medicaid Financing, 40–43.

109 Ibid., app. IV at 67 (citation omitted).

110 Ibid.

111 "Mark Friedman Biography," Fiscal Policy Studies Institute, http://resultsaccountability.com/mark-friedman-biography/ (last accessed December 8, 2014).

112 Mark Friedman, "The Cosmology of Financing: Financing Reform of Family and Children's Services," *Center for the Study of Social Policy,* June 28, 1994, Part II, http://www.fiscalpolicystudies.com/Documents/cosmology_of_financing.htm.

113 Carasso and Bess, "The Disposition of Federal Dollars in Florida's Social Services: Informing a Federal Funding Maximization Strategy," *Urban Institute* 32 (2003).

114 U.S. Government Accountability Office, GAO-05-836T, Medicaid: States' Efforts to Maximize Federal Reimbursements Highlight Need for Improved Federal Oversight 11 (2005).

115 U.S. Government Accountability Office, GAO/HEHS/OSI-00-69, Medicaid in Schools: Improper Payments Demand Improvements in HCFA Oversight 31 (2000).

116 Carasso and Bess, "The Disposition of Federal Dollars," 33.

117 Shaila Dewan, "Needy States Use Housing Aid Cash to Plug Budgets," *New York Times,* May 15, 2012, http://www.nytimes.com/2012/05/16/business/states-diverting-mortgage-settlement-money-to-other-uses.html?_r=1&pagewanted=all (accessed October 23, 2014).

118 "Summary of Governor Jindal's Overview of the FY 2009–2010 Executive Budget," news release, March 13, 2009, http://www.gov.state.la.us/index.cfm?md=news room&tmp=detail&catID=2&articleID=1063&navID=12.

119 Jeff Zeleny, "Gregg Ends Bid for Commerce Job," *New York Times*, February 13, 2009, at A1.

120 Kevin Landrigan, "Feds Might Demand $165m Payback: N.H. Official Warns Surplus at Risk over Medicaid 'Bonus,'" *Telegraph*, Nashua, New Hampshire, January 31, 2006.

121 Joint Standing Committee on Appropriations and Financial Affairs, *An Act to Make Supplemental Appropriations and Allocations for the Expenditures of State Government and to Change Certain Provisions of the Law Necessary to the Proper Operations of State Government for the Fiscal Years Ending June 30, 2002 and June 30, 2003*, LD 2080, 2d Sess. (Maine 2001), 48, http://www.maine.gov/legis/ofpr/afao2.pdf (accessed October 23, 2014).

122 State of Arizona, Joint Legislative Budget Committee, *Governor's Office of Strategic Planning and Budgeting—Report on Federal Revenue Maximization Initiative Part 9* (August 9, 2004), 2, http://www.azleg.gov/jlbc/jlbcag081704.pdf (accessed October 23, 2014).

123 Ibid., 3–4; see also Arizona, *Monthly Fiscal Highlights 1* (June 2005), 8, http://www. azleg.gov/jlbc/mfh-jun-05.pdf (accessed October 23, 2014) (*"Increased Title IV-E Administrative Claiming and Targeted Case Management*: The DCYF operating budget was reduced by $0.9 million in FY 2006 in anticipation of the additional IV-E revenue . . . *Title IV-E Funding for Out-of-Home Placement*: The DCYF Children Services budget was reduced by $0.5 million in FY 2006 in anticipation of the additional IV-E revenue.").

124 U.S. Government Accountability Office, *CMS Should Improve Reporting and Focus on Audit Collaboration with States*, GAO-12-627 (2012), http://www.gao.gov/assets/600/591601.pdf (accessed October 23, 2014).

125 Courier-Journal.com, "Editorial: The Cost of Cuts," July 7, 2013, http://archive. courier-journal.com/article/20130707/OPINION01/307070028/Editorial-cost-cuts (last accessed December 9, 2014).

126 *Mont. Code Ann.* § 53-1-610 (2009). ("The department of public health and human services shall seek federal funds to offset general fund expenditures to the maximum extent possible.")

127 Montana Office of Budget and Program Planning, *Public Health and Human Services 6901* (2005), B-9, http://budget.mt.gov/Portals/29/execbudgets/2005_budget/OBPPB.pdf (accessed December 9, 2014). ("The department is currently working on a "refinancing" project, which saves $3,000,000 general fund and increases $3,000,000 in federal funds each year of the biennium.")

128 Ibid., B-9 to B-10.

129 President Dwight D. Eisenhower, Farewell Address, January 17, 1961, http://www. americanrhetoric.com/speeches/dwightdeisenhowerfarewell.html (accessed October 23, 2014).

130 Adams, *The Iron Triangle: The Politics of Defense Contracting*, 24–26.

131 Kevin R. Kosar, Congressional Research Service, *Privatization and the Federal Government: An Introduction*, report prepared for members and committees of Congress, December 28, 2006, 11, http://www.fas.org/sgp/crs/misc/RL33777.pdf (accessed October 23, 2014).

132 House Energy and Commerce Committee Subcommittee on Health, *Hearing on Challenges Facing the Medicaid Program in the 21st Century*, 108th Cong., October 8, 2003, 58 (statement of Thomas Scully, Administrator, Centers for Medicaid and Medicare Services and Department of Health and Human Services), http://www.hhs.gov/asl/testify/t031008.html (accessed October 23, 2014).

133 Senate, 1965, S Rep. 89–404, 66, *as reprinted in* 1965 U.S.C.C.A.N. 1943, 2014.

134 Ibid. § 1396a(a)(30)(A).

135 *Federal Payments for Foster Care and Adoption Assistance, U.S. Code 42* § 674(a).

136 POMS, "SI § 00830.410 Foster Care Payments," Social Security Administration, https://secure.ssa.gov/apps10/poms.nsf/lnx/0500830410 (accessed September 15, 2014) ("Foster care payments made under title IV-E (both the Federal amount and State amount) are considered income based on need . . . . to the individual in care").

137 GAO, Medicaid Financing, note 12, 4–5. http://www.gao.gov/new.items/d05748.pdf.

138 Ibid., 23.

139 See ibid., 4 (describing conclusion that revenue maximization contingency fee in Georgia was paid directly out of the additional Medicaid reimbursements).

140 Ibid. § 1396b(a)(2)-(7); see also Ibid. § 674(a)(3) (stating the same requirement under Title IV-E).

141 Office of Management and Budget, Executive Office of the President, *Cost Principles for State, Local and Indian Tribal Governments*, Attachment B, § 33(a), no. A-87 (August 29, 1997) ("[C]osts of professional and consultant services . . . are allowable . . . when reasonable in relation to the services rendered and when not contingent upon recovery of the costs from the Federal Government."); see also U.S. Department of Health and Human Services, Office of the Inspector General, *Review of Mississippi's Retroactive Claim for Foster Care Administrative and Training Costs and Maintenance Payments*, A-04-98-00126, (2000), 3, http://oig.hhs.gov/oas/reports/region4/49800126.pdf (accessed October 23, 2014) (applying same conclusion to Title IV-E administrative costs).

142 *False Claims, U.S. Code 31* (2009) §§ 3729-3733; *False, Fictitious or Fraudulent Claims, U.S. Code 18* (2006) § 287.

143 *Civil Actions for False Claims, U.S. Code 31* (2010) § 3730; see also Timothy Stoltzfus Jost, *Our Broken Health Care System and How to Fix It: An Essay on Health Law and Policy*, 41 WAKE FOREST L. REV. 537, 568 (2006) ("[Q]ui tam provisions of the federal civil False Claims Act encourage knowledgeable insiders to expose secret fraud and corruption").

144 *Civil Actions for False Claims, U.S. Code 31* (2010 § 3729(b).

145 *Vt. Agency of Natural Res. v. United States ex rel. Stevens*, 529 U.S. 765 (2000).
146 *Cook County, Ill. v. United States ex rel. Chandler*, 538 U.S. 119 (2003).

CHAPTER 3

1 Candice N. Plotkin, "Study Finds Foster Kids Suffer PTSD," *The Harvard Crimson*, April 11, 2005.

2 Georgia Department of Human Resources Division of Family and Children Services, Education and Training Services Section, *Social Services IV-E Policy Trainer's Guide* (2006), http://dfcs.dhr.georgia.gov/sites/dfcs.dhs.georgia.gov/files/imported/DHR-DFCS/DHR_DFCS-Edu/Files/IV-E%20PG%20Final%20ver.12-06.pdf (accessed December 3, 2014).

3 Cynthia Andrews Scarcella et al., The Cost of Protecting Vulnerable Children V, Urban Institute, appendix A, http://www.urban.org/UploadedPDF/311314_vulnerable_children.pdf (accessed December 4, 2014).

4 U.S. Department of Health and Human Services, Administration for Children and Families, Administration on Children, Youth and Families, Children's Bureau, Numbers of Children in Foster Care on September 30th, by State, FY2004–FY2013, http://www.acf.hhs.gov/sites/default/files/cb/children_in_care_2013.pdf (accessed December 4, 2014).

5 National Resource Center for Family-Centered Practice and Permanency Planning, Hunter College School of Social Work, Foster Care Maintenance Payments, June 19, 2008, http://www.hunter.cuny.edu/socwork/nrcfcpp/downloads/foster-care-maintenance-payments.pdf (accessed December 4, 2014).

6 Joint Legislative Committee on Performance Evaluation and Expenditure Review (PEER), *Report to the Mississippi Legislature on the Department of Human Services' Use of Revenue Maximization Contracts* (2000), no. 413, http://www.peer.state.ms.us/reports/rpt413.pdf.

7 Georgia Medicaid Manual, "Assistance for Children in Placement," *Funding Sources* (2012) vol. II/MA, MT 45, sec. 2805-1-2, http://www.georgiamedicaidlaw.net/gamedicaid/2805.pdf (last accessed December 10, 2014).

8 National Council of Juvenile and Family Court Judges, *Child Welfare Finance Reform Policy Statement* (2011), http://www.chhs.ca.gov/CWCDOC/022813_PEI_Committee_childwelfarefinancereform_Courts.pdf.

9 Ibid.

10 Ibid.

11 DHHS Office of the Controller, *IV-E Foster Care Rate Setting User's Manual* (2013), http://www.ncdhhs.gov/control/fcf/FC_rate_setting_manual.pdf.

12 Susan Combs, Texas Comptroller of Public Accounts, "HHS 32: Increase Federal Health and Human Services Funding to Local Governments: Texas should increase the federal funding of local health and human services by helping local governments claim local expenditures," Window on State Government, http://www.cpa.state.tx.us/tpr/tpr4/c2.hhs/c232.html (accessed October 8, 2014).

13 Ibid.

14 Public Consulting Group, Technical Proposal for Kentucky Department for Community Based Services, SSI Eligibility Determination, May 26, 2010, 115 (on file with author).

15 Fred Grimm, "Creating Juvenile Zombies, Florida-Style," *Miami Herald*, May 28, 2011.

16 David Sessions, "Psychotropic Drug Abuse in Foster Care Costs Government Billions," *Politics Daily*, http://www.politicsdaily.com/2010/06/17/psychotropic-drug-abuse-in-foster-care-costs-government-billions/ (accessed December 1, 2014).

17 Ibid.

18 Adam Carasso and Roseana Bess, *Final Report to Florida Philanthropic Network on the Disposition of Federal Dollars in Florida's Social Services: Informing a Federal Funding Maximization Strategy*, (Urban Institute, 2003), 56–57, http://www.urban.org/UploadedPDF/410822_federal_dollars.pdf.

19 Cynthia Andrews Scarcella and Roseana Bess, eds., *The Cost of Protecting Vulnerable Children IV: How Child Welfare Funding Fared during the Recession* (Urban Institute, 2004), 25, http://www.urban.org/UploadedPDF/411115_VulnerableChildrenIV.pdf.

20 479 NAC 2-001.08.

21 Daniel L. Hatcher, "Foster Children Paying for Foster Care," 27 CARDOZO L. REV. 1797 (2006). (Article provided foundational research and material for this chapter of the book.)

22 "Westchester, Putnam Police Briefs, D.A.: Social Worker Stole Death Benefits," *Journal News*, January 25, 2011, http://www.lohud.com/article/20110126/NEWS01/101260328/Westchester-Putnam-police-briefs (accessed October 23, 2014).

23 Ibid.

24 Ibid.

25 Lorraine Ahearn, "At Eleventh Hour, Judge Saves Boy in Foreclosure," *Greensboro News & Record*, December 18, 2005.

26 *In re J.G.*, 86 N.C. App. 498–501 (2007).

27 Kevin P. Mahon, Westchestergov.com, agreement letter to Board of Acquisition and Contract, July 1, 2010, http://aandc.westchestergov.com/data/FinalResolution/12244.pdf.

28 Ahearn, "At Eleventh Hour, Judge Saves Boy in Foreclosure," 500–501.

29 Ibid. at 507–508.

30 Charisse S. Johnson, "Use of a Child's Resources," administrative letter FSCWS-17-07 to County Directors of Social Services, North Carolina Department of Health and Human Services Division of Social Services, December 18, 2007, http://info.dhhs.state.nc.us/olm/manuals/dss/csm-05/man/FSCWS_AL_17_07.htm.

31 MAXIMUS, "Spotlight on Iowa SSI Advocacy," http://www.maximus.com/so-child-welfare (accessed on November 17, 2014).

32 Public Consulting Group, "Social Security Advocacy Management Services— SSAMS™ Offerings for Foster Care Agencies," http://www.publicconsultinggroup. com/humanservices/SSI_SSDI/ssi_for_fostercare.html (accessed October 16, 2014).

33 Ibid.

34 Internal email to Greg Holland, Maryland Department of Human Resources, from Fateen J. Bullock, director, Benefits and Eligibility Advocacy Services, MAXIMUS, January 10, 2013 (on file with author).

35 MAXIMUS, SSI/SSDI Assessment Report, Maryland Department of Human Resources, February 22, 2013, 3 (on file with author).

36 Maryland Department of Human Resources, *MAXIMUS Benefits & Eligibility Advocacy Services*, SSI/SSDI Assessment Report, February 2013 (on file with author).

37 Ibid., 5.

38 Ibid., 12.

39 Ibid.

40 Internal email to Greg Holland, Maryland Department of Human Resources, from Fateen J. Bullock, Director, Benefits & Eligibility Advocacy Services, MAXIMUS, January 2, 2013 (on file with author).

41 MAXIMUS, Maryland SSI Advocacy Pilot Project Work Plan, September 2012 (on file with author).

42 MAXIMUS, SSI/SSDI Assessment Report, 12–13.

43 F.M. Blake, A Division of Public Consulting Group, Inc., Cost Proposal, FY09 & FY10 SSI Screening and Determinations for Children, Commonwealth of Kentucky, April 28, 2008, 3 (on file with author).

44 McDowell, Stromatt & Associates, Technical Proposal, FY09 & FY10 DCBS-SSI Eligibility for Children, May 3, 2008, 8 (on file with author).

45 Public Consulting Group, Technical Proposal, SSI Eligibility Determination, Kentucky Dept. for Community Based Services, May 26, 2010, 31 (on file with author).

46 F.M. Blake, A Division of Public Consulting Group, Inc., Technical Proposal, FY09 & FY10 SSI Screening and Determinations for Children, Commonwealth of Kentucky, April 28, 2008, 11 (on file with author).

47 Ibid., 15.

48 Ibid., 16.

49 Public Consulting Group, SSI Eligibility Determination, Kentucky Department for Community Based Services, Letter accompanying proposal, May 26, 2010, 4 (on file with author).

50 Ibid., Technical Proposal, 83–84.

51 Ibid.

52 Ibid., 84.

53 Ibid.

54 Shirley Baack, Nebraska Department of Health and Human Services, internal email regarding public records request and attaching copy of statute 43-907 "that

allows DHHS to use the SSI and SSA funds of State Wards to reimburse foster care . . . ," June 6, 2013 (on file with author).

55 479 NAC 2-001.08B2.

56 Shirley Baack, Nebraska Department of Health and Human Services, internal email including spreadsheet showing the amount of state use of foster children's Social Security funds as cost reimbursement, June 6, 2013 (on file with author).

57 MAXIMUS, Inc., MAXIMUS SSI Advocacy Project, Presentation for Director Thomas Pristow, Nebraska Department of Health and Human Services, Division of Children and Family Services, June 12, 2012, 10 (on file with the author).

58 Ibid., 13.

59 MAXIMUS, Inc., Proposal to Provide Appropriate Application Title II (SSA) and Title XVI (SSI) for the Nebraska Department of Health and Human Services, Division of Children and Family Services, Technical Proposal, RFP #38688-03, October 20, 2008, A.2–5 (on file with author).

60 Public Consulting Group, SSI/SSDI Assessment Report, Division of Family and Children's Services, Georgia Department of Human Services, November 3, 2009 at 16 (on file with author).

61 Accenture, Georgia SHINES: Child Welfare Automation, http://www.accenture.com/us-en/Pages/success-georgia-shines-child-welfare-automation-summary.aspx (accessed December 1, 2014).

62 Department of Family and Children's Services, Georgia Department of Human Services, Administration Policies and Procedures Manual, § 2403.1 Restricted Funds–Children, October 2009 (on file with author).

63 Public Consulting Group, SSI/SSDI Assessment Report, 3.

64 Ibid., 24, 25.

65 Roger Munns, Iowa Department of Human Services Public Information Officer, Letter to Daniel L. Hatcher, June 13, 2013 (on file with author).

66 MAXIMUS, Inc., Bid Proposal for Iowa Department of human Services SSI Advocacy Project, § K Cost Proposal, February 12, 2009, 3 (on file with author).

67 MAXIMUS, Inc., Bid Proposal for Iowa Department of human Services SSI Advocacy Project, Letter Accompanying Technical Proposal, February 12, 2009, 2 (on file with author).

68 Public Consulting Group, Social Security Advocacy Assessment, State of Florida, Department of Children and Families, September 14, 2012, 28.

69 Ibid., 28, 29.

70 Ibid., 5.

71 Ibid.

72 Ibid.

73 Ibid., 6.

74 MAXIMUS, Bid Proposal for Iowa Department of Human Services SSI Advocacy Project, Technical Proposal, C-2 (on file with author).

75 Memorandum from Carnitra D. White, Executive Director, Maryland Social Services Administration, to directors of local offices, regarding Supplemental Security Income (SSI) Project, September 11, 2012 (on file with author). Maryland has since received a federal waiver of the rules, so the state can claim both IV-E and SSI for foster children.

76 In the Matter of J.G., 2006 WL 6086103, 2 (N.C.App.) (Brief of Amicus Curiae North Carolina Association of County Commissioners).

77 Ibid., 3.

78 Commonwealth of Kentucky, Contract with McDowell, Stromatt & Associates, SSI Eligibility Determinations for Children, June 24, 2008, 9 (on file with author).

79 Ibid.

80 MAXIMUS, Inc., MAXIMUS SSI Advocacy, Important Facts for Youth in Foster Care (on file with the author).

81 MAXIMUS, Inc., Bid Proposal for Iowa Department of Human Services SSI Advocacy Project, Technical Proposal, February 12, 2009, E-11 (on file with author).

82 Public Consulting Group, SSI/SSDI Assessment Report, Division of Family and Children's Services, Georgia Department of Human Services, November 3, 2009 at 13 (on file with author).

83 Public Consulting Group, GA DFCS SSI Assessment—Site Visit Summary, Thursday, September 24, 2009 (on file with author).

84 Ibid.

85 Margaret Bitz, Unit Administrator, Nebraska Department of Health and Human Services, internal email regarding SSI, October 11, 2012 (on file with author).

86 Program Operations Manual System (POMS), "GN 00502.110 Taking Applications in the RPS, TN 35 (07–08): B3," Social Security Administration, http://policy.ssa.gov/poms.nsf/ lnx/0200502110 (accessed October 23, 2014) (hereinafter "POMS").

87 Ibid. §§ 404.2021(c), 416.621(c).

88 What happens to your monthly benefits while we are finding a suitable representative payee for you?, *Code of Federal Regulations*, title 20, sec. 404.2011 (2005).

89 Social Security Administration, Office of the Inspector General, *Financial-Related Audit of the Baltimore City Department of Social Services—An Organizational Representative Payee for the Social Security Administration*, A-13-00-10066 (2001), 4–8, http://www.ssa.gov/oig/ ADOBEPDF/A-13-00-10066.pdf.

90 Social Security Administration, Office of the Inspector General, *Analysis of Information Concerning Representative Payee Misuse of Beneficiaries' Payments*, A-13-01-11004 (2002), http://www.ssa.gov/oig/ADOBEPDF/A-13-01-11004.pdf.

91 MAXIMUS, Technical Proposal in Response to Maryland Department of Human Resources, Social Services Administration, Small Procurement Solicitation for Consultation Services, DHR Agency Control No. SSA/CS 13-001 S, June 22, 2012, 5 (on file with author).

92 F.M. Blake, A Division of Public Consulting Group, Inc., Technical Proposal, FY09 & FY10 SSI Screening and Determinations for Children, Commonwealth of Kentucky, April 28, 2008, 14 (on file with author).

93 Commonwealth of Kentucky, Contract with McDowell, Stromatt & Associates, 11–12.

94 I have been involved in much of the litigation, both as lead counsel for a former foster child named Alex and as counsel for advocacy organizations filing an amicus brief in support of the foster child in another case (*In re Ryan W.*)

95 *Wash. State Dep't of Soc. & Health Servs. v. Guardianship Estate of Keffeler*, 537 U.S. 371, 378, 382 (2003).

96 *Washington State Dep't of Social & Health Services v. Guardianship Estate of Keffeler*, 537 U.S. 371 (2003).

97 *In re Ryan W.*, 434 Md. 577 (2013) (The author of this book was co-counsel for amici supporting the foster child's appeal).

98 *Social Security Act, U.S. Code* 42 (2006), § 672(a)(1).

99 Ibid., § 675(4)(A).

100 *Connor B. v. Patrick*, 771 F. Supp. 2d 142 (D. Mass. 2011).

101 SSA, Office of the Inspector General, *Hawaii Dep't Of Human Services—An Organizational Representative Payee for the Social Security Administration*, A-09-08-28045 (2008), 5, (emphasis added) (citing *Code of Federal Regulations*, title 45, sec. 92.24 (2012)), http://oig.ssa.gov/sites/default/files/audit/full/html/A-09-08-28045.html (accessed October 23, 2014).

102 Use of Benefit Payments, *Code of Federal Regulations*, title 20, sec. 404.2040(a) (2012).

103 47 Fed. Reg. 30,468, 30,470 (July 14, 1982).

104 Social Security Program Operation Manual System (POMS) GN 00602.030.

105 POMS, "§GN 00602.001 Use of Benefits," Social Security Administration, https://secure.ssa.gov/apps10/poms. nsf/lnx/0200602001 (site now discontinued).

106 Social Security Administration, Training Organizational Representative Payees, Unit 4, http://www.ssa.gov/payee/LessonPlan-2005-2.htm (accessed November 29, 2014).

107 Ibid., Unit 4.

108 Consumer Financial Protection Bureau, Managing Someone Else's Money: Help for Representative Payees and VA Fiduciaries, October 2013, http://files.consumerfinance.gov/f/201310_cfpb_lay_fiduciary_guides_representative.pdf (accessed November 29, 2014).

109 Ibid.

110 Social Security Administration, Representative Payee Program Fact Sheet, http://www.ssa.gov/payee/factsheetengl.htm (accessed November 29, 2014).

111 Maryland Senate Bill No. 914, Maryland 434th Session of the General Assembly, 2014 (The author of this book testified in support of the bill).

112 Ibid. Hearing before Senate Judicial Proceedings Committee, February 27, 2014, http://mgaleg.maryland.gov/webmga/frmMain.aspx?pid=billpage&tab=subject3&id=sb0914&stab=01&ys=2014RS (accessed December 4, 2014). As of the time of this writing, the agency has not yet supported the legislation to protect foster children's resources. The hope is that, if the legislation is introduced again in 2016, the

Maryland agency will change its mind and decide to truly protect the children's best interests.

113 *Armstrong v. United States*, 364 U.S. 40, 49 (1960).

CHAPTER 4

1 Monitor Staff, "No Pride in Taxing State's Hospital Beds," *Concord Monitor*, May 1, 2011, http://www.concordmonitor.com/article/254529/no-pride-in-taxing-states-hospital-beds?CSAuthResp=1339288174%3Ae3hpcr3lh2npm9vpfpdrhqta1 3%3ACSUserId%7CCSGroupId%3Aapproved%3A022D7C75109B46B1CD4DE4E 81DEA9114&CSUserId=94&CSGroupId=1 (accessed October 16, 2014); Monitor Staff, "With Revenue Down, Medicaid Enhancement Tax Creates Headaches," April 14, 2013, http://www.concordmonitor.com/news/politics/5546218-95/ with-revenue-down-medicaid-enhancement-tax-creates-headaches (accessed December 21, 2014).

2 Dr. Marjorie Kanof, U.S. GAO, *Medicaid Financing: Long-Standing Concerns about Inappropriate State Arrangements Support Need for Improved Federal Oversight*, GAO-08-255T (2007), http://www.gao.gov/assets/120/118488.pdf (emphasis added) (accessed October 15, 2014).

3 Ibid., emphasis added.

4 Kathryn G. Allen, U.S. Government Accountability Office, *Medicaid: Intergovernmental Transfers Have Facilitated State Financing Schemes*, GAO-04-574T (2004), http://www.gao.gov/new.items/d04574t.pdf (accessed October 15, 2014).

5 Kathryn G. Allen, U.S. Government Accountability Office, *Medicaid: Intergovernmental Transfers Have Facilitated State Financing Schemes*, GAO-04-574T, (2004), http://www.gao.gov/assets/120/110702.pdf (accessed October 15, 2014).

6 Kathryn G. Allen, U.S. Government Accountability Office, *Medicaid: States' Efforts to Maximize Federal Reimbursements Highlight Need for Improved Federal Oversight*, GAO-05-836T (2005), http://www.gao.gov/assets/120/111839.pdf (accessed October 15, 2014).

7 Kathryn G. Allen, U.S. Government Accountability Office, *Medicaid: Improved Federal Oversight of State Financing Schemes Is Needed*, GAO-04-228 (2004), http://www.gao.gov/assets/250/241469.pdf (accessed October 15, 2014).

8 Ibid.

9 Peggy Archer, Oregon Legislative Fiscal Office, *Budget Information Brief/2001-4: Medicaid Upper Payment Limit* (Salem, 2001), http://www.oregonlegislature.gov/ lfo/Documents/bb2001_4.pdf (accessed October 24, 2014).

10 Ibid.

11 Dr. Marjorie Kanof, U.S. Government Accountability Office, *Medicaid Financing: Long-Standing Concerns about Inappropriate State Arrangements Support Need for Improved Federal Oversight*, GAO-08-255T (2007), http://www.gao.gov/assets/120/118488.pdf (accessed October 15, 2014).

12 Susan Combs, Texas Comptroller of Public Accounts, Certification Revenue Estimate 2008–09 (estimating 439.3 million in general fund revenue from the

disproportionate share hospital program), http://www.texastransparency.org/
State_Finance/Budget_Finance/Reports/Certification_Revenue_Estimate/
cre0809/cre08.pdf (accessed November 30, 2014); Susan Combs, Texas Comptroller of Public Accounts, Certification Revenue Estimate 2010–11 (estimating
595 million in general fund revenue from the disproportionate share hospital
program and upper payment limit program), http://www.texastransparency.org/
State_Finance/Budget_Finance/Reports/Certification_Revenue_Estimate/cre1011/
text.php (accessed November 30, 2014); Susan Combs, Texas Comptroller of
Public Accounts, Certification Revenue Estimate 2012–13 (estimating 669 million
in general fund revenue from the disproportionate share hospital program and
upper payment limit program), http://www.texastransparency.org/State_Finance/
Budget_Finance/Reports/Certification_Revenue_Estimate/cre1213/text.php (accessed November 30, 2014).

13 Harvey Rice, "State Diverts Funds Meant for Hospitals," *Houston Chronicle*, April
1, 2013, Section: B Health Care.

14 Ibid.

15 Ibid.

16 Ibid.

17 U.S. Government Accountability Office, *Medicaid: More Transparency of and
Accountability for Supplemental Payments Are Needed*, GAO-13-48 (2012), http://
www.gao.gov/assets/660/650322.pdf (accessed October 15, 2014).

18 Ibid.

19 Ibid., FN 19.

20 Wisconsin Health Care Association (WHCA)/Wisconsin Center for Assisted
Living (WiCAL), *Background Paper: Funding Sources to Support Nursing Home
Resident Care* (2007), http://archives.whcawical.org/whca-docs/032007wn-a.pdf
(accessed October 15, 2014).

21 Daniel L. Hatcher, "Romney's Medicaid Shell Game," *Boston Globe*, October 12,
2012. (My op-ed provided material and background for this section of the book.)

22 Commonwealth of Massachusetts, "Executive Summary: Highlights," Governor's
Budget Recommendation House 1 Fiscal Year 2004, http://www.mass.gov/bb/
fy2004h1/execsumm/ (accessed October 22, 2014).

23 "Medicaid Money Laundering," *Wall Street Journal*, May 19, 2008, http://online.
wsj.com/article/SB121115735476802403.html (accessed October 22, 2014).

24 Chris Fletcher, "Valley News: Why Big Hospitals Are Suing N.H.," *New Hampshire
Center for Public Policy Studies*, August 6, 2011, http://www.nhpolicy.org/news/
valley-news-why-big-hospitals-are-suing-nh (accessed October 22, 2014).

25 Commonwealth of Massachusetts, "Budget Recommendations: FFP for the
Uncompensated Care Trust Fund," Governor's Budget Recommendation House 1
Fiscal Year 2004, http://www.mass.gov/bb/fy2004h1/outsec/h280.htm (accessed
October 22, 2014). Emphasis added.

26 Commonwealth of Massachusetts, "Budget Recommendations: FFP for Disproportionate Share Hospital Payments to DMH/DPH Facilities," Governor's Budget

Recommendation House 1 Fiscal Year 2004, http://www.mass.gov/bb/fy2004h1/outsec/h281.htm (accessed October 22, 2014). Emphasis added.

27 Commonwealth of Massachusetts, "Nursing Home Assessment to the General Fund," Governor's Budget Recommendation House 1 Fiscal Year 2004, http://www.mass.gov/bb/fy2004h1/outsec/h144.htm (accessed October 22, 2014); Commonwealth of Massachusetts, "Pharmacy Assessment to the General Fund," Governor's Budget Recommendation House 1 Fiscal Year 2004, http://www.mass.gov/bb/fy2004h1/outsec/h147.htm (accessed October 22, 2014).

28 Public Consulting Group, Jim Waldinger, Health Care Reform Subject Matter Expert, http://www.publicconsultinggroup.com/health/sme/JimWaldinger.html (accessed November 30, 2014.

29 U.S. Government Accountability Office, *Medicaid Financing: States' Use of Contingency-Fee Consultants to Maximize Federal Reimbursements Highlights Need for Improved Federal Oversight*, GAO-05-748 (2005), http://www.gao.gov/assets/250/246870.pdf (emphasis added) (accessed November 30, 2014)

30 Ibid.

31 Missouri Hospital Association, *The Hospital Federal Reimbursement Allowance*, white paper submitted to the Missouri Department of Economic Development, October 8, 2010, http://www.ded.mo.gov/Content/MO%20Hospital%20Assn%2c%20THE%20HOSPITAL%20FEDERAL%20REIMBURSEMENT%20AL-LOWANCE.pdf (accessed October 22, 2014).

32 1992 Mo. Legis. Serv. H.B. 1744, (L.1992, H.B. No. 1744(§ 208.420). Emphasis added.

33 Ibid., § 208.435. Emphasis added.

34 Ibid., § 208.400. Emphasis added.

35 Missouri Hospital Association, *The Hospital Federal Reimbursement Allowance*.

36 Ibid.

37 Ibid.

38 Ibid.

39 Ibid.

40 Alabama Medicaid Pharmacy Study Commission, *Medicaid: A Time for Change* (2012), slides, http://www.medicaid.alabama.gov/documents/2.0_Newsroom/2.2_Boards_Committees/2.2.1_Med_Adv_Comission/2.2.1_Advisory_Commission_Presentation_11-1-12.pdf (accessed October 23, 2014).

41 Kathryn G. Allen and Robert H. Hast, U.S. General Accounting Office, *Medicaid: Poor Oversight and Improper Payments Compromise Potential Benefit*, GAO/T-HEHS/OSI-00-87 (2000), http://www.gao.gov/assets/110/108362.pdf (accessed October 15, 2014).

42 U.S. Department of Health and Human Services, Office of Inspector General, *Review of Maine's Medicaid Retroactive Claims for School-Based Health Services—January 2001 Through June 2003*, A-01-04-00004 (2005), https://oig.hhs.gov/oas/reports/region1/10400004.pdf.

43 William J. Scanlon, U.S. General Accounting Office, *Medicaid: Questionable Practices Boost Federal Payments for School-Based Services*, GAO/T-HEHS-99-148, (1999), http://www.gao.gov/assets/110/107966.pdf (accessed October 15, 2014).

44 Robert H. Hast, Office of Special Investigations, U.S. General Accounting Office, "Gratuities Provided to Officials Responsible for the Procurement of Michigan School-Based Medicaid Consulting Services, B-286188," letter to William V. Roth, Jr. and Daniel Patrick Moynihan, September 8, 2000, http://www.gao.gov/assets/100/90080.pdf.

45 Ibid.

46 Thomas P. DiNapoli, Office of the New York State Comptroller, "Special Education Contractors Misusing Taxpayer Dollars: Multiple Felony Arrests Stemming from Audits," news release, June 25, 2012, http://www.osc.state.ny.us/press/releases/june12/062512.htm (accessed October 22, 2014).

47 Ibid.

48 Ibid.

49 Emma G. Fitzsimmons, "Contractor Who Ran Special Education Pre-K Programs Is Charged with Fraud," *New York Times*, November 7, 2013.

50 Ibid.

51 Kathryn G. Allen and Robert H. Hast, U.S. General Accounting Office, *Medicaid: Poor Oversight and Improper Payments Compromise Potential Benefit*, GAO/T-HEHS/OSI-00-87 (2000), http://www.gao.gov/assets/110/108362.pdf (accessed October 15, 2014).

52 Ibid.

53 State of New Jersey, *Special Education Medicaid Initiative (SEMI): Provider Handbook* (Public Consulting Group, 2011), http://www.nj.gov/treasury/administration/pdf/semi-handbook.pdf.(accessed October 24, 2014).

54 Christopher D. Cerf, Department of Education, "Special Education Medicaid Initiative SY13–14 Revenue Projections," letter to Chief School Administration, Charter School Lead Person, School Business Administrators, and Directors of Special Education, January 29, 2013, http://www.state.nj.us/treasury/administration/pdf/SpecialEducationMedicaidInitiative.pdf (accessed December 12, 2014).

55 Ibid.

56 N.J. Admin. Code tit. 6A, 6A:23A-5.3.

57 Christopher D. Cerf, Department of Education, "Special Education Medicaid Initiative SY14–15 Revenue Projections," letter to Chief School Administration, Charter School Lead Person, School Business Administrators, and Directors of Special Education, January 28, 2014, http://education.state.nj.us/broadcasts/2014/JAN/28/10825/SEMI%20Broadcast.pdf (accessed October 24, 2014).

58 State of New Jersey, Department of the Treasury, *Semi Parental Consent Best Practices*, http://www.state.nj.us/treasury/administration/pdf/semi-parental-consent-best-prectices.pdf (accessed October 24, 2014).

59 Ibid.

60 State of New Jersey, Department of the Treasury, *General Provisions*, http://www. state.nj.us/treasury/omb/publications/14approp/pdf/genprov.pdf (accessed October 24, 2014).

61 Ibid.

62 Daniel R. Levinson, Department of Health and Human Services, Office of Inspector General, *Review of New Jersey's Medicaid School-Based Health Claims Submitted by Maximus, Inc.*, A-02-07-01051 (2010), https://oig.hhs.gov/oas/reports/region2/20701051.pdf (accessed November 30, 2014).

63 Ibid.

64 Daniel R. Levinson, Department of Health and Human Services, Office of Inspector General, *Review of New Jersey's Medicaid School-Based Health Claims Submitted by Public Consulting Group, Inc.*, A-02-07-01052 (2010), https://oig.hhs.gov/oas/reports/region2/20701052.pdf (accessed October 15, 2014).

65 Tony Gicas, "Extra Revenue for Schools," *NorthJersey.com*, November 30, 2012, http://www.northjersey.com/news/181487561_Extra_revenue_for_schools.html (accessed October 22, 2014).

66 Ibid.

67 William J. Scanlon, U.S. General Accounting Office, *Medicaid: Questionable Practices Boost Federal Payments for School-Based Services*, GAO/T-HEHS-99-148 (1999), http://www.gao.gov/assets/110/107966.pdf (accessed November 30, 2014).

68 Ibid.

69 Ibid.

70 Senate Committee on Finance, U.S. Department of Health and Human Services, Office of Inspector General, *Testimony of: George M. Reeb, Assistant Inspector General for the Centers for Medicare & Medicaid Audits*, June 28, 2005, https://oig.hhs.gov/testimony/docs/2005/50628-reeb-fin.pdf (accessed October 24, 2014).

71 Ibid.

72 Ibid.

73 Families for Better Care, "New York," Nursing Report Cards, http://nursinghomereportcards.com/state/ny/ (accessed October 22, 2014). Emphasis added.

74 Senate Committee on Finance, U.S. Department of Health and Human Services, Office of Inspector General, *Testimony of: George M. Reeb, Assistant Inspector General for the Centers for Medicare & Medicaid Audits*, June 28, 2005, https://oig.hhs.gov/testimony/docs/2005/50628-reeb-fin.pdf (accessed October 24, 2014).

75 U.S. Department of Health and Human Services, Office of Inspector General, *Adequacy of New York State's Medicaid Payments to A. Holly Patterson Extended Care Facility*, A-02-03-01004 (2005), Appendix B, http://oig.hhs.gov/oas/reports/region2/20301004.pdf (accessed October 24, 2014).

76 Ibid.

77 Senate Committee on Finance, U.S. Department of Health and Human Services, Office of Inspector General, *Testimony of: George M. Reeb, Assistant Inspector General for the Centers for Medicare & Medicaid Audits*, June 28, 2005, https://oig.hhs.gov/testimony/docs/2005/50628-reeb-fin.pdf (accessed October 24, 2014).

78 U.S. General Accounting Office, Nursing Homes: CMS's Special Focus Facility Methodology Should Better Target the Most Poorly Performing Homes, Which Tended to Be Chain Affiliated and For-Profit, GAO-09-689, August 2009 at 15, http://www.gao.gov/assets/300/294408.pdf (accessed November 30, 2014).

79 Associated Press, "Many Indiana Nursing Homes Understaffed," *Journal Gazette*, March 8, 2010, http://www.journalgazette.net/article/20100308/NEWS07/100309573/-1/NEWS09 (accessed October 22, 2014).

80 Ibid.

81 Families for Better Care, "Indiana," Nursing Report Cards, http://nursinghomereportcards.com/state/in/ (accessed October 22, 2014).

82 "Indiana Nursing Home Medicaid Reimbursement Update," H.O.P.E., September 2011, http://www.hoosierownersandproviders.org/Uploads/1109.pdf (last accessed December 22, 2014).

83 Christopher D. Atkins, "List of Appropriations," Regular Session of the 2013 Indiana General Assembly, State Budget Agency (2013), http://www.in.gov/sba/files/AP_2013_0_0_2_Budget_Report.pdf (accessed October 15, 2014).

84 Regular Session of the 2011 Indiana General Assembly, State Budget Agency, *Adam M. Horst, List of Appropriations* (2011), http://www.in.gov/sba/files/ap_2011_all.pdf (accessed October 15, 2014).

85 Indiana State Budget Agency, *General Fund and Rainy Day Fund Summaries* (2011), http://www.in.gov/sba/files/FY_2011_Close-Out_Surplus_Statement.pdf (accessed October 15, 2014).

86 Heather Gillers, Tim Evans, Mark Nichols, and Mark Alesia, "Crisis of Care Among State Nursing Homes, 1 in 10 Indiana Nursing Homes is Rated Among the Worst in the U.S.," *Indystar.com*, March 7, 2010, http://www.indystar.com/article/20100309/NEWS14/3070442/Crisis-care-among-state-nursing-homes (accessed October 22, 2014).

87 Families for Better Care, "Maryland," Nursing Report Cards, http://nursinghomereportcards.com/state/md/ (accessed October 22, 2014).

88 Ibid.

89 Kevin Spradlin, "Nursing Home Administrators Say Tax Would Penalize Elderly," *Cumberland Times-News*, February 24, 2010, http://www.times-news.com/news/local_news/nursing-home-administrators-say-tax-would-penalize-elderly/article_3408dba9-311a-5a4c-b186-9cf49c6fa20a.html (accessed October 22, 2014).

90 MD HEALTH GEN § 19-310.1, amended by Acts 2012, 1st Sp. Sess., c. 1, § 1, eff. June 1, 2012.

91 MD HEALTH GEN § 19-310.1, amended by Acts 2010, c. 484, § 3, eff. June 1, 2010.

92 Ibid. (emphasis added).

93 Ibid.

94 U.S. Government Accountability Office, Medicaid: States Reported Billions More in Supplemental Payments in Recent Years, GAO 12-694, July 2012 at 18, http://www.gao.gov/assets/600/592785.pdf (accessed November 30, 2014).

95 Indiana State Budget Agency, General Fund: Combined Statement of Unappropri-
    ated Reserve, http://www.in.gov/sba/files/ap_2011_0_0_51_reserve.pdf (accessed
    November 30, 2014).
96 State of North Carolina, General Fund Monthly Financial Report, May 31, 2013,
    http://www.osc.nc.gov/pdfs/May_2013_General_Fund_Monthly_Report.pdf (ac-
    cessed November 29, 2014).
97 http://www.window.state.tx.us/taxbud/cre-current/text.html.
98 Bob Norberg, "California Hospital Group Proposes Ballot Initiative for Medi-Cal
    Provider Free," *California Healthline*, October 10, 2013, http://www.california-
    healthline.org/capitol-desk/2013/10/california-hospital-group-proposes-ballot-
    initiative-for-medi-cal-provider-fee (accessed October 22, 2014).
99 Florida Agency for Health Care Administration, *Florida Medicaid Intergovern-
    mental Transfer Technical Advisory Panel Report* (2011), http://ahca.myflorida.
    com/Medicaid/igt/docs/Final%20_IGT_TAP_Report_010611.pdf (accessed Octo-
    ber 22, 2014).

CHAPTER 5

 1 See, generally, Daniel L. Hatcher, *Child Support Harming Children: Subordinating
    the Best Interests of Children to the Fiscal Interests of the State*, 42 WAKE FOREST
    L. REV. 1029 (2007); Daniel L. Hatcher, *Collateral Children: Consequence and
    Illegality at the Intersection of Foster Care and Child Support*, 74 BROOKLYN L.
    REV. 1333 (2009). (Both articles provided research background and material for
    this chapter of the book.)
 2 Department of Health and Human Services, Notices, "Office of Child Support
    Enforcement; Privacy Act of 1974; System of Records," *Federal Register* 75, no. 139
    (July 21, 2010): 42453, http://www.gpo.gov/fdsys/pkg/FR-2010-07-21/pdf/2010-
    17738.pdf (accessed November 3, 2014).
 3 For simplicity, this chapter refers to custodial parents as mothers and noncusto-
    dial parents as fathers, although certainly recognizing that the situation is often
    reversed.
 4 *Harvey v. Marshall*, 389 Md. 243 (2005). The author of this book was co-counsel
    for the appellant.
 5 Ibid.
 6 If a foster child is not eligible for IV-E payments, a state is not required by federal
    law to seek child support payments from the parents. However, even without the
    federal mandate, several states have established their own procedures that require
    parents of children in state-funded foster care to make child support payments in
    order to repay the state costs.
 7 *In re T.D.P.*, 164 N.C. App. 287 (2004).
 8 *Virginia v. Autry*, 441 A.2d 1056, 1060 (Md. 1982) (citing 1781 Md. Laws, ch. 13, § 1).
 9 William Blackstone, *Commentaries on the Laws of England*, vol. 1 (Chicago: Cal-
    laghan and Company, 1871), 446–447.
10 33 *Vt. Stat. Ann.* § 4106(f).

11 *Powers v. Office of Child Support*, 173 Vt. 390 (2002).

12 Ibid. at 398.

13 *Department of Revenue, Child Support Enforcement Division v. Pealatree*, 996 P.2d 84 (2000).

14 *Harvey v. Marshall*, 389 Md. 243 (2005). The author of this book was co-counsel for the appellant.

15 Ibid.

16 Ibid.

17 *Harvey*, 389 Md. at 251–254.

18 Ibid.

19 Ibid., 252–254.

20 Ibid.

21 *Harvey v. Marshall*, 158 Md.App. 355, 385 (2005).

22 Ibid.

23 Ibid.

24 *Harvey v. Marshall*, Brief of Appellee, Md. Ct. of Appeals, September Term 2004, No. 109 at 26; *Harvey v. Marshall*, Brief of Appellee, Md. Ct. of Special Appeals, September Term 2003, No. 532 at 22.

25 Office of Child Support Enforcement, U.S. Department of Health and Human Services, "The Story Behind the Numbers: Who Owes the Child Support Debt?" 1 (2004), http://www.acf.hhs.gov/programs/cse/pol/IM/2004/im-04-04.htm.

26 Joseph DiPrimio, Executive Director, Child Support Enforcement Administration, Maryland Department of Human Services, Testimony in Opposition to House Bill 550, February 14, 2014 (on file with author).

27 Ibid.

28 See House Committee on Ways and Means, *Testimony of: Harry J. Holzer, Ph.D., Professor at Georgetown University and Visiting Fellow at the Urban Institute, Georgetown University Public Policy Institute*, January 24, 2007, http://waysand-means.house.gov/hearings.asp?formmode=view&id=5398 (site now discontinued).

29 Ho-Po Crystal Wong, "Does Stricter Child Support Enforcement Create More Criminal Dads? A Study of the Effect of Child Support Enforcement Policy on Crimes" (November 16, 2014), available at SSRN: http://ssrn.com/abstract=2526438 or http://dx.doi.org/10.2139/ssrn.2526438 (accessed December 5, 2014).

30 U.S. Department of Health and Human Services, Office of Inspector General, *Client Cooperation with Child Support Enforcement: Challenges and Strategies to Improvement*, OEI-06-98-0004 (2000), 7, http://oig.hhs.gov/oei/reports/oei-06-98-00041.pdf (accessed November 3, 2014) [hereinafter Challenges and Strategies].

31 See Maria Cancian, Daniel R. Meyer, and Jen Roff, *The Effects of Child Support Pass-Through and Disregard Policies,* Report to the Wisconsin Department of Workforce Development (2006).

32 Ibid.

33 Challenges and Strategies at 16.

34 Ibid.

35 *In re T.D.P.*, 164 N.C. App. 287 (2004), *affirmed per curiam, In re T.D.P.*, 359 N.C. 405 (2004).

36 Ibid.

37 U.S. Department of Health and Human Services, Office of Inspector General, *Child Support for Children in IV-E Foster Care*, OEI-04-91-00530 (1992), http:// oig.hhs.gov/oei/reports/oei-04-91-00530.pdf (accessed November 3, 2014).

38 Andrea J. Sedlak and Diane D. Broadhurst, U.S. Dept. of Health and Human Services, Administration for Children and Families, National Center on Child Abuse and Neglect, *Executive Summary of the Third National Incidence Study of Child Abuse and Neglect* (1996), http://www.childwelfare.gov/pubs/statsinfo/nis3. cfm (accessed November 3, 2014).

39 Administration for Children and Families, U.S. Department of Health and Human Services, National Survey of Child and Adolescent Well-Being: One Year in Foster Care: Wave 1 Data Analysis Report 108–113 (2003).

40 *Social Security Act, U.S. Code* 42 (2014), § 671(a)(17).

41 U.S. Department of Health and Human Services, Administration for Children and Families, Child Welfare.

42 See, e.g., *Md. Code Regs.* 07.02.11.26(C) (Requiring that the "local department shall: (1) Initiate child support for every child in out-of-home placement; and (2) Pursue support enforcement activity for both absent parents unless" the parents legal rights have been terminated); *Neb. Admin. R. & Regs.* Title 466, Ch. 21, § 002.01J1 ("In all ADC and foster care IV-D cases in which there is not a court order for child support, the case must be referred to the county/authorized attorney to obtain an order for support"); Tex. Admin. Code Title 40, § 700.1108(a) ("Unless parental rights are terminated, the Texas Department of Protective and Regulatory Services (PRS) must ask the county or district attorney to include a request for child support and health insurance in every petition for managing conservatorship and substitute-care placement, including court-ordered placements").

43 *Social Security Act, U.S. Code* 42 (2014), § 671(a) (15).

44 U.S. Department of Health and Human Services, Office of Inspector General, *Child Support for Children in IV-E Foster Care*, OEI-04-91-00530 (1992), http:// oig.hhs.gov/oei/reports/oei-04-91-00530.pdf (accessed November 3, 2014).

45 Ibid.

46 Ibid., appendix E.

47 Ibid., iii.

48 *Matter of Adoption of J.W.M.*, 532 N.W.2d 372, 380 (N.D. 1995) (dissenting opinion discussing reliance on unpaid child support as grounds for termination of parental rights in petition for adoption).

49 *N.C. Gen. Stat. Ann.* § 7B-1111(a) (3).

50 *In re D.L.T.*, 283 Ga. App. 223 (2007).

51 Ibid., 225.

52 Ibid.

53 E.g., *South Carolina Dept. of Social Services v. Phillips*, 301 S.C. 308, 391 S.E.2d 584 (S.C. Ct. App. 1990); South Carolina *Dept. of Social Services v. Parker*, 336 S.C. 248, 519 S.E.2d 351 (S.C. Ct. App. 1999), *rehearing denied* (Aug 28, 1999).

54 E.g., *In re C.M.*, 275 Ga. App. 719, 721 (2005); *In re A.R.A.S.*, 278 Ga. App. 608, 613 (2006).

55 *In re C.M.*, 275 Ga. App. at 721.

56 *In re A.R.A.S.*, 278 Ga. App. at 613.

57 *In re E.F.C.K.*, 175 N.C. App. 419 (2006).

58 *In the Matter of H.J.A. and T.M.A.* 754 S.E.2d 257 (N.C. Ct. App. 2014) (unpublished opinion).

59 *M.L.B. v. S.L.J.*, 519 U.S. 102, 119 (1996).

60 *Troxel v. Granville*, 530 U.S. 57, 65 (2000).

61 *Reno v. Flores*, 507 U.S. 292, 301–302 (1993).

CHAPTER 6

1 Lisa Chedekel, "Use of Antipsychotics in Nursing Homes Stirs Concerns, Reforms," *Hartford Courant*, February 4, 2013, http://articles.courant.com/2013-02-04/health/hc-psychotropic-drugs-nursing-homes-20130203_1_antipsychotics-home-regulators-home-residents (accessed November 3, 2014).

2 Howard Gleckman, "Dementia Patients Still Getting Dangerous Antipsychotic Drugs in Nursing Homes," *Forbes*, November 20, 2013, http://www.forbes.com/sites/howardgleckman/2013/11/20/dementia-patients-still-getting-dangerous-antipsychotic-drugs-in-nursing-homes/ (accessed November 3, 2014).

3 Lucette Lagnado, "Prescription Abuse Seen in U.S. Nursing Homes," *Wall Street Journal*, December 4, 2007, http://online.wsj.com/news/articles/SB119672919018312521?mod=djem_jiewr_hc&mg=reno64-wsj&url=http%3A%2F%2Fonline.wsj.com%2Farticle%2FSB119672919018312521.html%3Fmod%3Ddjem_jiewr_hc (accessed November 3, 2014).

4 Sam Roe, "Psychotropic Drugs Given to Nursing Home Patients Without Cause," *Chicago Tribune*, October 27, 2009, http://articles.chicagotribune.com/2009-10-27/health/chi-nursing-home1-psychotropics-oct27_1_nursing-home-psychotropic-drugs-antipsychotic-drugs/4 (accessed November 3, 2014).

5 Ibid.

6 Ibid.

7 Ibid.

8 Ibid.

9 Fred Grimm, "Creating Juvenile Zombies, Florida-Style," *Miami Herald*, May 28, 2011 (emphasis added).

10 Ibid.

11 Michael LaForgia, "Huge Doses of Potent Antipsychotics Flow into State Jails for Troubled Kids," *Palm Beach Post*, May 24, 2011, http://www.palmbeachpost.com/news/news/state-regional/huge-doses-of-potent-antipsychotics-flow-into-stat/nLsbf/ (accessed November 3, 2014).

12 Ibid.

13 Kris Hundley, "Suicide of Foster Child, 7, Prompts Review of DCF Drug Policy," *In Memory of Gabriel Myers*, May 9, 2009, http://gabrielmyers.wordpress.com/2009/05/09/suicide-of-foster-child-7-prompts-review-of-dcf-drug-policy/ (accessed November 3, 2014).

14 Gregory D. Kutz, U.S. Government Accountability Office, *HHS Guidance Could Help States Improve Oversight of Psychotropic Prescriptions*, GAO-12-270T (2011), http://gao.gov/assets/590/586570.pdf (accessed November 3, 2014).

15 U.S. Government Accountability Office, *Report to Congressional Requesters: Concerns Remain about Appropriate Services for Children in Medicaid and Foster Care*, GAO-13-15 (2012), http://www.gao.gov/assets/660/650716.pdf (accessed November 3, 2014).

16 Mike Ward, "Advocates Question Number of Foster Children on Psych Drugs," *Statesman.com*, January 30, 2013, http://www.statesman.com/news/news/state-regional/advocates-question-number-of-foster-children-on-ps/nWBYG/?__federated=1 (accessed November 3, 2014).

17 Alan Judd, "Foster Care Fraught with Private Abuses, Public Excuses," *Atlanta Journal-Constitution*, April 29, 2010, http://www.ajc.com/news/news/local/foster-care-fraught-with-private-abuses-public-exc/nQfHs/ (accessed November 3, 2014).

18 Ibid.

19 Ibid.

20 Ibid.

21 Christina Jewett and Sam Roe, "Doctor Gives Risky Drugs at High Rate," *Chicago Tribune*, November 10, 2009, http://articles.chicagotribune.com/2009-11-10/news/chi-drugs-doctor-reinsteinnov10_1_medicaid-records-show-mentally-ill-patients-patient-deaths/2 (accessed November 3, 2014).

22 Christina Jewett and Sam Roe, "In Chicago's Nursing Homes, a Psychiatrist Delivers High-Risk Meds, Cut-Rate Care," ProPublica and *Chicago Tribune*, November 10, 2009, http://www.propublica.org/article/michael-reinstein-chicago-clozapine (accessed November 3, 2014).

23 Jewett and Roe, "Doctor Gives Risky Drugs at High Rate."

24 Ibid.

25 Christina Jewett and Sam Roe, "Doctor-Drugmaker Ties: Psychiatrist Dr. Michael Reinstein Received Nearly $500,000 from Antipsychotic Drug's Manufacturer," *Chicago Tribune*, November 11, 2009, http://articles.chicagotribune.com/2009-11-11/news/0911100746_1_antipsychotic-drug-psychotropic (accessed November 3, 2014).

26 Ibid.

27 Christopher N. Osher and Jennifer Brown, "Drug Firms Have Used Dangerous Tactics to Drive Sales to Treat Kids," *Denver Post*, April 14, 2014, http://www.denverpost.com/investigations/ci_25561024/drug-firms-have-used-dangerous-tactics-drive-sales (accessed November 3, 2014).

28 Ibid.

29 Ibid.

30 Ibid.

31 Michael LaForgia, "Dosed in Juvie Jail: Drug Firms Pay State-Hired Doctors," *Palm Beach Post*, May 24, 2011, http://www.palmbeachpost.com/news/news/dosed-in-juvie-jail-drug-firms-pay-state-hired-doc/nLsb8/ (accessed November 3, 2014).

32 Ibid.

33 Karen De Sa, "The Rx Alliance that Drugs Our Kids," *San Jose Mercury News*, November 23, 2014.

34 U.S. Department of Justice, Office of Public Affairs, "Nation's Largest Nursing Home Pharmacy and Drug Manufacturer to Pay $112 Million to Settle False Claims Act Cases," news release, 09-1186, November 3, 2009, http://www.justice.gov/opa/pr/2009/November/09-civ-1186.html (accessed November 3, 2014).

35 Brady Dennis, "Johnson & Johnson Agrees to Pay $2.2 Billion in Drug-Marketing Settlement," *Washington Post*, November 4, 2013, http://www.washingtonpost.com/national/health-science/johnson-and-johnson-agrees-to-pay-22-billion-in-drug-marketing-settlement/2013/11/04/a7092342-456a-11e3-b6f8-3782ff6cb769_story.html (accessed November 3, 2014).

36 U.S. Department of Justice, Office of Public Affairs, "Abbott Labs to Pay $1.5 Billion to Resolve Criminal & Civil Investigations of Off-label Promotion of Depakote," news release, 12-585, May 7, 2012, http://www.justice.gov/opa/pr/2012/May/12-civ-585.html (accessed November 3, 2014).

37 Michael S. Schmidt and Katie Thomas, "Abbott Settles Marketing Lawsuit," *New York Times*, May 7, 2012, http://www.nytimes.com/2012/05/08/business/abbott-to-pay-1-6-billion-over-illegal-marketing.html?_r=0 (accessed November 3, 2014).

38 U.S. Department of Justice, Office of Public Affairs, "GlaxoSmithKline to Plead Guilty and Pay $3 Billion to Resolve Fraud Allegations and Failure to Report Safety Data," news release, 12-842, July 2, 2012, http://www.justice.gov/opa/pr/2012/July/12-civ-842.html (accessed November 3, 2014).

39 U.S. Department of Justice, Office of Public Affairs, "Pharmaceutical Giant AstraZeneca to Pay $520 Million for Off-label Drug Marketing," news release, 10-487, April 27, 2010, http://www.justice.gov/opa/pr/2010/April/10-civ-487.html (accessed November 3, 2014).

40 U.S. Department of Justice, "Eli Lilly and Company Agrees to Pay $1.415 Billion to Resolve Allegations of Off-label Promotion of Zyprexa," news release, 09-038, January 15, 2009, http://www.justice.gov/opa/pr/2009/January/09-civ-038.html (accessed November 3, 2014).

41 Gardiner Harris and Alex Brenson, "Lilly Said to Be Near $1.4 Billion U.S. Settlement," *New York Times*, January 14, 2009, http://www.nytimes.com/2009/01/15/business/15drug.html (accessed November 3, 2014).

42 Washington State Office of the Attorney General, "Pfizer Inc. to Pay $2.3 Billion in Historic Medicaid Fraud Settlement," news release, September 2, 2009, http://www.atg.wa.gov/pressrelease.aspx?&id=23742#.U8VTRdwirwI (accessed November 3, 2014).

43 U.S. Department of Justice, "Bristol-Myers Squibb to Pay More Than $515 Million to Resolve Allegations of Illegal Drug Marketing and Pricing," news release, 07-782, September 28, 2007, http://www.justice.gov/opa/pr/2007/September/07_civ_782.html (accessed November 3, 2014).

44 "Non-Profit vs. For-Profit Nursing Homes: Is There a Difference in Care?" Center for Medicare Advocacy, http://www.medicareadvocacy.org/non-profit-vs-for-profit-nursing-homes-is-there-a-difference-in-care/ (accessed November 3, 2014).

45 HCR Manor Care, Carlyle Closing, December 21, 2007, http://www.hcr-manorcare.com/about-hcr-manorcare/corporate-matters/carlyle-closing/ (accessed November 30, 2014).

46 Heather Gillers, Tim Evans, Mark Nichols, and Mark Alesia, "Cash Flows in to HHC Nursing Homes, Care Lags," *Indystar.com*, May 10, 2010, http://archive.indystar.com/article/20100511/NEWS14/5160304/Cash-flows-HHC-nursing-homes-care-lags (accessed November 3, 2014).

47 Ibid.

48 Indiana State Government, *Senate Bill No. 309: Digest of SB 309* (2001), http://www.in.gov/legislative/bills/2001/ES/ES0309.1.html (accessed November 5, 2014).

49 Indiana State House, Legislative Services Agency, Office of Fiscal and Management Analysis, *Fiscal Impact Statement* (2001), http://www.in.gov/legislative/bills/2001/PDF/FISCAL/SB0309.003.pdf (accessed November 3, 2014).

50 Indiana State Government, Conference Committee Report, *Digest for EHB 1866*, (2001), http://www.in.gov/legislative/bills/2001/HCCP/CC186604.001.html (accessed November 3, 2014).

51 Frank O'Bannon, Indiana State Government, "Governor Vetoes HEA 1866," news release, May 11, 2001, http://www.in.gov/apps/utils/calendar/presscal?PF=gov&Clist=4&Elist=34726 (accessed November 3, 2014).

52 Gillers et al., "Cash Flows in to HHC Nursing Homes, Care Lags."

53 Ibid.

54 Ibid.

55 Ibid.

56 Ibid.

57 J. K. Wall, "Feds Scrutinize Nursing Home Buying Spree," *Indianapolis Business Journal*, April 27, 2013, http://www.ibj.com/feds-scrutinize-nursing-home-buying-spree/PARAMS/article/41005 (accessed November 3, 2014).

58 Ibid.

59 Gillers et al., "Cash Flows in to HHC Nursing Homes, Care Lags."

60 Ibid.

61 Ibid.

62 "Wishard to Get $40M Donation, New Name: Hospital to Be Renamed for Sidney, Lois Eskenazi," *Indy Channel*, June 22, 2011, http://www.theindychannel.com/news/wishard-to-get-40m-donation-new-name (accessed November 3, 2014).

63 Wall, "Feds Scrutinize Nursing Home Buying Spree."

64 John Russell, "Eskenazi Hospital Prepares to Open," *Indystar.com*, November 16, 2013, http://www.indystar.com/story/news/2013/11/16/eskenazi-hospital-prepares-to-open/3609921/ (accessed November 3, 2014).

65 Ibid.

66 Ibid.

67 Heather Gillers, Tim Evans, Mark Nichols and Mark Alesia, "Cash flows in to HHC nursing homes, care lags," *Indystar.com*, May 10, 2010, http://www.indystar.com/article/20100511/NEWS14/5160304/Cash-flows-HHC-nursing-homes-care-lags (accessed November 3, 2014).

68 Ibid.

69 American Civil Liberties Union, *In for a Penny: The Rise of America's New Debtors' Prisons* (2010), 6, https://www.aclu.org/files/assets/InForAPenny_web.pdf#page=6 (accessed November 3, 2014).

70 John Gibeaut, "Get Out of Jail—But Not Free: Courts Scramble to Fill Their Coffers by Billing Ex-Cons," *ABA Journal*, July 1, 2012, http://www.abajournal.com/magazine/article/get_out_of_jailbut_not_free_courts_scramble_to_fill_their_coffers_by_billin/ (accessed November 3, 2014).

71 42 *PA Code* § 9730.1 (2012), http://law.justia.com/codes/pennsylvania/2010/title-42/chapter-97/9730-1/ (accessed November 3, 2014).

72 Ibid.

73 Ibid.

74 Clackamas County Circuit Court, "Collections," Oregon Judicial Department, http://courts.oregon.gov/Clackamas/pages/collections.aspx (accessed November 3, 2014).

75 "About AllianceOne: Company Overview," Alliance One, http://www.allianceoneinc.com/About_Us.html (accessed November 3, 2014).

76 Clackamas County Circuit Court, "Collections."

77 Joseph P. Smith, "Bridgeton Hires Private Business to Collect Fines," *Daily Journal*, July 9, 2012, http://archive.thedailyjournal.com/article/20120710/NEWS01/307100036/Bridgeton-hires-private-business-collect-fines (accessed November 3, 2014).

78 Nicholas Huba, "Brick Targets Unpaid Court Fines," *Asbury Park Press*, June 13, 2014, http://www.app.com/story/news/local/brick-point-pleasant/2014/06/13/brick-jackson-court-fees/10504327/ (accessed November 3, 2014).

79 Ibid.

80 Alicia Bannon, Mitali Nagrecha, and Rebekah Diller, *Criminal Justice Debt: Barrier to Reentry* (Brennan Center for Justice at New York University School of Law,

2010), 2, http://brennan.3cdn.net/c610802495d901dac3_76m6vqhpy.pdf (accessed November 3, 2014).

81 Joseph Shaprio, "As Court Fees Rise, the Poor Are Paying the Price," *NPR*, May 19, 2014, http://www.npr.org/2014/05/19/312158516/increasing-court-fees-punish-the-poor (accessed November 3, 2014).

82 ACLU, *In for a Penny* at 13, https://www.aclu.org/files/assets/InForAPenny_web.pdf (accessed November 30, 2014).

83 Farlex, "MAXIMUS Reports Record Third Quarter Revenue of $141.7 Million and EPS of $0.43," The Free Library, http://www.thefreelibrary.com/MAXIMUS+Reports+Record+Third+Quarter+Revenue+of+%24141.7+Million+and . . .-a0106153591 (accessed October 16, 2014).

84 Human Rights Watch, Profiting from Probation: America's Offender-Funded Probation Industry, 2014 at 3, http://www.hrw.org/sites/default/files/reports/us0214_ForUpload_0.pdf (accessed November 30, 2014).

85 "Electronic Home Monitoring, City of Mountlake Terrace," http://www.cityofmlt.com/cityServices/police/electronicHomeMonitoring.htm (accessed November 3, 2014).

86 Ames Alexander, Joseph Neff, and Karen Garloch, "Senator: Hospitals Profited on Drugs for Poor, Uninsured," *Charlotte Observer*, April 3, 2013, http://www.charlotteobserver.com/2013/04/03/3956004/senator-3-nc-nonprofit-hospitals.html#.U81UNtwirwI (accessed November 3, 2014).

87 Andrew Pollack, "Dispute Develops over Discount Drug Program," *New York Times*, February 12, 2013.

88 Ryan Grim, "Billy Tauzin Rides Again, This Time Battling Against Big Pharma (Update)," *Huffington Post*, August 13, 2013, http://www.huffingtonpost.com/2013/08/13/billy-tauzin-drugs_n_3719468.html (accessed November 3, 2014).

89 Danielle Paquette, "End-of-Life Care: And Industry with Soaring Profits, Funded by Taxpayers," *Washington Post*, August 21, 2014.

90 Ibid.

91 Peter Waldman, "Preparing Americans for Death Lets Hospices Neglect End of Life," *Bloomberg*, July 22, 2011, http://www.bloomberg.com/news/2011-07-22/preparing-americans-for-death-lets-for-profit-hospices-neglect-end-of-life.html (accessed November 3, 2014).

92 "Kids for Cash Trial: Former PA Judge Ciavarella Claims Money Was 'Finder's Fee,'" *International Business Times*, February 14, 2011, http://www.ibtimes.com/kids-cash-trial-former-pa-judge-ciavarella-claims-money-was-finders-fee-266837 (accessed November 30, 2014).

CHAPTER 7

1 I had the opportunity to work with Congressman Stark's office in drafting and supporting the Foster Children Self Support Act.

2 The bill was introduced under the sponsorship and leadership of Senator Jamie Raskin and Delegate Kathleen Dumais in 2014, and by Senator Raskin and Del-

egate Geraldine Valentino-Smith in 2015. I worked with the lawmakers in drafting and supporting the state legislation.

3 I served as lead counsel for Alex.

4 I also served as co-counsel for several advocacy organizations filing an amicus brief in support of Ryan's case.

5 Michael B. Sauter, "Alexander E.M. Hess and Thomas C. Frohlich, 24/7 Wall St.: America's Richest States," *USA Today*, September 21, 2013, http://www.usatoday.com/story/money/business/2013/09/21/americas-richest-states/2845525/ (accessed November 11, 2014).

6 U.S. Department of Health and Human Services, Office of Child Support Enforcement, *FY2013 Preliminary Report* (2014), Table P-30, http://www.acf.hhs.gov/programs/css/resource/fy2013-preliminary-report-table-p-30 (accessed November 11, 2014).

7 Senate Finance Committee, *Social Security Amendments of 1965*, 89th Cong., 1st sess. 1965, S. Rep. 89-404, 78; 245–46.

8 Jackie Kucinich, "Rubio: War on Poverty Has Been Lost," *Washington Post*, January 8, 2014, http://www.washingtonpost.com/blogs/post-politics/wp/2014/01/08/rubio-war-on-poverty-has-been-lost/ (accessed November 11, 2014).

9 Robert Greenstein, "Commentary: Ryan 'Opportunity Grant' Proposal Would Likely Increase Poverty and Shrink Resources for Poverty Programs Over Time," *Center on Budget and Policy Priorities*, July 24, 2014, http://www.cbpp.org/cms/index.cfm?fa=view&id=4176 (accessed November 11, 2014).

10 Daniel L. Hatcher, "Romney's Medicaid Shell Game," *Boston Globe*, October 12, 2014, http://www.bostonglobe.com/opinion/2012/10/12/podium-medicaid/X5KHn9vVJjfRPgDAtxku3M/story.html?camp=pm (accessed November 11, 2014).

11 Brené Brown, *Daring Greatly: How the Courage to Be Vulnerable Transforms the Way We Live, Love, Parent, and Lead.* New York: Gotham, 2012.

SELECTED BIBLIOGRAPHY

Personal Responsibility and Work Opportunity Reconciliation Act of 1996. Pub. L. No. 104-193. § 101–116, 110 Stat. 2105 (1996).

Harvey v. Marshall, 884 A.2d 1171 (Md. 2005).

Harvey v. Marshall, 158 Md.App. 355 (2005).

In re Gault, 387 U.S. 1 (1967).

In re J.G., 652 S.E.2d 266 (N.C. Ct. App. 2007).

In Re Ryan W., 434 Md. 577 (2013).

Myers v. Baltimore County Dept. of Social Services, Brief of Appellant, 2010 WL 4890061 (Md.App.) (Appellate Brief).

Myers v. Baltimore County Dept. of Social Services, Reply Brief of Appellant, 2011 WL 3575944 (Md.App.) (Appellate Brief).

Wash. State Dep't of Soc. & Health Servs. v. Guardianship Estate of Keffeler, 537 U.S. 371 (2003).

Joint Legislative Committee on Performance Evaluation & Expenditure Review (PEER).

Report to Mississippi Legislature: The Department of Human Services' Use of Revenue Maximization Contracts, no. 413. December 6, 2000.

Social Security Administration, *Training Organizational Representative Payees,* Lesson Plan, http://www.ssa.gov/payee/LessonPlanORGTGNGUIDEfinalnumber10.htm#SSILIMIT:

U.S. Congress. House. Committee on Ways and Means. *2004 Green Book: Background Material and Data on the Programs Within the Jurisdiction of the Committee on Ways and Means,* 108th Cong., 2004. Committee Print.

U.S. Department of Health and Human Services, Office of the Assistant Secretary for Planning and Evaluation. *Federal Foster Care Financing: How and Why the Current Funding Structure Fails to Meet the Needs of the Child Welfare Field.* 2005.

U.S. Department of Health and Human Services, Office of Inspector General. *Client Cooperation with Child Support Enforcement: Challenges and Strategies to Improvement.* 2000.

U.S. Government Accountability Office. GAO-05-748, *Medicaid Financing: States' Use of Contingency-Fee Consultants to Maximize Federal Reimbursements Highlights Need for Improved Federal Oversight.* 2005.

———. GAO-05-836T, *Medicaid: States' Efforts to Maximize Federal Reimbursements Highlight Need for Improved Federal Oversight.* 2005.

———. GAO-04-228, *Medicaid: Improved Federal Oversight of State Financing Scheme-*
sIs Needed. 2004.

———. GAO/HEHS/OSI-00-69, *Medicaid in Schools: Improper Payments Demand*
Improvements in HCFA Oversight. 2000.

———. GAO/T-HEHS-99-148, *Medicaid: Questionable Practices Boost Federal Payments*
for School-Based Services. 1999.

Adams, Gordon. *The Iron Triangle: The Politics of Defense Contracting.* Studies/Council
on Economic Priorities. New Brunswick, NJ: Transaction Publishers, 1981.

Adler, Libby S. *The Meanings of Permanence: A Critical Analysis of the Adoption and*
Safe Families Act of 1997, 38 HARV. J. ON LEGIS. 1 (2001).

Ahearn, Lorraine. "At Eleventh Hour, Judge Saves Boy in Foreclosure." *Greensboro*
News & Record, December 18, 2005.

Appell, Annette R. *Protecting Children or Punishing Mothers: Gender, Race and Class in*
the Child Protection System [An Essay], 48 S.C. L. REV. 577 (1997).

Appell, Ruth. *Representing Children Representing What?: Critical Reflections on Lawyer-*
ing for Children, 39 COLUM. HUM. RTS. L. REV. 573 (2008).

Baicker, Katherine and Douglas Staiger, *Fiscal Shenanigans, Targeted Federal Health*
Care Funds, and Patient Mortality, 120 Q.J. ECON. 345 (2005).

Benedetto, Michele. *An Ounce of Prevention: A Foster Youth's Substantive Due Process*
Right to Proper Preparation for Emancipation, 9 U.C. DAVIS J. JUV. L. & POL'Y
381 (2005).

Boyer, Bruce A. *Jurisdictional Conflicts Between Juvenile Courts and Child Welfare*
Agencies: The Uneasy Relationship Between Institutional Co-Parents, 54 MD. L. REV.
377 (1995).

Brito, Tonya L. *The Welfarization of Family Law*, 48 U. KAN.L. REV. 229 (2000).

Cahn, Naomi. *State Representation of Children's Interests*, 40 FAM. L.Q. 109 (2006).

Cammett, Ann. *Deadbeats, Deadbrokes, and Prisoners*, 18 Geo. J. on Poverty L. & Pol'y
127 (2011).

Carasso, Adam and Roseana Bess. *The Disposition of Federal Dollars in Florida's Social*
Services: Informing a Federal Funding Maximization Strategy. Urban Institute, 2003.

Chambers, David L. *Fathers, the Welfare System, and the Virtues and Perils of Child-*
Support Enforcement, 81 VA. L. REV. 2575 (1995).

Chou, Cristina Chi-Young. *Renewing the Good Intentions of Foster Care: Enforcement*
of the Adoption Assistance and Child Welfare Act of 1980 and the Substantive Due
Process Right to Safety, 46 VAND. L. REV. 683 (1993).

Curtis, George B. *The Checkered Career of Parens Patriae: The State as Parent or Ty-*
rant?, 25 DEPAUL L. REV. 895 (1976).

Custer, Lawrence B. *The Origins of the Doctrine of Parens Patriae*, 27 EMORY L.J. 195 (1978).

Czapanskiy, Karen Syma. *To Protect and Defend: Assigning Parental Rights When Par-*
ents Are Living in Poverty, 14 WM. & MARY BILL RTS. J. 943 (2006).

DeVault, Esme Noelle. *Reasonable Efforts Not So Reasonable: The Termination of the*
Parental Rights of a Developmentally Disabled Mother, 10 ROGER WILLIAMS U. L.
REV. 763 (2005).

Diller, Matthew. *Form and Substance in the Privatization of Poverty Programs*, 49 UCLA L. REV. 1739 (2002).

Dohrn, Bernardine. *Seize the Little Moment: Justice for the Child 20 Years at the Children and Family Justice Center*, 6 NW. J. L. & SOC. POL'Y 334 (2011).

Dowd, Nancy E. *Fatherhood and Equality: Reconfiguring Masculinities*, 45 SUFFOLK U. L. REV. 1047, 1048 (2012).

Edelman, Peter, Harry J. Holzer, and Paul Offner. *Reconnecting Disadvantaged Young Men.* Washington, DC: Urban Institute Press, 2006.

Fernandes-Alcantara, Adrienne L. et al. *Child Welfare: Social Security and Supplemental Security Income (SSI) Benefits for Children in Foster Care.* Report for Congress. RL 33855. Washington, DC: Congressional Research Service, 2011.

Fineman, Martha A. *The Vulnerable Subject: Anchoring Equality in the Human Condition*, 20 YALE J.L. & FEMINISM 1, 9–15 (2008).

———. *The Vulnerable Subject and the Responsive State*, 60 EMORY L.J. 251, 257 (2010).

Fondacaro, Mark R. et al. *Reconceptualizing Due Process in Juvenile Justice: Contributions from Law and Social Science*, 57 HASTINGS L.J. 955 (2006).

Fontana, Jacqueline M. *Cooperation and Good Cause: Greater Sanctions and the Failure to Account for Domestic Violence*, 15 WIS. WOMEN'S L.J. 367 (2000).

Fraidin, Matthew I. *Stories Told and Untold: Confidentiality Laws and the Master Narrative of Child Welfare*, 63 ME. L. REV. 1 (2010).

Gilman, Michele Estrin. *Legal Accountability in an Era of Privatized Welfare*, 89 CALIF. L. REV. 569 (2001).

Gordon, Daniel I. *Organizational Conflicts of Interest: A Growing Integrity Challenge*, 35 PUB. CONT. L.J. 25 (2005).

Gordon, Robert M. *Drifting Through Byzantium: The Promise and Failure of the Adoption and Safe Families Act of 1997*, 83 MINN. L. REV. 637, 679 (1999).

Guggenheim, Martin. *Somebody's Children: Sustaining the Family's Place in Child Welfare Policy*, 113 HARV. L. REV. 1716 (2000).

———. *What's Wrong with Children's Rights.* Cambridge, MA: Harvard University Press, 2005, 63–65.

Harris, Deborah. *Child Support for Welfare Families: Family Policy Trapped in Its Own Rhetoric*, 16 N.Y.U. REV. L. & SOC. CHANGE 619 (1988).

Hansen, Drew D. *The American Invention of Child Support: Dependency and Punishment in Early American Child Support Law*, 108 YALE L.J. 1123 (1999).

Hatcher, Daniel L. *Foster Children Paying for Foster Care*, 27 CARDOZO L. REV. 1797 (2006).

———. *Child Support Harming Children: Subordinating the Best Interests of Children to the Fiscal Interests of the State*, 42 WAKE FOREST LAW REV. 1029 (2007).

———. *Collateral Children: Consequence and Illegality at the Intersection of Foster Care and Child Support*, 74 BROOK. L. REV. 1333 (2009).

———. *Poverty Revenue: The Subversion of Fiscal Federalism*, 52 ARIZ. L. REV. 675 (2010).

———. *Purpose vs. Power: Parens Patriae and Agency Self-Interest*, 42 N. MEX. L. REV. 159 (2012).

Heclo, Hugh. "Issue Networks and the Executive Establishment." in Vol. 88, *The New American Political System*, Anthony King, ed. Washington, DC: American Enterprise Institute for Public Policy Research, 1978.

Huang, Chien-Chung and Hillard Pouncy. "Why Doesn't She Have a Child Support Order?: Personal Choice or Objective Constraint." *Family Relations* 54, no. 547 (2005).

Huberfeld, Nicole. *Bizarre Love Triangle: The Spending Clause, Section 1983, and Medicaid Entitlements,* 42 U.C. DAVIS L. REV. 413 (2008).

Huntington, Clare. *Rights Myopia in Child Welfare,* 53 UCLA L. REV. 637 (2006).

Kelly, Lisa. *If Anybody Asks You Who I Am: An Outsider's Story of the Duty to Establish Paternity,* 6 YALE J.L. & FEMINISM 297 (1994).

Krause, Harry D. *Child Support in America: The Legal Perspective.* Lexis Law Pub. Charlottesville: Michie Co., 1981.

Levesque, Roger J. R. *Targeting "Deadbeat" Dads: The Problem with the Direction of Welfare Reform,* 15 HAMLINE J. PUB. L. & POL'Y 1 (1994).

Maldonado, Solangel. *Deadbeat or Deadbroke: Redefining Child Support for Poor Fathers,* 39 U.C. DAVIS L. REV. 991 (2006).

McLanahan, Sarah et al. "Fragile Families, Welfare Reform, and Marriage." *Welfare Reform and Beyond: The Future of the Safety Net.* R. Haskins, I. Sawhill, K. Weaver, and A. Kane, eds. Washington, DC: Brookings Institution, November 2001.

Minow, Martha. *Public and Private Partnerships: Accounting for the New Religion,* 116 HARV. L. REV. 1229 (2003).

Murphy, Jane C. *Legal Images of Fatherhood: Welfare Reform, Child Support Enforcement, and Fatherless Children,* 81 NOTRE DAME L. REV. 325 (2005).

Musgrave, Richard A. *The Theory of Public Finance: A Studying in Public Economy.* New York: McGraw-Hill, 1959.

Oates, Wallace E. *Fiscal Federalism.* The Harbrace Series in Business and Economics. HBJ Accounting Series. New York: Harcourt Brace Jovanovich, 1972.

———. *The Political Economy of Fiscal Federalism.* Lexington, MA: Lexington Books, 1977.

———. "Toward A Second-Generation Theory of Fiscal Federalism." *International Tax and Public Finance* 12, no. 349 (2005).

Ramsey, Sarah H. *Children in Poverty: Reconciling Children's Interests with Child Protective and Welfare Policies: A Response to Ward Doren and Roberts,* 61 MD. L. REV. 437 (2002).

Roberts, Dorothy. *Shattered Bonds: The Color of Child Welfare.* New York: Basic Civitas Books, 2002.

Rodden, Jonathan A., *Hamilton's Paradox: The Promise and Peril of Fiscal Federalism.* Cambridge Studies in Comparative Politics. New York: Cambridge University Press, 2005.

Rose-Ackerman, Susan. *Cooperative Federalism and Co-Optation,* 92 YALE L.J. 1344 (1983).

Rosenbaum, Sara. *Medicaid at Forty: Revisiting Structure and Meaning in a Post-Deficit Reduction Act Era,* 9 J. HEALTH CARE L. & POL'Y 5 (2006).

Sankaran, Vivek S. *Innovation Held Hostage: Has Federal Intervention Stifled Efforts to Reform the Child Welfare System?,* 41 U. MICH. J.L. REFORM 281 (2007).

Scarcella, Cynthia Andrews, et al. *The Cost of Protecting Vulnerable Children IV: How Child Welfare Funding Fared During the Recession.* Urban Institute, 2004.

Schuele, Donna. *Origins and Development of the Law of Parental Child Support,* 27 J. FAM. L. 807 (1989).

Schwartz, Sonya, Shelly Gehshan, Alan Weil, and Alice Lam. "Moving Beyond the Tug of War: Improving Medicaid Fiscal Integrity." *National Academy for State Health Policy* (2006).

Seymour, John. Parens Patriae *and Wardship Powers: Their Nature and Origins,* 14 OXFORD J. LEGAL STUD. 159 (1994).

Super, David A. *Rethinking Fiscal Federalism,* 118 HARV. L. REV. 2544 (2005).

tenBroek, Jacobus. *California's Dual System of Family Law: Its Origin, Development, and Present Status, Part I,* 16 STAN. L. REV. 257 (1964).

Woodhouse, Barbara Bennett. *Hidden in Plain Sight: The Tragedy of Children's Rights From Ben Franklin to Lionel Tate.* Princeton: Princeton University Press, 2008.

———. *The Courage of Innocence: Children as Heroes in the Struggle for Justice,* 2009 U. ILL. L. REV. 1567 (2009).

INDEX

Abbott Laboratories, 191

Abilify, 192

ABLE Act. *See* Achieving a Better Life Experience Act

abused and neglected children: in poverty, 167–68; vulnerability of, 14–15, 167–68. *See also* foster children

Achieving a Better Life Experience Act (ABLE Act), 101

administrative costs, 71–72, 163–64

Adoption and Safe Families Act (ASFA), 171

adoption assistance, 72

agencies. *See* human service agencies

A. Holly Paterson Extended Care Facility, *136*, 136–38

aid programs: fiscal federalism and, 28–29; grant-in-aid programs, 33–35; poverty industry undermining, 3–4; statutory purpose of, clarified and enforced, 217–18; strengthening of, 7; structural improvements to, 219–21

Alabama, 66–67

Alaska, 153

Albany County nursing home, 135–36, *136*

Alliance One Credit Company, 199–200

American Senior Communities, 195

anti-psychotic medications, 75, 184–88, 192

Arizona, 50

Asbury Park Press, 201

AseraCare, 205

ASFA. *See* Adoption and Safe Families Act

Ashcroft, John, 123–25

asset limit, SSI, 100–101

AstraZeneca, 189–90, 192

Atlanta Journal-Constitution, 188

audits: failure of, 141–42; improved, 220; OIG, 16–17; by poverty industry, 51–52

Baltimore City Office of Child Support Enforcement, 145, 154

Baltimore County Department of Social Services (BCDSS), 11–12, 97

bastardy acts, 147–51, 156

BCDSS. *See* Baltimore County Department of Social Services

Bearden v. Georgia, 202

bed taxes: Medicaid and, 119–26, 133, 139–40; nursing homes and, 133, 139

bipartisanship, in poverty industry, 112, 208

Blagojevich, "Rod," 38

Blake, Fred, 85

Bridgeton, NJ, 200

Bristol Myers Squibb, 192

Brown, Jerry, 142

budget: cuts, 25–27, 52; fiscal federalism and, 26

burial spaces, 87

California: foster care in, 191; Medicaid in, 142

CASA. *See* court-appointed special advocate

caseworkers: children's best interests and, 23; child support and, 166, 172; reunification and, 172

United States (U.S.): bastardy acts, 147–51, 156; CMS, 30, 37, 43, 47, 141, 218; Department of Justice, 30–31; federalism in, 32–33; *parens patriae* in, 18–19. *See also* Supreme Court, U.S.

University of Massachusetts Medical School (UMMS), 44

Upper Payment Limits (UPLs): Medicaid and, 115–19, *116*, 133–35, 137; nursing homes and, 133–35, 137

U.S. *See* United States

VA benefits. *See* Veteran's Assistance benefits

Vermont, 151–53

Veteran's Assistance (VA) benefits, 65, 73, 210–13

volunteer representative payee programs, 96

vulnerability, 221

vulnerable populations: abused and neglected children, 14–15, 167–68; agencies' purpose and, 13, 17–19, 26–27, 90–91, 98, 110, 147–58, 166, 208–17, 221; agencies' self-interest and, 13, 18–27, 90–91, 110, 147, 151–58, 166, 221; disabled poor, 15–16; exploitation of, 1–7; impoverished, fragile families, 13–14, 160, 167–68; interdependence of, 7, 17, 221; *parens patriae* and, 17–21, 23, 25,

27, 103, 208–9; strength of, 6; unmet needs of, 1–3. *See also* elderly poor; foster children

wardships, 18, 24–25

Washington Post, 205

Washington State: court fees and fines in, 202–3; electronic monitoring in, 204; Medicaid in, 45

Washington State Dep't of Social & Health Services v. Guardianship Estate of Keffeler, 102

welfare cost recovery, 144–46; bastardy acts and, 147–51, 156; conflicting purpose in, 148–57; culture of conflict in, 158–61; family economics impacted by, 162–63; history of, 149–51; impact of, 157–64; poverty increased by, 161; public economics impacted by, 163–64; societal costs of, 161; with tax refunds, 160

WellCare, 30–31

women, mental illness in, 16

Woodhouse, Barbara Bennett, 23–24

Yaple, Mike, 132–33

Zone Program Integrity Contractors (ZPICs), 43

Zyprexa, 192

ABOUT THE AUTHOR

Daniel L. Hatcher is Professor of Law at the University of Baltimore, teaching the Civil Advocacy Clinic and other courses. He previously worked at the Maryland Legal Aid Bureau and Children's Defense Fund. He has represented foster children and impoverished adults, testified before Congress and the Maryland General Assembly, and written several publications regarding the issues in this book.

Printed and bound by CPI Group (UK) Ltd, Croydon, CR0 4YY

09/06/2025

14685810-0001